The Moral Psychology
of Envy

MORAL PSYCHOLOGY OF THE EMOTIONS

Series Editor: Mark Alfano, Macquarie University

How do our emotions influence our other mental states (perceptions, beliefs, motivations, intentions) and our behavior? How are they influenced by our other mental states, our environments, and our cultures? What is the moral value of a particular emotion in a particular context? This series explores the causes, consequences, and value of the emotions from an interdisciplinary perspective. Emotions are diverse, with components at various levels (biological, neural, psychological, social), so each book in this series is devoted to a distinct emotion. This focus allows the author and reader to delve into a specific mental state, rather than trying to sum up emotions en masse. Authors approach a particular emotion from their own disciplinary angle (e.g., conceptual analysis, feminist philosophy, critical race theory, phenomenology, social psychology, personality psychology, neuroscience) while connecting with other fields. In so doing, they build a mosaic for each emotion, evaluating both its nature and its moral properties.

Other titles in this series:

The Moral Psychology of Anger, edited by Myisha Cherry and Owen Flanagan
The Moral Psychology of Contempt, edited by Michelle Mason
The Moral Psychology of Compassion, edited by Justin Caouette and Carolyn Price
The Moral Psychology of Disgust, edited by Nina Strohminger and Victor Kumar
The Moral Psychology of Gratitude, edited by Robert Roberts and Daniel Telech
The Moral Psychology of Admiration, edited by Alfred Archer and André Grahle
The Moral Psychology of Regret, edited by Anna Gotlib
The Moral Psychology of Hope, edited by Claudia Blöser and Titus Stahl
The Moral Psychology of Amusement, edited by Brian Robinson
The Moral Psychology of Boredom, edited by Andreas Elpidorou
The Moral Psychology of Love, edited by Berit Brogaard and Arina Pismenny
The Moral Psychology of Hate, edited by Noell Birondo
The Moral Psychology of Envy, edited by Sara Protasi

The Moral Psychology of Envy

Edited by Sara Protasi

ROWMAN & LITTLEFIELD
Lanham • Boulder • New York • London

Published by Rowman & Littlefield
An imprint of The Rowman & Littlefield Publishing Group, Inc.
4501 Forbes Boulevard, Suite 200, Lanham, Maryland 20706
www.rowman.com

Copyright © 2022 by The Rowman & Littlefield Publishing Group, Inc.

All rights reserved. No part of this book may be reproduced in any form or by any electronic or mechanical means, including information storage and retrieval systems, without written permission from the publisher, except by a reviewer who may quote passages in a review.

British Library Cataloguing in Publication Information Available

Library of Congress Cataloging-in-Publication Data

Library of Congress Cataloging-in-Publication DataNames: Protasi, Sara, 1978- editor.
  Title: The moral psychology of envy / edited by Sara Protasi.
  Description: Lanham : Rowman & Littlefield, [2022] | Series: Moral psychology of the emotions | Includes bibliographical references and index.
  Identifiers: LCCN 2022018680 (print) | LCCN 2022018681 (ebook) | ISBN 9781538160060 (cloth) | ISBN 9781538172124 (paperback) | ISBN 9781538160077 (ebook)
  Subjects: LCSH: Envy. | Envy--Moral and ethical aspects.
  Classification: LCC BF575.E65 M67 2022 (print) | LCC BF575.E65 (ebook) | DDC 152.4/8--dc23/eng/20220621
  LC record available at https://lccn.loc.gov/2022018680
  LC ebook record available at https://lccn.loc.gov/2022018681

Contents

Introduction: Striving to Be Better, Sulking in a Corner, Stealing the Spotlight, Spoiling Someone's Joy: The Many Faces of Envy   1
Sara Protasi

Chapter 1: A Sociocultural Perspective on Envy: On Covetous Desire, the Evil Eye, and the Social Regulation of Equality   23
Patricia M. Rodriguez Mosquera

Chapter 2: How Envy and Being Envied Shape Social Hierarchies   41
Jens Lange and Jan Crusius

Chapter 3: On the Epistemic Effects of Envy in Academia   61
Felipe Romero

Chapter 4: "I Could Have Been You": Existential Envy and the Self   77
Íngrid Vendrell Ferran

Chapter 5: Envy, Compassion, and the Buddhist (No)Self   93
Christina Chuang

Chapter 6: Let the Donkeys Be Donkeys: In Defense of Inspiring Envy   111
Maria Silvia Vaccarezza and Ariele Niccoli

Chapter 7: Malicious Moral Envy   129
Vanessa Carbonell

Chapter 8: "You're Just Jealous!": On Envious Blame   147
Neal A. Tognazzini

Chapter 9: The Fact of Envy: Trends in the History of Modern Economics   163
Miriam Barkovsky

Chapter 10: The Politics of Envy: Outlaw Emotions in Capitalist
  Societies   181
  Alfred Archer, Alan Thomas, and Bart Engelen

Chapter 11: To Envy an Algorithm   199
  Alison Duncan Kerr

Chapter 12: The Envious Consumer   217
  Niels van de Ven

Index   237

About the Contributors   247

Introduction

Striving to Be Better, Sulking in a Corner, Stealing the Spotlight, Spoiling Someone's Joy: The Many Faces of Envy

Sara Protasi

A tiny child is eating a huge ice cream: a big crunchy waffle replete with smooth, bright-colored yumminess melting quickly in the summer heat. Their little chubby fingers get wet, and the caretaker's impatient call to hurry up only makes the child clumsier—in a fatal second, the cone slips from the child's grip and falls face-down on the dirty pavement.

The child's cry resonates in the torrid air, far-reaching in the neighborhood, a moment that will consolidate into a sad childhood memory through numerous retellings. Behind a fence, a peeking face turns from intensely yearning and covetous to smiling with schadenfreude: "ah, that serves them right! If I can't have ice cream, why should other children?" the little voyeur's expression suggests.

Envy is the malignant gaze, the evil eye that mars other people's good fortune, a blight of relations and ruin of societies—so the common thinking goes, shaped by millennia of religious and cultural condemnation of this emotion.

That common thinking shaped how I thought about envy when I was a child myself: I feared this deadly sin, seeing it as a corrupting force to be repressed, denied, and hidden at all costs, except in the secrecy of the confessional. I could have never admitted envy, even to my best friend—*especially* to my best friend, who might have been the target of it![1]

But when I started thinking about envy years later, as a graduate student, I realized that envy had propelled me to achieve worthy objectives and meet high expectations. I remembered how, as a passionate but mediocre dance student, envy for superior peers had motivated me to practice more intelligently and effortfully. Those better dancers had s*how*n me both that I *could* improve myself and *how* I could do it. (And no, in case you were wondering, that wasn't just admiration!)[2]

My personal experience fueled an intellectual journey through historical accounts of this emotion and lead to the discovery that it had been unjustly maligned . . .

ENVY IS SAID IN MANY WAYS, IN DIFFERENT TRADITIONS

As I looked into the envy literature in philosophy and psychology, I discovered that some scholars had come to the same conclusion: that envy wasn't necessarily vicious, counterproductive, or irrational. In both fields, these dissenting voices argued that envy could be *emulative* and *benign*, leading to self-betterment and achievement, void of malice or hostility toward the envied.

In philosophy, this minority view had existed for a long time, arguably since Aristotle's discussion of *phthonos* and *zēlos* in *Rhetoric* (II.10–11). Aristotle defines these two emotions as pains felt at the good fortune of others who are perceived as equals. But *phthonos* is concerned with the other's success, rather than with the possibility of acquiring the lacked good, while *zēlos* is concerned with the good itself, which agents see as obtainable and deserved. Consequently, *phthonos* is a despicable emotion felt by ignoble people bent on stopping others from having and enjoying goodness, while *zēlos* is a noble emotion that motivates to pursue excellence.

The distinction between these two emotions has been exaggerated, in my view, by commentators of Aristotle's, especially Christian (e.g., Aquinas) but also modern ones, who, in their eagerness to reject envy, have interpreted *zēlos* (often translated as "emulation," not an emotion term at all) as different *in kind* from *phthonos* (always translated as "envy"). (For a longer discussion, see Protasi 2021, esp. 169–73.) Several philosophers in history (e.g., Descartes, Hobbes, and Butler) have talked about envy and emulation, but few have defended envy *qua* envy.[3] In the contemporary debate, some concede that envy is hostile toward the envied but reject the implication that this hostility is always harmful, because envy helps to recognize and redress injustice (La Caze 2001 and Frye 2016), while others argue that envy is excusable or reasonable (Green 2013 and Bankovsky 2018, both after

Rawls 1971). Krista Thomason (2015) vindicates the moral value of feeling envy, independently from its consequences, while Gabriele Taylor (1988, 2006) distinguishes between three kinds of envy (admiring, emulative, and destructive), thus joining Aristotle in recognizing that envy has subtypes. Many philosophical accounts of envy, however (with the notable exception of Aaron Ben-Ze'ev work, e.g., 1990, 2000) haven't engaged much with contemporary empirical discussions.

While influential texts appeared in sociology, anthropology, and psychology in the 1960s and 1970s (e.g., Schoeck 1969; Foster 1972; Silver and Sabini 1978), a *systematic* empirical investigation of envy, especially in social psychology, started in the 1980s and 1990s (e.g., see works authored collaboratively and individually by W. Gerrod Parrott, Judith Rodin, Peter Salovey, and Richard H. Smith). The 2000s saw another increase in scholarly interest in envy (see figure 0.1, panel a). However, compared to other self-conscious emotions such as shame, guilt, and embarrassment, envy remains relatively underexplored, as shown in figure 0.1, panel b.[4]

The last two decades' boom in the study of envy coincided with the rising popularity of benign envy. A notion of nonmalicious or admiring envy could already be found in some of the aforementioned early classics (Foster 1972; Silver and Sabini 1978; Parrott 1991). But as recently as 2007, two authoritative reviews still concurred with each other that benign envy could only be a "weak" (Miceli and Castelfranchi 2007, 456) and "sanitized" (Smith and Kim 2007, 47) version of envy *proper*, insofar as it lacked what was deemed the essential feature of ill-will toward the envied. As such, accepting the notion of benign envy risked "obscur[ing] the nature of envy" (Smith and Kim 2007, 47) with the consequence of "missing the important differences between envy and admiration or emulation" (Miceli and Castelfranchi 2007, 475). But Niels van de Ven and collaborators' germinal studies (2009, 2011) disrupted this consensus, and the tide has turned since. The notion of benign envy, *qua* genuine envy, has become much more mainstream, even though space for debate remains (e.g., see the adversarial review by Crusius et al. 2020).

DISSENTING VOICES MEET IN THE MIDDLE, SOMEWHAT ELEVATED

I was writing my dissertation during those transitional years (2010–2014), so I witnessed this momentous shift with excitement. But even as I appreciated the empirical vindication of my intuitions and life experiences, I noticed how philosophical references in psychology articles were sparse and often only present in the introductory section. Much like philosophy theorized about a psychological phenomenon without delving deeply in the scientific evidence,

a) Publications about envy

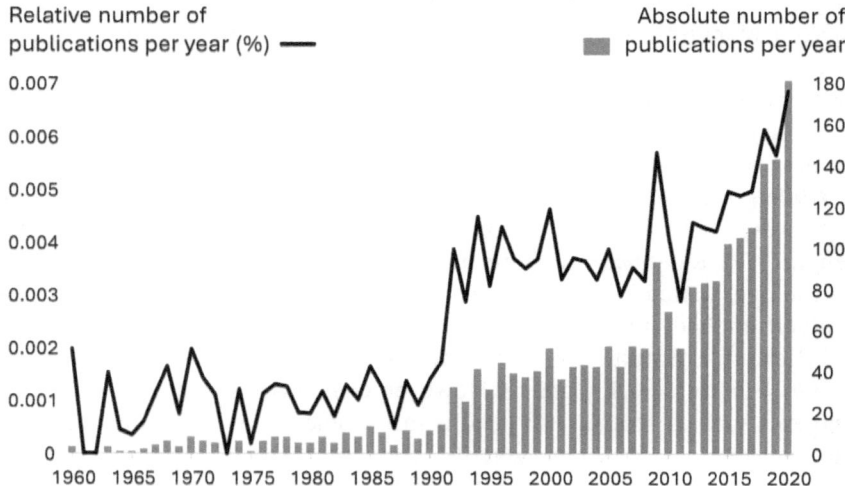

b) Publications about envy and other self-conscious emotions

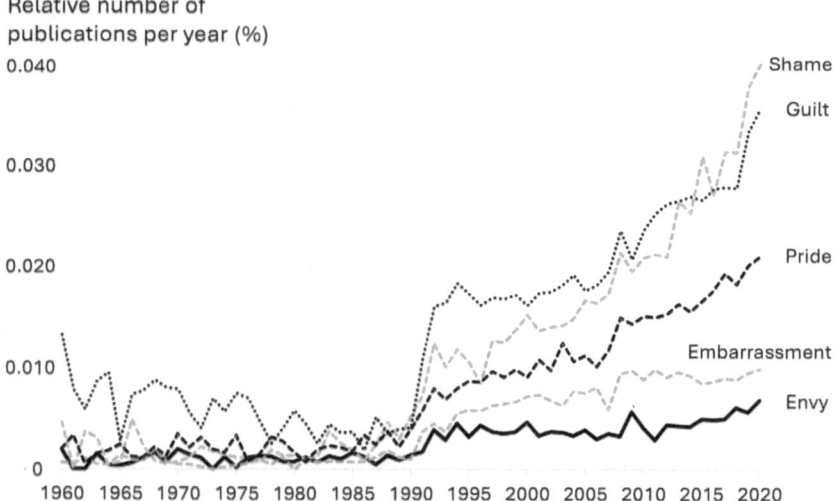

Figure 0.1 Trends in envy publications. Panel (a) shows the number of publications on envy per year as indexed by Web of Science Core Collection (SCI-EXPANDED; SSCI) from 1960 to 2020. The absolute number of publications corresponds to the number of yearly publications found in a "topic" search that includes title, abstract, and (automatically generated) keywords. The relative number of publications represents the percentage of publications on envy in all publications indexed by Web of Science of that year to normalize for general publication trends. Panel (b) shows the relative number of publications for envy and other self-conscious emotions using the same metric as in Panel (a).

so psychology studied (and to an extent experimented on) an ethical phenomenon without engaging significantly with philosophical perspectives.

As a result, these parallel investigations had *converged* on the same conclusion that there are (at least) two types of envy, benign and malicious, but *diverged* with regard to the kind of factors responsible for this envy's dual nature. Philosophers had individuated *focus of concern*—what agents are concerned with and value—as the main, though perhaps not the only, factor responsible for the type of envy we experience. When we are concerned with lack of the envied *object*, we tend to be motivated to pursue it, and thus to *level up* (push ourselves to the envied's level). When we are concerned with the *envied* having the envied object, we tend to be motivated to take it from them or destroy it altogether, and thus to *level down* (pull the envied down to our level). Psychologists instead had realized that a crucial factor in whether we feel benign or malicious envy is *perception of control over the outcome*: when the envier feels capable to improve their situation, they level up; when, instead, they feel "helpless" and "hopeless" (Miceli and Castelfranchi 2007) they level down.

My own taxonomy of envy emerged from intersecting these two variables into a two-by-two model, according to which there are four types of envy (or subtypes, depending on one's ontological commitments): emulative, inert, aggressive, and spiteful (Protasi 2021). I'm not committed to all the details of my view, but I strongly believe in the *interdisciplinary impetus* that produced it.

This volume represents a further attempt to move the study of envy in this direction (see also Lange and Protasi 2021). I invited psychologists and philosophers from a variety of subfields; some share their latest take on a topic they studied extensively, while others are new to envy and provide novel and refreshing insights. Almost all the chapters were first workshopped, then subject to a round of peer review among contributors, with additional comments from me. This process was fruitful—I believe—to introduce the authors to approaches and ideas that may have been unfamiliar to them. (I am thankful to contributors for bearing with my incessant bibliographic suggestions.) The authors conduct research at institutions across the world and come from different cultural and linguistic communities—such diversity being particularly important when thinking about a culturally complex emotion such as envy.

A ROADMAP (SOME POSSIBLE ITINERARIES)

In the next section, I provide detailed summaries of chapters following a narrative that makes sense to me; however, many different pathways are possible, so here's a roadmap to help the reader orient themselves:

Disciplines: Readers looking for chapters authored by *psychologists* should read chapters 1, 2, and 12; all others are authored by *philosophers*, but chapters 4 and 5 engage substantively with psychological literature and topics, chapter 9 provides an *history of economics* perspective, and chapters 4, 5, and 6 contain material of interest to the *historian of philosophy*.
Domains: Chapters 4, 5, 6, 7, and 8 focus on the *personal and ethical* sphere. Chapters 9 and 10 discuss *political* interactions. Chapter 3, 11, and 12 concern what Martha Nussbaum (2016) has called the "Middle Realm" of interpersonal yet non-intimate apolitical relations. Finally, chapters 1 and 2 provide bird's-eye views that look at envy at a *sociocultural* and *collective* level.
Varieties: Most chapters accept that there are different varieties of envy, but the ones whose arguments and analyses rely on that assumption the most are chapters 2, 3, 4, 5, 6, 7, 11, and 12.
Verdict: Is envy good or bad?! Chapters 4, 5, 7, and 8 mostly concern *negative* aspects of envy, while chapters 3, 6, 10 highlight its *positive* aspects. Chapters 1, 2, 9, 11, and 12 strive to be *neutral*.

Of course, there are endless possible ways of reading this volume, and I hope you'll create your own adventure! You might have noticed that I have not provided a *definition* of envy. That's no accident, since different authors define envy differently, even though there's lots of overlap. While no chapter is devoted *primarily* to analyzing the nature of envy *tout court*, I invite readers interested in definitional questions to look at the many excellent reviews of the psychological literature: Miceli and Castelfranchi (2007); Smith and Kim (2007); Van de Ven (2016); Lange et al. (2018); and Crusius et al. (2020). For reviews of the philosophical literature, see D'Arms (2017) and (Protasi) 2021.

THE STOPS: CHAPTER SYNOPSES

Envy's complexity is foregrounded in this volume, which starts with Patricia M. Rodriguez Mosquera's chapter: "A Sociocultural Perspective on Envy: On Covetous Desire, the Evil Eye, and the Social Regulation of Equality." Rodriguez Mosquera is a psychologist whose work demonstrates the importance of studying emotions in their social and cultural context. Her chapter elegantly reviews research in cultural anthropology and psychology, and analyzes this deeply relational emotion within the context of cultural networks of values, norms, and practices, which, on the one hand, fear and condemn envy and, on the other, consider it necessary for the social regulation of wealth, status, and power.

"Envy is as ubiquitous to social life as social comparison is," states Rodriguez Mosquera (24), and proceeds to present well-established relations between envy and social comparison processes, and envy's cognitive appraisals. She then reviews the influential work of cultural anthropologist George Foster, whose aforementioned 1972 paper is a rich and fascinating classic. Rodriguez Mosquera usefully summarizes central concepts he develops, such as the "limited good" (the cultural worldview according to which good fortune is scarce and distributed unequally); his understanding of envy along the two axes of fear and competition; the cultural practices of concealment, denial, symbolic sharing, and true sharing. She then presents ethnographic accounts by Amitav Ghosh, Richard Eves, Carolina Izquierdo and Allen Johnson, and Shu-Yuan Yang, which enrich and complicate the picture of envy. These studies were conducted in Mexico, Egypt, Papua New Guinea, Peru, the Philippines, Spain, and the United States, and include diverse economic and sociocultural systems, ranging from small preindustrial hunter-gatherer and subsistence agriculture communities to large, highly industrialized countries. Depending on economic and social factors, envy arises within or between households and social groups; it deters excessive accumulation of wealth and maintains social equality, or stimulates achievement and competition; it is feared and shunned, or hoped for and cultivated; it stems from perceptions of scarcity and limit, or of abundance and growth; it is connected with desire for keeping the status quo, or for changing it.

Rodriguez Mosquera concludes the chapter with an analysis of studies she and her collaborators conducted on Spanish and American subjects, showing that being envied is an *ambivalent* emotional experience, characterized by a mixture of pleasure and displeasure, and conditioned by cultural differences. Her *multicultural* portrait of envy confirms that, while being a cross-cultural emotion with stable defining features, envy is multifaceted and highly flexible with regard to its situational antecedents, motivational tendencies, and behavioral consequents.

As Rodriguez Mosquera highlights, the experience of being envied has been under-investigated in psychology. The second chapter, "How Envy and Being Envied Shape Social Hierarchies" by Jens Lange and Jan Crusius, contributes to filling this lacuna. Just like Rodriguez Mosquera (and Niels van de Ven, also a contributor to the volume), Lange and Crusius are central figures in the aforementioned psychological "boom" on envy; they have played a fundamental role in establishing the legitimacy of benign envy, for instance, by creating a dispositional benign and malicious envy scale (Lange and Crusius 2015). Here, they argue that envy regulates social hierarchies, in two ways: first, persons with higher social status elicit envy in those who have less; second, these lower-rank persons' envy elicits responses in higher-ranked persons. Thus, envying and being envied occurs in a dynamic relationship, whose complexity they astutely unravel in their contribution.

Lange and Crusius start from uncontroversial features of envy: the envier believes that the envied possesses something valuable that they lack, whether it's an object, an achievement, an advantage, a trait, or the like. This lack negatively impacts the envier's self-evaluation, and evidence shows that "the object's relevance often means higher social rank of the advantaged person" (42). Envy is a response to a threat to the fundamental social need for status and motivates people to overcome rank differentials. Envy is, thus, contrary to the traditional perception of envy as maladaptive, *functional*. But Lange and Crusius are careful to explain that this doesn't mean that envy is *always* adaptive, or good for one's well-being, either individually or collectively.

I can't do justice in this limited space to Lange and Crusius's nuanced and detailed analysis of the dynamic between envier and envied, but I'll mention that they divide it into four steps: first, rank is displayed and communicated by higher-status people; second, envy is manifested in lower-status people's emotional expressions and behavioral cues; third, in response to being envied, higher-ranked persons react with either approach or avoidance behavior; fourth, these responses may change the position of higher-ranked persons, starting the circle anew. Jointly, these four steps constitute the process through which envy and being envied shape social hierarchies. Of particular interest to scholars of social relations, in general, might be their discussion of two different strategies to attain social rank (prestige and dominance) and their interaction with kinds of envy (unsurprisingly, obnoxious higher-ranked people who communicate a domination strategy elicit malicious envy).

Each social circle we inhabit comes with its own envy dynamic, but envying and being envied in the ivory tower might be unexpectedly productive—or so Felipe Romero cleverly argues in chapter 3, "On the Epistemic Effects of Envy in Academia." Romero brings to the volume his interdisciplinary expertise in the social epistemology of research, approaching envy from a decision theoretic perspective. As abstract and detached as that may sound, I should warn you that some examples will feel unnervingly familiar!

After providing his account of envy and highlighting four possible strategies available to the envier (self-destruction, destruction, emulation, and construction), Romero considers traditional arguments against envy's negative consequences. First, he concedes that envy can decrease psychological well-being, and then moves to the idea that envy is collectively disadvantageous because it leads to a suboptimal allocation of resources. (Both of these lines of argument are developed in subsequent chapters.) Romero aims to show that this latter worry doesn't apply to academic envy, insofar as it's primarily concerned with contribution of knowledge. "Academics get rewarded for producing *epistemic goods*: scientific findings, theories, arguments, models, experimental designs, etc." (67). Priority rules determine who is considered most meritorious and who is awarded professional recognition and prestige in the form of eponymy and prizes, and, relatedly, material goods such as grants and better working conditions. Romero admits that this reward system is imperfect and that non-epistemic factors may influence and distort assessment of merit and prestige attributions; however, it's sustained by the academic community by taking tangible outputs such as publications as reliable indicators of epistemic value. Perceived disadvantage with regard to epistemic goods compared to a colleague in one's league is thus what triggers *academic envy*.

Epistemic goods, however, are public, non-exclusive, and cannot be destroyed, according to Romero, and thus, unlike in other workplaces where destructive and self-destructive envious behavior may actually reduce envy, the most effective strategies to overcome one's disadvantage and reduce envy in academia are collectively advantageous. I can't get into details here, but this is a very engaging part of the chapter, since Romero considers possible behaviors motivated by envy and shows their effectiveness, or lack thereof, including burning your envied colleague's car (please don't try this at home). He concludes by deriving some implications for the design of epistemic institutions and warning that it may be difficult to restructure institutions to reduce envy without severe epistemic drawbacks.

Romero's overall luminous approach to envy and its unexpected benefits for our intellectual community contrasts starkly with the dark portrait Íngrid Vendrell Ferran paints in chapter 4, "'I Could Have Been You': Existential Envy and the Self." Vendrell Ferran is an established scholar of the emotions in the continental tradition, who has written extensively about envy. Here, she draws from the rich phenomenological tradition, in particular Max Scheler, María Zambrano, and Walter Biemel, and from Miguel de Unamuno's existentialist works, to investigate the notion of *existential envy*, a globalizing form of envy where the object of envy is another person's entire being.[5]

While all envy derives from comparing oneself to a similar other, whose perceived superiority is in a domain relevant to our identity, this phenomenon is amped up in existential envy: after an initial stage in which the envier targets aspects of the envied that are relevant to the self, they become increasingly obsessed with the other's whole being. Existential envy arises when "strong feelings of an insurmountable inferiority, powerlessness, and despair appear connected to the counterfactual thought: 'I could have been you!'" (77). Because becoming another person is impossible, existential envy leads both to intense hostility toward the envied and a diminution in self-worth.

Aptly weaving together empirical evidence and philosophical accounts from the continental and analytic traditions, Vendrell Ferran distinguishes between different types of negative feelings felt by existential enviers, such as sense of disempowerment (already discussed by Salice and Montes Sánchez 2019), disadvantage, and helplessness and hopelessness. She also discusses three types of comparison, namely between the envier and the envied's *empirical selves*, where the envier compares biographical, social, and psychological actual features of themselves and the rival; between the envied's empirical self and the envier's *ideal self*, which is "configured by ideals, desires, and imaginings about the kind of person she would like to be" (84); and between the envier's own empirical and ideal selves, where the envier experiences a painful discrepancy between who they are and who they could have been and would like to be. This latter self-comparison is a moment of self-disclosure, which could be productive, but which, due to the perception that these possibilities are now foreclosed, becomes a source of pain, and of hostility toward the envied. This feeling of being so close yet so far away to one's ideal self explains the peculiar intensity of existential envy, which, Vendrell Ferran concludes, is also linked to low self-esteem, self-reproach, and self-deception.

The blurring of identity between the envier and the envied, lamented as a dangerous path to self-devouring envy by Vendrell Ferran, is instead prescribed as an antidote to envy altogether by Christina Chuang in chapter 5, "Envy, Compassion, and the Buddhist (No)Self." One of Chuang's research programs is comparative ethics between early modern philosophy (Hume, Hutcheson, and Spinoza) and Asian philosophy (Mencius and the ethical doctrines in the *Bhagavad Gita*). Her comparative expertise allows her to note that Western compassion, which is often prescribed as a remedy to envy, cannot address the root cause of the problem, because envy and compassion both presuppose a strong sense of the self.

Chuang starts by observing that envy and compassion (or pity)[6] are conceived as opposites in the Western philosophical tradition (as exemplified by Aristotle, *Rhetoric* II.9 1386b16, and Spinoza, *Ethics* IIId23–d24). While envy is a malevolent emotion caused by another person's good fortune, which motivates to rejoice of that person's misfortune, compassion is a benevolent emotion caused from another person's misfortune, which motivates to rejoice at another person's good fortune. However, they are both responses to the good or bad fortune of a similar and close other, whom we aren't indifferent to, but who's *distinct* from us. Against this understanding, she proposes a Buddhist-inspired approach that conceives of the self as flexible, impermanent, and interdependent. In Buddhism, clinging to the notion of self is the source of selfish desires and attachments, and ultimately of all suffering. The Buddhist compassionate person is motivated by a universal concern for humankind. *All suffering* is relevant to *all creatures* without mediation through a particular self, and yet not blindly: Buddhist compassion is infused with wisdom and knowledge of the true sources of our misery. Chuang's full picture of the *Bodhisattva* is more complex, but I need to save space for her original application of Buddhist compassion to envy management in clinical settings, in particular to cognitive behavioral therapy (CBT) approaches. Identifying dysfunctional thinking patterns is a crucial step in CBT, and the list of maladaptive beliefs connected to envy—Chuang highlights—is imbibed with egocentric considerations, attachment to values antithetical to Buddhism (such as high status), and inability to accept one's limitations and cultivate humility. After considering whether emulative envy could be spared Buddhist condemnation (the predictable answer is: no), the chapter ends with a thoughtful discussion of how self-compassion can be a balm for the peculiar sting of inert envy.[7]

Those who aren't persuaded by this radical change in how we think about the self and who feel more positive about envy might find Maria Silvia Vaccarezza and Ariele Niccoli's chapter "Let the Donkeys Be Donkeys: In Defense of Inspiring Envy" (chapter 6) uplifting. Vaccarezza and Niccoli situate envy in the context of an *exemplarist* account of moral progress, according to which we educate our character thanks, in part, to feeling appropriately toward moral exemplars. Following Linda Zagzebski (2010, 2015, 2017), philosophers have attributed a central role to *admiration* and other positive-affect emotional attitudes (adoration, elevation, awe, gratitude, and inspiration) for moral exemplars. Adding envy to this lofty list promises to provoke much eyebrow-raising, but Vaccarezza and Niccoli point out that encountering moral exemplars can trigger also negative-affect emotions such as shame, guilt, and envy, and have argued in past work that these unavoidable emotions can be valuable both intrinsically and instrumentally.

Here, they expand their argument by defending the role of *inspiring envy*. This is a form of benign envy that involves a desire to emulate a morally superior, envied person. However, inspiring envy is prone to the risk of *literal emulation*, risk which they illustrate brilliantly with Aesop's fable *The Donkey and the Pet Dog*: when a donkey attempts to gain favor by imitating a puppy (such as leaping toward the master and putting his feet on his shoulders) catastrophe and ruin for the poor donkey ensue. Outside of the allegory, literal emulation can lead to either complete failure, which causes painful feelings of powerlessness and lack of self-worth, and/or to a form of conformism, which jeopardizes moral integrity and practical autonomy. To avoid this self-defeating outcome, the authors set out to "identify under what conditions envy can fuel a process of affective and motivational transformation" (116). They appeal to an Aristotelian notion of practical wisdom, whereby the practically wise person inspires an *analogical* form of emulation, which defies attempts at literal emulation and encourages active and autonomous moral deliberation and self-improvement. Choosing the right person to emulate is shown to be an essential first step in this transformative journey: one should choose a person who acknowledges their shortcomings and strives to respond to reasons. Such a person is also more likely to respond constructively and compassionately to being envied. (Remember I told you there are many possible pathways to walk through in here? Consider juxtaposing inspiring to existential envy . . .)

Vaccarezza and Niccoli's fascinating analysis of a fruitful relation between envied and envier in the context of moral education finds a sharp and enlightening counterpoint in Vanessa Carbonell's chapter on "Malicious Moral Envy" (chapter 7) Carbonell's research is at the intersection of normative ethics, moral psychology, metaethics, and applied ethics. She has investigated moral agents, both ordinary and extraordinary (what Susan Wolf has dubbed "moral saints") and is interested in what moral agents are like and what morality demands of them.

Her chapter starts with a captivating case study: former US president Donald Trump's apparent envy for prominent immunologist Anthony Fauci. Carbonell convincingly argues that Trump felt for Fauci *malicious moral envy*, which she characterizes as an aversive reaction to a rival's moral properties or accomplishments, accompanied by a tendency to level-down the target by morally tarnishing or sabotaging them. (For some readers, the experience of reading Carbonell's description of Trump's feelings may provide a useful case study for a germane topic, namely schadenfreude—but maybe I'm projecting.) Independently from the particular case, Carbonell makes a compelling argument for malicious moral envy's existence in general. For someone whose self-esteem is bound up with their moral identity, it's natural to feel envy toward morally superior people. Sometimes, they'll be motivated to self-improve, as discussed by Vaccarezza and Niccoli, but, as Carbonell remarks, "self-improvement is hard and costly. If you cannot solve your problem by leveling yourself up, a remaining option is to level the person down. The motivation to tarnish moral standouts, to cut down the 'tall poppy,' is probably more common than we like to admit" (134). But there seems to be a tension: good people don't steal, spoil, sabotage, or engage in other behaviors malicious envy recommends. If the envier did any of those, they'd become *morally worse*! So, malicious moral envy seems self-defeating and puzzling: Does the envier want to be good or not? After considering some debunking explanations (such as that malicious enviers only envy moral virtue's *rewards*, including good reputation, or that they are simply akratic), Carbonell invites the reader to assume that malicious moral envy cannot be explained away so easily, because this assumption casts light on fraught features of morality. Drawing on previous explorations of moral sainthood and moral ambivalence, she suggests that *mild* malicious moral envy may help agents navigate the socially complex and constantly changing landscape of moral requirements.

Even though I contrasted Carbonell's chapter with Vaccarezza and Niccoli's, both of these chapters defend envy's potential to contribute positively to our ethical lives. Neal Tognazzini curbs our enthusiasm with "'You're Just Jealous!': On Envious Blame" (chapter 8): he uses his competence on moral responsibility and the ethics of blame to anatomize a seemingly deflective response to criticism ("You're just jealous!"), all the while charming the reader with case studies from pop-culture.

Wait, what's the difference between envy and jealousy?—you might be wondering. Tognazzini starts from this distinction, often obfuscated in everyday language. He adopts the view according to which envy is an aversive reaction to a *lack* of a valued object, while jealousy is an aversive reaction to a *loss* of a valued object. Through light-hearted, yet carefully dissected, examples, Tognazzini demonstrates that, even though speakers tend to use "jealous," sometimes they mean "envious." Tognazzini then asks: Assume the accusation is warranted and the criticism is truly motivated by envy or jealousy; intuitively, that seems problematic, but why?

The first explanation is based on the idea of criticism as a form of *testimony*, where envy might undermine the credibility of the blamer. He appeals to standard distinctions in the epistemology of testimony: when we wonder whether to believe someone, we consider two main factors, namely whether the speaker is sincere and competent. By analogy, "accusing a critic of jealousy or envy might be an attempt to impugn either the critic's sincerity or their competence" (152). However, this notion of criticism may be too "thin": criticisms often aren't just assertions (providing reasons to believe certain claims) but also rebukes (providing reasons to engage in certain actions). In this "expanded testimonial model," Tognazzini fruitfully compares "You're just jealous" with "Look who's talking!" and introduces a sophisticated taxonomy of *hypocritical* blamers. All of these varieties of hypocrisy, however, can be reduced to failures of sincerity or of competence and, thus, the expanded testimonial model accommodates also rebukes. Nevertheless, Tognazzini briefly considers an alternative model, in which envious blame is interpreted as an *abuse of power*: the blamer is just trying to knock a rival down, weaponizing blame as a "status-leveler" (159). On either model, accusing a critic of "jealousy" equates to painting them as ill-suited to moral conversations, because insincere, incompetent, or abusive. Tognazzini assumes a familiar stance—condemning envy as ethically perilous—through the novel connection with the moral psychology of blame.

Miriam Bankovsky's work sits at the intersection of political philosophy, political science, and economics. While her current main research project concerns how the family has been conceptualized in the history of economic thoughts, she isn't new to our topic, having published a prize-winning article on economic envy in 2018. (I'm putting to test here Romero's hypothesis that academic envy augments epistemic goodness.) In chapter 9, "The Fact of Envy: Trends in the History of Modern Economics," she outlines four concepts of envy that appear in modern economics and reflects on their significance for moral psychology. Economists haven't discussed envy as an individual moral disposition but, rather, as a matter of fact that's morally neutral, whose effects are studied because of their implications for production, consumption, and the distribution of resources. This consequentialist approach (broadly construed) doesn't preclude normative conclusions, which span over a variety of domains, from political institutions and business organizations to the family.

The first concept Bankovsky analyzes is envy in the welfarist tradition, according to which envy is a *mere preference for the "bundle" of goods* that another agent has. This technical notion was introduced so that theories of distributive justice would be efficient (in the sense of getting the most utility out of a given set of resources), thereby permitting for "objective" interpersonal comparisons of utility, while preserving the possibility of satisfying agent preferences in a fair and equitable way. The second concept is envy as a *negative consumption externality*, developed by behavioral economists, according to which envy decreases the agent's well-being and can be represented as a disutility. The third concept is envy as a *disposition* whose effects can be manipulated to achieve certain objectives. Behavioral and experimental economics from the 1980s onward studied how envious people behaved in real life, either through lab simulations or via anthropological and sociological studies, but also included manipulation of incentives to see whether envy could support certain social positive objectives. Finally, the fourth and perhaps oddest concept is that of envy as a *commodity in families*, where children's envy is moderated by a parent who seeks to maximize familial income.

This chapter will prove to be an invaluable resource for those who approach moral psychology from an interdisciplinary perspective but who, like me, aren't well versed in economics, since Bankovsky explains complex notions in a simple yet precise way. It also helps the reader situate the discussion of class envy that takes place in the following contribution.

Alfred Archer, Alan Thomas, and Bart Engelen have collaborated on two ambitious and wide-ranging interdisciplinary research programs: one (with Niels van de Ven) aimed to identify moral exemplars and their role in moral education; the other investigates how inequality affects well-being, with particular attention to the role played by shame, envy, and anxiety. Their chapter "The Politics of Envy: Outlaw Emotions in Capitalist Societies" (chapter 10) stems from this latter program and tackles a classic topic: the idea that economic egalitarians adopt a "politics of envy." The usual response to this damning accusation is to deny either that egalitarianism is motivated by envy, or that envy is always malicious. But our contributors' original and thought-provoking answer is that *both sides of the political spectrum* promote envy, but one type of envy is dictated by the emotional regimes of capitalistic societies, while the other is an outlaw emotion that helps us recognize injustice.

After a brisk review of the empirical literature on envy and the philosophical debate on envy and egalitarianism, Archer, Thomas, and Engelen introduce the notion of *emotional regime* (the "set of normative emotions and the official rituals, practices, and emotives that express and inculcate them"; Reddy 2001, 129), and ask: what is the emotional regime of capitalist societies? They define a capitalist society as one in which a minority controls the major means of production, so that they monopolize the terms on which other people labor for a wage. How could this system be popular?! Even accounting for material incentives and fear of unemployment or poverty, more seems to be needed "to generate the kind of active engagement and voluntary sacrifices that are increasingly required from all wage earners" (185). Scholars have suggested a variety of ideals contributing to such a support, and the authors themselves have a book in progress on a comprehensive account of capitalistic emotional regimes. Here, they focus on envy, admiration, and emulation for the rich. Drawing on Adam Smith's analysis in *The Theory of Moral Sentiments*, they show that in a society where the rich flaunt their wealth, they receive more attention and social approval.[8] Hoping to become rich is a crucial drive to engage in the labor market, and admiration and envy for the rich play a key role in ensuring the stability of capitalist societies. Thus, those who endorse capitalism cannot condemn the "politic of envy" without hypocrisy. Envy for the rich is an *outlaw emotion* (Jaggar 1989), which rejects the emotional dictates of capitalism.

Envy for a richer person is a typical case of envy. A much less typical one is explored by Alison Duncan Kerr in "To Envy an Algorithm" (chapter 11). Kerr is the author (with Justin D'Arms 2008) of an authoritative and opinionated review of envy in the philosophical tradition, but has turned to investigating artificial intelligence. Her chapter begins with the engrossing and heartbreaking story of professional Go player Lee Sedol's crushing defeat at the hands—or should I say circuits—of computer program Alpha Go. Kerr asks: Is it possible to feel fitting envy toward an *artificial intelligence*?

AI's presence is ubiquitous and deeply embedded, if often unnoticed, in our reality, but we rarely emotionally interact with most of it. However, once Kerr presents the details of Sedol and AlphaGo's match, it's hard to doubt the intensity of the feelings that Sedol experienced: he went from being quite confident in his victory to so dejected that he decided to retire from professional

Go play. But while it's not hard to imagine that one could feel envy toward a non-sentient being (much great sci-fi is premised on the possibility of feeling anger and love and lust toward robots—not to mention news about AI "girlfriends"[9]), it's questionable whether that envy can be *appropriate*. Thus, Kerr carefully reviews the traditional assessments of envy (whether it can be fitting, warranted, beneficial, and moral), to show that envy for AIs meets at least the first two conditions and, in some varieties, even the latter two. She contrasts Sedol's envy for AlphaGo with cases in the vicinity (anger at vending machines—which can be intense but is unfitting—and jealousy at a dog—which may be fitting but also enjoys a possibility for reciprocity that is unmatched in emotions toward AIs) and then proceeds to argue that this type of envy is not only understandable but also fitting. Sedol and AlphaGo were arguably genuine competitors (as perceived by the sentient beings involved in the competition), and being the best at Go was likely to be, for Sedol, a self-relevant goal of the sort that usually induces envy toward superior others. The paper ends with an absorbing analysis of the different stages that Sedol's envy might have gone through. Adopting my taxonomy of envy (Protasi 2016, 2021), she argues that Sedol might have first felt emulative, then inert envy.

Ending this volume with envy toward AIs would have been apt, a nod at a posthuman future nicely contrasting with our initial journey among diverse human communities, some of which are still immersed in traditional preindustrial ways of life. But I decided to give Niels van de Ven the last word with his chapter "The Envious Consumer" (chapter 12) given that his research was central in advancing the functional approach to envy in social psychology, and given also that his chapter nicely summarizes much of the empirical evidence on envy that is relevant to the moral psychology of envy.

"All you need is envy"—this is how a global marketing agency starts a report on how brands can position themselves to sell more products. But it has to be the *right* kind of envy! Benign envy is considered a central motivation to buy goods, and thus marketers aim to increase it in consumers, while malicious envy increases dissatisfaction with the brand or product, and so marketers aim to decrease it. Thus, the chapter begins with a general overview of benign envy, and then proceeds to discuss some studies in marketing research in particular. It's interesting to see how investigations into this specific field shed light on general connections between envy and self-esteem, and envy and competition, among others. Van de Ven goes on to review evidence concerning many topics that are discussed throughout the volume, such as the circumstances that give rise to each type of envy and whether people want to be envied. Particularly relevant to the political dimensions of envy is his remark that, while envy usually thrives in small differences, that doesn't mean that we never envy the super-rich, who "still sets a standard for others that 'trickles down' to people's desires at lower levels of income" (222).

This desire to emulate the rich and engage in conspicuous consumption and thus increase one's social status—a phenomenon that we've seen analyzed in critical terms by Archer, Thomas, and Engelen—leads Van de Ven to discuss positional goods, which derive their value from their relative position in a ranking, which include not only status and consumer products but also grades in school, intelligence, fitness, attractiveness, and more.[10] The essay ends with suggestions about how some empirical evidence might aid political philosophers as they ask normative questions about envy and inequality (such as *whether* envy for the rich is rational or justified, or whether it should be repressed or encouraged).

FINAL THOUGHTS, AND MUCH GRATITUDE

Envy, as perhaps all emotions, has many faces, many shades, many ways of manifesting itself and moving us. It can push us to strive to be better and pursue higher and harder achievements, as Lange and Crusius, Romero, Vaccarezza and Niccoli, and Van de Ven, especially, highlight. It can send us sulking in a corner and wallow in despair, as Vendrell Ferran, Chuang, and Kerr warn us about. It can motivate us to steal the spotlight, as Carbonell describes in the Trump case study, but also to sabotage the envied and take away envied goods, including richness amassed without merit, as Archer, Thomas and Engelen suggest. It can tempt us into spoiling someone's joy, as the superstition of the evil eye in many cultures attest to, as Rodriguez Mosquera illustrates. Its effects can be barely noticeable, as in the clouding of moral judgment analyzed by Tognazzini, or it can impact a family, a firm, or an entire economic system, as recounted by Bankovsky.

But, in all its forms, envy is a painful and powerful passion that derives from the necessary mechanism of social comparison, from the human tendency to look obliquely at what our peers are, have and are doing: how do we stack up against one another? Even if it makes us uncomfortable to feel it, because it reminds of others' superior standing, envy is normal and functional. Shunning our envious feelings altogether may be impossible (unless one reforms one's conception of the self as dramatically as Chuang invites us to do), but we can shape them and channel them toward its most productive and fruitful expressions and forms.

And sometimes contrary emotions, such as gratitude (Klein 1957) are appropriate instead. I'm grateful to series editor Mark Alfano for entrusting me with a component of his ambitious and important project on the moral psychology of the emotions; he strikes the perfect balance between attentive and prompt, on the one hand, and relaxed and reassuring, on the other. I'm also grateful to the rest of the editorial team at Rowman and Littlefield, including Dhara Snowden, Frankie Mace and Deni Remsberg. Finally, I'm immensely grateful to all the contributors for having shared their expertise and insights on envy; for having increased my awareness of its drawbacks and faults, but also of its benefits and virtues; for having widened the scope of my knowledge of envy notions across space, time and traditions; and for having collaborated with each other generously. They graciously forgave my occasional organizational mishaps, and tolerated the deluge of correspondence (and its *emphatic* **formatting**!) I subjected them to. Most importantly, I thank them all for the conscientiousness and integrity with which they approached each phase of the workshopping and revision process. I appreciate that writing for an edited volume is a peculiar process, to which one is invited on the basis of one's competence, but that also requires submitting to requests for changes one may not always agree with. I endeavored to walk a fine line between respecting the contributors' voices and views, and attempting to help them achieve the best possible version of their arguments. While I can't be sure I was able to reach this outcome, I'm really happy with the quality of the chapters you are about to read.[11]

NOTES

1. For a discussion of the role envy plays in loving relationships, see Protasi (2021, chapter 4). Vendrell Ferran's analysis of existential envy in this volume is also illuminating with regard to a certain type of intense friendships, especially same-gender ones.

2. For the difference between emulative or benign envy and admiration, see Van de Ven, Zeelenberg, and Pieters (2009, 2011, 2012); Van de Ven (2017); and Protasi (2019, 2021).

3. For a review of many historical accounts of envy, see Protasi (2021, appendix).

4. Figures, titles, and methodological explanation were provided by Jan Crusius, who very kindly and generously searched for these data for my sake.

5. Thinking about envy as involving a desire to be the other person is also present in the psychoanalytic tradition. Particularly relevant to the phenomenon described by Vendrell Ferran is the Lacanian analysis of Margaret Atwood's novel *The Robber Bride* by Joan Wyatt (1988), which is intended as a contribution in feminist psychoanalytic scholarship.

6. Whether pity or compassion are different emotions is a vexed question. Neither Aristotle nor Spinoza draw the distinction.

7. The suggestion that compassion and love may be antidotes to envy isn't new, but Chuang's more radical solution is, in my view, more appealing, since it bypasses entirely what I've called the paradox of love and envy (namely that the same conditions in which love thrives also give rise to envy; see Protasi 2017 and Protasi 2021,

chapter 4). Of course, it comes at the obvious cost of a significant alteration of how we understand our mind and/or requires an arduous spiritual training.

8. It's worth noting that, while Smith assumes these are features of "mankind," in fact they are socially and culturally specific, as the anthropological research reviewed in Rodriguez Mosquera's chapter shows: not in all unequal societies the rich boast their fortune, for fear of arousing envy that is *too* malicious and destructive.

9. For example, Kayla Kibbe's "Men in China Are Falling in Love with their AI Girlfriend," *InsideHook*, December 23, 2020, https://www.insidehook.com/daily_brief/tech/men-in-china-falling-in-love-with-ai-girlfriend.

10. In a forthcoming paper (Protasi 2022) I argue that positional goods are much more widespread than we realize, and also that social comparison plays a huge role in assessment of goodness. Consequently, envy plays a fundamental role in safeguarding our happiness.

11. I thank Jan Crusius, Gen Eickers, Barrett Emerick, Shen-yi Liao, Kengo Miyazono, and Birgitte Necessary for their very helpful and prompt feedback on previous versions of this introduction. It is dedicated to the memory of Maria Miceli, a brilliant researcher and a kind mentor.

REFERENCES

Aristotle. (fourth c. BCE) 2007. *On Rhetoric: A Theory of Civic Discourse*, trans. and ed. G. A. Kennedy. New York: Oxford University Press.

Bankovsky, Miriam. 2018. "Excusing Economic Envy: On Injustice and Impotence." *Journal of Applied Philosophy* 35 (2): 257–79.

Ben-Ze'ev, Aaron. 1990. "Envy and jealousy." *Canadian Journal of Philosophy* 20 (4): 487–516.

———. 2000. *The Subtlety of Emotions*. Cambridge, MA: MIT Press.

Crusius, Jan, Manuel F. Gonzalez, Jens Lange, and Yochi Cohen-Charash. 2020 "Envy: An Adversarial Review and Comparison of Two Competing Views." *Emotion Review* 12 (1): 3–21.

D'Arms, Justin. 2017. "Envy," *The Stanford Encyclopedia of Philosophy* (Spring 2017 Edition), Edward N. Zalta (ed.), https://plato.stanford.edu/archives/spr2017/entries/envy/

D'Arms, Justin, and Alison Duncan Kerr. 2008. "Envy in the Philosophical Tradition," in *Envy: Theory and Research*, edited by Richard H. Smith, 39–59. New York: Oxford University Press.

La Caze, Marguerite. 2001. "Envy and Resentment." *Philosophical Explorations* 4 (1): 31–45.

Frye, Harrison P. 2016. "The Relation of Envy to Distributive Justice." *Social Theory and Practice* 42 (3): 501–24.

Foster, George M. 1972. "The Anatomy of Envy: A Study in Symbolic Behavior." *Current Anthropology* 13: 165–202.

Green, Joshua E. 2013. "Rawls and the Forgotten Figure of the Most Advantaged: In Defense of Reasonable Envy toward the Superrich." *American Political Science Review* 107 (1): 123–38.

Klein, Melanie. 1957. *Envy and Gratitude: A Study of Unconscious Forces*. New York: Basic Books.

Lange, Jens, and Sara Protasi. 2021. "An Interdisciplinary Perspective on the Value of Envy." *Review of Philosophy and Psychology*: 1–20. https://doi-org.ezproxy.ups.edu:2443/10.1007/s13164-021-00548-3.

Lange, Jens, Lisa Blatz, and Jan Crusius. 2018. "Dispositional Envy: A Conceptual Review." In *The SAGE Handbook of Personality and Individual Differences*, edited by Virgil Zeigler–Hill and Todd Shackelford, 424–40. Los Angeles: SAGE.

Miceli, Maria, and Cristiano Castelfranchi. 2007. "The envious mind." *Cognition and Emotion* 21 (3): 449–79.

Nussbaum, Martha. 2016. *Anger and Forgiveness: Resentment, Generosity, Justice*. New York: Oxford University Press.

Parrott, W. Gerald. 1991. "The Emotional Experiences of Envy and Jealousy." In *The Psychology of Envy and Jealousy*, edited by Peter Salovey, 3–30. New York: Guilford Press.

Parrott, W. Gerrod, and Richard H. Smith. 1993. "Distinguishing the Experiences of Envy and Jealousy." *Journal of Personality and Social Psychology* 64: 906–20.

Protasi, Sara. 2016. "Varieties of Envy." *Philosophical Psychology* 29 (4): 535–49.

———. 2017. "Invideo et amo: On Envying the Beloved." *Philosophia* 47: 1765–84.

———. 2019. "Happy Self-Surrender and Unhappy Self–Assertion." In *The Moral Psychology of Admiration*, edited by Alfred Archer and André Grahle, 45–60. London: Rowman & Littlefield International.

———. 2021. *The Philosophy of Envy*. Cambridge; New York: Cambridge University Press.

———. 2022. "The Things We Envy: Fitting Envy and Human Goodness." In *Fittingness*, edited by Christopher Howard and Richard Rowland. New York: Oxford University Press.

Rawls, John. *A Theory of Justice*. Cambridge, MA: Harvard University Press.

Salice, Alessandro, and Alba Montes Sánchez. 2019. "Envy and Us." *European Journal of Philosophy* 27 (1): 227–42.

Schoeck, Helmut. 1969. *Envy: A Theory of Social Behaviour*. San Diego: Harcourt, Brace & World.

Silver Silver, Maury, and John Sabini. 1978. "The Social Construction of Envy." *Journal for the Theory of Social Behaviour* 8: 313–32.

Smith, Richard H., and Sung Hee Kim. 2007. "Comprehending Envy." *Psychological Bulletin* 133: 46–64.

Smith, Richard H., W. Gerrod Parrott, Ed F. Diener, Richard H. Hoyle, and Sung Hee Kim. 1999. "Dispositional Envy." *Personality and Social Psychology Bulletin* 25: 1007–20.

Spinoza, Baruch. (1677) 1949. *Ethics*, ed. and trans. J. Gutmann. New York: Hafner Publishing Company.

Taylor, Gabriele E. 1988. "Envy and Jealousy: Emotions and Vices." *Midwest Studies in Philosophy* 13: 233–49.
———. 2006. *Deadly Vices*. Oxford: Oxford University Press.
Thomason, Krista K. 2015. "The Moral Value of Envy." *The Southern Journal of Philosophy* 53 (1): 36–53.
Van de Ven, Niels. 2016. "Envy and Its Consequences: Why It Is Useful to Distinguish Between Benign and Malicious Envy." *Social and Personality Psychology Compass* 10 (6): 337–49.
———. 2017. "Envy and Admiration: Emotion and Motivation Following Upward Social Comparison." *Cognition and Emotion* 31 (1): 193–200.
van de Ven, Niels, Marcel Zeelenberg, M., and Rik Pieters. 2009. "Leveling Up and Down: The Experiences of Benign and Malicious Envy." *Emotion* 9: 419–29. DOI: 10.1037/a0015669.
———. 2011. "Why Envy Outperforms Admiration." *Personality and Social Psychology Bulletin* 37: 784–95.
———. 2012. "Appraisal patterns of envy and related emotions." *Motivation and Emotion* 36: 195–204.
Zagzebski, Linda. 2010. "Exemplarist Virtue Theory." *Metaphilosophy* 41 (1–2): 41–57.
———. 2015. "Admiration and the Admirable." *Aristotelian Society* 89 (1): 205–21.
———. 2017. *Exemplarist Moral Theory*. Oxford: Oxford University Press.

Chapter 1

A Sociocultural Perspective on Envy

On Covetous Desire, the Evil Eye, and the Social Regulation of Equality

Patricia M. Rodriguez Mosquera

The Spanish philosopher Miguel de Unamuno elevated envy to the realm of morality and the sacred by defining envy as the experience of *hambre espiritual* (i.e., spiritual hunger, Unamuno 1998, 56). Moreover, the philosopher's classification of envy as a type of "hunger" evokes images of intense and unfulfilled desires. Thus, for Unamuno, envy is akin to a physiological craving, and, at the same time, an emotional experience that transcends ordinary life. Although Unamuno wrote about envy in the context of early twentieth-century Spanish culture, his definition of envy is supported by research in both psychology and cultural anthropology. Indeed, a key characteristic of the subjective experience of envy is an intense desire for an object, attribute, or skill that another possesses. In addition, many cultures place envy in the realm of the sacred and magical by promoting beliefs on the power of the gaze, or evil eye, through which envious feelings operate to harm others.[1]

This chapter presents a sociocultural approach to envy based on extant research on culture and envy in cultural anthropology and psychology. It starts with a short section on the cognitive, affective, and motivational structure of envy as an individual emotional experience. Next, research on envy in cultural anthropology is discussed, starting with the pioneering work by Foster in the 1960s and reviewing subsequent work till the present day. The following section focuses on research on sociocultural influences on envy in psychology, which is scarce compared to ethnographic work on envy. Finally, the chapter ends with some conclusions about the multiple facets of envy across cultures.

ENVY AS A PSYCHOLOGICAL EXPERIENCE: ON THE NATURE OF COVETOUS DESIRE

Envy is as ubiquitous to social life as social comparison is. Research in psychology has consistently shown that social comparison processes are *necessary* for envy to occur (for an overview, see Smith and Kim 2007). Both upward and downward social comparison processes are relevant to envy, with the former being associated with feeling envious of another and the latter with feeling that one is the target of another person's envy. Most research in psychology, however, has focused on envy as the consequence of an upward social comparison that is unflattering to the self with the resulting feelings of envy toward another person (for exceptions, see Lee et al. 2018; Liu et al. 2019; Liu, Zhu, and Lam 2020; Parrott and Rodriguez Mosquera 2008; Romani, Grappi, and Bagozzi 2016; Scott et al. 2015; and Van de Ven, Zeelenberg, and Pieters 2010). This research has not taken a cultural perspective on envy but has, rather, focused on understanding the cognitive, affective, motivational, and behavioral profile of envy as an individual emotional experience.

In terms of envy's cognitive profile, this research has demonstrated that three cognitive appraisals are necessary for envy to be felt. First, the cognitive appraisal of lacking an object or quality that another person has. Second, the cognitive appraisal that the object or attribute one lacks is self-relevant (i.e., important for the person's self-image or/and social status). Third, the cognitive appraisal of coveting what another possesses, which gives envy its affective signature as *covetous desire*. Further, in relation to envy's motivational structure, research in psychology has distinguished between a *benign* and a *malicious* form of envy. Malicious envy is characterized by ill-will motivations, for example, wanting to harm the envied other or the coveted object, whereas benign envy is characterized by more prosocial motivations, such as wanting to be close to the envied other (Lange and Crusius 2015; Parrott and Smith 1993; Smith et al. 1999; Van de Ven, Zeelenberg, and Pieters 2009; for a philosophical approach on types of envy, see Protasi 2021). Importantly however, Lange, Paulhus, and Crucius (2018) found that both types of envy are associated with socially undesirable behaviors, with the difference being that malicious envy is associated with more blatantly aggressive behaviors such as taking revenge in nasty ways.[2]

Cultural anthropological work on envy will be discussed next. This work also defines envy as a covetous emotion rooted in social comparison processes. However, ethnographic work on envy has not distinguished between two types of envy at the level of individual experience since its focus has been on envy's meanings and social consequences in particular cultures.

ENVY AND THE "LIMITED GOOD"

In cultural anthropology, George M. Foster pioneered work on envy with his field work in the Spanish-speaking community of Tzintzuntzan, Mexico, between 1958 and 1963. According to Foster, all cultures need to deal with the social reality that success and achievement are inherently relational and breed social competition and envy. Thus, Foster viewed envy as a pan-cultural emotion and developed the concept of the "limited good" to explain how the emotion operates across cultures (Foster 1965a, 1965b, 1967, 1972).

The *limited good* is a cultural ethos, or world view. At the heart of this ethos is the cultural belief that wealth, resources, status, power, and more generally good fortune, are not unlimited and available in equal quantities to all individuals. Consequently, an increase in the wealth or status of an individual or family is believed to happen at the expense of the wealth/status of others in a community. The serious implication of these zero-sum beliefs is that the good fortune of some can disrupt a community's social structure, especially if the social structure is based on cultural values that promote egalitarianism. In his ethnographic work in Tzintzuntzan, Foster documented how the threat of other's *envidia*—the Spanish term for envy-deters the accumulation of wealth and other resources by one individual or family in the community. In other words, in Tzintzuntzan, the ethos of the limited good served to maintain social equality in wealth, resources, and status by encouraging the fear of others' envy, a fear central to Foster's *fear axis of envy* (Foster 1965b, 1972).

Foster defined the fear axis of envy in terms of the cultural practices (or "cultural forms," Foster 1972, 175) that individuals in a culture use to *reduce* actual or potential envy in others, in particular, *concealment, denial, symbolic sharing*, and *true sharing*. Concealment refers to hiding behaviors, for example, not discussing one's good health with others or not displaying an object believed to be wanted by others (e.g., jewelry; a property). Concealment as a cultural practice is intimately related to the evil eye, a cultural expression of the fear of envy important to many cultures (Dundes 1992). The evil eye symbolizes the power of an individual's gaze that is infused with envious feelings. At the heart of the evil eye is the belief that gazing at a coveted object, or at the person who possesses the coveted object, can cause misfortune or illness to the person who is envied. Further, denial includes modesty and other behaviors aimed at reducing the worth of an object in the eyes of others, for example, denying the beauty or financial value of an object as an attempt to symbolically express that the object is not worth the envy of others. Symbolic sharing involves two types of behavior: verbal offers to share and giving a token (e.g., a gift) that stands in place for the coveted object. Finally, true sharing means to literally give away part, or all, of the coveted object to others. This latter coping strategy is only used when concealment, denial, or symbolic sharing have failed.

Although Foster proposed that the limited good ethos and associated fear of envy should be present across societies, he did expect differences in terms of their economic origins. His expectations for less wealthy societies were confirmed by his ethnographic work in Tzintzuntzan where the limited good ethos was rooted in the hardships involved in trying to ensure that one's basic needs are covered. Thus, the real scarcity of resources in Tzintzuntzan fueled its inhabitants' fear of envy when they accumulated wealth or possessed a valued object. For wealthier societies, however, Foster expected the greater availability of material resources to increase a cultural emphasis on competition and achievement in social relations. This cultural emphasis would, in turn, create a social reality in which individuals would expect that everyone wants to succeed and therefore envies others' success. Moreover, Foster expected this cultural emphasis on competition and achievement to also create an additional envy axis based on the *enjoyment* of others' envy: the *competitive axis of envy*. Although Foster did not provide systematic ethnographic support for these expectations about envy in wealthier societies, psychological research to be presented in a later section has shown the connection between cultural values and the enjoyment of being envied.

Foster pioneered work on envy in cultural anthropology and placed envy as an important object of inquiry for cultural anthropologists. Later ethnographic research has mostly focused on Foster's fear axis of envy, revealing new ways in which the fear of others' envy operates across cultures. This later cultural anthropological work has also discovered the limitations of Foster's concept of the limited good by showing that the zero-sum ethos is not a pan-cultural phenomenon, starting with the work by Amitav Ghosh that will be discussed next.

ENVY, ASPIRATIONS, AND THE POSSIBILITY OF GROWTH

Amitav Ghosh's field work in the Egyptian village of Naçaawy (a pseudonym), province of Beheira, revealed new cultural facets of envy, or *hasad* in Arabic, the language spoke in Naçaawy (Ghosh 1983). At the time of Ghosh's field work, the village of Naçaawy had a population of 1,700 living in 250 households. The most important social unit in this community was a household, which typically included extended family. In Naçaawy, despite a strong cultural emphasis on cooperation, reciprocity, and egalitarianism, social status based on landholding created two social groups: those who had enough resources to be self-sufficient and those who needed the support of others. These two social groups were referred to by the inhabitants of Naçaawy as the "comfortable people" and the "needy people," respectively (Ghosh 1983, 212). Importantly, this social structure determined the objects that were seen as worthy of others' envy and the cultural practices believed to be effective to prevent this envy.

Owning land allowed households to cultivate it for profit (i.e., to sell in local markets) as well as for feeding their household, what enabled a household to be self-sufficient and, at the same time, accumulate wealth to invest in livestock. Because livestock could also be sold for profit, having livestock represented the possibility for a household's wealth to grow, thereby making livestock the preeminent *object* of *hasad* in Naçaawy. Furthermore, *hasad* was culturally viewed to be an inter-group, and not a within-group phenomenon, in Naçaawy. That is, envy was expected among households, but not among members of the same household. This cultural perspective on envy deterred competition and ensured cooperation among family members. In other words, removing envy from the familial sphere protected the economic productivity of the household.

Furthermore, envy among households was not only expected; it was also feared. In fact, the envy of other households for one's livestock was feared to such an extent that houses were built in Naçaawy to allow for the cultural practice of *concealment*. In particular, houses were built with very small windows to protect them from prying eyes and the interior of houses—where livestock was always kept—could never be seen when entering a house. Interestingly, it was those with more wealth and status, the landowners or "comfortable ones" (Ghosh 1983, 212) that were most suspected of being competitive with each other and feel envious of each other. To reduce potential competition among the "comfortable" households, there was a strong cultural norm in Naçaawy against feeling envy toward others. This strong cultural norm was sustained by cultural practices that aimed to let others know that one does not envy them, for example, by avoid complimenting another. Moreover, envy was elevated in Naçaawy to the realm of morality because of envy's cultural associations with the *moral emotions* of hate and resentment. Indeed, a shared cultural belief in this community was that feeling frequent envy leads to resentment and hate toward others. Taken together, these cultural beliefs, norms, and practices about envy served to reduce competition in social relations and preserved the stability of Naçaawy's social structure.

Ghosh's research on envy supports, challenges, and extends Foster's work on envy (Foster 1972). First, Ghosh's findings regarding concealment align with Foster's findings on this cultural practice. In both ethnographies, *concealment* emerged as the preferred cultural practice to manage the envy of others. Second, in Foster's ethnographic work in Tzintzuntzan, the fear of others' envy was maintained by a *zero-sum view* of wealth and resources. In contrast, fear of envy was maintained in Naçaawy by the opposite cultural view that greater wealth and resources are *potentially available for all*. Third, the fact that a limited good ethos was not present in Naçaawy's also means that envy had a more positive cultural meaning in Naçaawy than in Tzintzuntzan. Although Ghosh reported a real concern for the regulation of others' envy in social interactions in Naçaawy, others' envy also represented *possibilities for improvement* and *aspirations*. Thus, Ghosh's research also extends Foster's research by documenting envy's positive consequences for the self and one's family.

Finally, Ghosh's work also showed that the aspirational side of envy was made possible by a stable economy, what raises important questions about how culture and economic systems interact to affect envy. What could happen if economic changes disrupt the everyday life of cultural communities? Would cultural meanings and practices surrounding envy be affected? Would economic changes increase, or perhaps decrease, the fear of others' envy? The cultural anthropological work discussed in the next section provides answers to these important questions.

ENVY AS A RESPONSE TO ECONOMIC CHANGES

Richard Eves studied envy among the Lelet, a rural subsistence farming community in inland Papua New Guinea (Eves 2000). At the time of Eves' field work, the Lelet community had approximately 500 people living across four different villages. The sociopolitical history of the Lelet is different than those of other inland villages in Papua New Guinea. In particular, the Lelet resisted pressures to move to the coast, as other inland communities did, and successfully managed to market their produce at major towns in the region. This led to the Lelet becoming progressively more prosperous than coastal communities since the 1980s. Eves discovered an association between the Lelet's new-found economic prosperity and an *increased worry about being envied* and being harmed by envy, especially by those living in coastal communities. However, what explains this connection between an increase in a community's wealth and an increase in the fear of others' envy?

Eves explained this link in terms of economic changes and prosperity interfering with the Lelet's cultural traditions. In particular, an increase in wealth made it difficult for the Lelet to engage in traditional cultural practices of *concealment* and *giving* (gift exchange) to regulate the potential envy of others. Among the Lelet, wealth was expected to only be displayed in specific social contexts characterized by clear cultural norms for social interaction, for example, funerals. Furthermore, giving among the Lelet also occurred in carefully controlled ways and by only giving as much as it was possible for a recipient to return. This cultural practice of giving aimed at avoiding shame in the recipient of a gift. However, the community's economic prosperity led to the possession of new objects (e.g., cars) and to less social control over the display of these objects and a greater social inequality in acts of giving and receiving.

Carolina Izquierdo and Allen Johnson (2007) also related an increase in the fear of others' envy to economic changes experienced by the Matsigenka community of the Peruvian Amazon, an Arawakan-speaking community. This ethnographic research was based on illness narratives collected in field work in the 1970s and in 1996 to 2004. At the time of the second field work, the total population of the Matsikenga was between 10,000 and 12,200 individuals. Izquierdo and Johnson's research focused on the Matsigenka communities of Shimaa and Kamisea, with each community having an average population of 250 to 300 individuals. In addition to facing economic changes, the Matsigenka also faced a major demographic change when Evangelical missionary outreach led to the creation of larger settlements, which required the Matsigenka to create new forms of social organization (e.g., the creation of communal meeting places and formalized political structures). An additional change the Matsikenga faced was the presence of oil companies operating in the Peruvian Amazon region, which introduced new forms of employment, a cash economy, and new diseases. Izquierdo and Johnson documented how these changes led to increased stress among the Matsikenga about the well-being and future of their communities, and they investigated how this increased stress affected the cultural life and practices of the Matsikenga.

To this end, Izquierdo and Johnson collected 136 illness narratives provided by 95 community members (53 adults, 36 children, and 6 adolescents; for details of other methods used see Izquierdo and Johnson 2007). Analyses of these narratives revealed three ways in which increased stress expressed itself in changes in cultural life. First, there was an increase in competition for resources among community members. Second, there was an increase in the *fear of others' envy* due to the acquisition of new possessions brought by the cash economy (e.g., radios) and the difficulty of *concealing* these possessions in a small community. Third, there was an increase in accusations of the *evil eye* and *sorcery*. Furthermore, sorcery was viewed as a direct consequence of envy, and both envy and sorcery became to be seen as the major cause of illness and death among the Matsikenga. For example, some of the respondents shared that "When somebody wants something that you have, they want it and then they make you sick" (Izquierdo and Johnson 2007, 434). Interestingly, there is no word for envy in the Matsikenga language, which led respondents to use the Spanish word *envidia* to explain the origin of illness in their narratives.

Importantly, although the Matsikenga initially conceived of envy (and the evil eye and sorcery) as an emotion that was only possible to be felt by outsiders (for example, oil companies' employees), the community gradually became to fear the envy of other community members. This increased fear undermined social cohesion within the community and was interpreted by Izquierdo and Johnson as a response to the increased stress caused by the multiple changes and challenges the community had to face.

In sum, both Eves (2000) and Izquierdo and Johnson (2007) identified the economic changes a community faces as an antecedent of an increased concern with the envy of others in social relations. Moreover, they also identified the explanation for this association between economic changes and increased fear of envy: *interference* with traditional cultural practices of *concealment*. Furthermore, the cultural importance of concealment to prevent others' envy among the Lelet and Matsikenga align with Ghosh's (1983) and Foster's (1972) findings on this cultural practice. Finally, Izquierdo and Johnson emphasized that the economic—and other—changes the Matsikenga faced were not chosen by them, but largely imposed by outside pressures, and mostly colonization pressures. Thus, envy is also an important emotion to consider in the context of politics, a dimension that is central to Yang's ethnography that will be discussed next.

ENVY AND EMPOWERMENT

Yang's field work among the Bugkalot reveals a cultural view of envy as *empowering*, as a motivator for economic and societal change (Yang 2013). Yang conducted field work in Gingin, a Bugkalot village in the Philippines, in 2005 and in 2006 to 2008. At the time of Yang's field work, the Bugkalot community was organized in clusters of sixty-five persons living in ten households. Households included extended family and was the main unit of social organization among the Bugkalot. As it was the case in the Egyptian community studied by Ghosh (1983), the Bugkalot endorsed strong egalitarian values and norms for households, with each family member equally contributing to the household economy and equally sharing in the profits of the household. This egalitarianism extended to cultural practices around food, with food being equally distributed among all household members.

The Bugkalot faced changes similar to those experienced by the Matsikenga (Izquierdo and Johnson 2007) and the Lelet (Eves 2000) as they were forced to adapt from an economy mostly based on cultivation, hunting, and fishing into a market economy that started around the 1970s. An additional change was the arrival of settlers into the community, who competed with the Bugkalot for the cultivation of land. In addition, the creation of extractive industry also interfered with traditional modes of subsistence as wage earning became an important source of livelihood, especially among men, displacing the importance of hunting. Moreover, these economic changes were accompanied by a process of "othering" by the settlers toward the Bugkalot that included viewing their culture as a threat to capitalist development (for details on this process see Yang 2013). Thus, these economic and demographic changes also posed a threat to the survival and continuity of Bugkalot culture. Importantly, envy played a key role in the way that the Bugkalot responded to these changes and threats.

In particular, the Bugkalot viewed their relationship with the settlers as an inter-group relationship characterized by discrimination and prejudice by the settlers and they challenged these negative views about their culture by asserting themselves as agents—rather than passive recipients—of the economic changes their community faced. Most importantly, the Bugkalot viewed *apet* and *gamak*, the Bugkalot words for "envy" and "desire," respectively, as the motivating forces behind their community's pursuit of success during economic changes. This cultural view on envy as a main motivator for aspiring to do better was central to Bugkalot culture. In fact, the Bugkalot had long viewed *apet* (envy) as the cause of *liget*, which can be translated as "anger/energy/passion" (Yang 2013, 204), a highly valued emotional experience that was culturally construed as a *motivator* for all types of achievements. Not surprisingly, therefore, *apet* was seen among the Bugkalot as the most effective means to correct social inequality because of its empowering motivational value.

Thus, the Bugkalot mobilized the cultural meaning of envy in their community to assert themselves politically in response to the changes placed by outsiders and external political forces. In other words, cultural views on envy were used as an "interpretative framework" (Yang 2013, 219) to understand and cope with political changes, economic changes, and prejudice. This cultural view on envy as empowering is reminiscent of the aspirational connotations of envy in the Egyptian village of Naçaawy studied by Ghosh (1983). Taken together, Yang's (2013) and Ghosh's (1983) research clearly demonstrate that envy has positive consequences for individuals and cultures. Moreover, their findings also align with psychological research on the motivational benefits of benign envy as discussed in this chapter's previous section on envy as a psychological experience.

ENVY AND CULTURE IN PSYCHOLOGICAL RESEARCH: THE PLEASURE AND DISPLEASURE OF BEING ENVIED

Psychological research on culture and envy is scarce. A search at the time of writing in *psychinfo*, a major database for psychological research using the terms "culture" and "envy"/ "envied" in title or abstract, yielded only eight articles that examined culture and envy. A first article published in 1993, by Hupka, Otto, Tarabrina, and Reidl, examined cross-cultural variations in the associative meanings of the emotion terms envy, jealousy, anger, and fear among 389 German, Russian, and US college students (254 women, 135 men). Across the three samples, the nouns most frequently associated with envy were money, prestige, property, revenge, selfishness, status, and wealth. Hupka, Zaleski, Otto, Reidl and Tarabrina (1997) published related work on associations between color terms and the emotion terms envy, anger, fear, and jealousy among 661 college students (336 women, 220 men) from Germany, Mexico, Poland, Russia, and the United States. In a later cross-cultural study, Kim and Hupka (2002) asked 304 US and Korean college students (180 women, 124 men) to free associate words with several emotion terms including envy, which was most frequently associated with jealousy, hatred/hate, and greed in both cultural samples.

Later work in psychology focused on cultural influences in the development of the envy concept among children. Specifically, Jensen de Lopez and colleagues asked 131 children ages three, four, and five years old (61 girls, 70 boys) from Zapotec (Mexico) and Denmark to respond to a story that depicted the hostile reaction of a child who wanted an object that another child had. Results showed that culture did not influence the children's interpretation of the story, with four-and five-year-old participants explaining the child's hostile reaction in terms of the child not having the desired object (for information on a second study see Jensen de Lopez et al. 2012). A different approach to study envy in relation to culture was taken by Wu, Bai, and Fiske (2018) who examined evaluations of rich people among Chinese and US participants. Wu and colleagues' third study among 196 US and Chinese college students (US sample 41 percent female and Chinese sample 48 percent female) was especially important as it measured both implicit and explicit stereotypes about rich people. Results showed that both US and Chinese participants reported positive implicit evaluations, but ambivalent self-reported explicit evaluations, of the rich.

More recently, Wenninger, Kreus, and Krasnova (2019) asked 182 German college students (57.1 percent female) and 176 (70.5 percent female) college students from Hong Kong about their envy toward their friends' postings in

Facebook and the strategies they used to manage their envy. The study also measured individualistic and collectivistic cultural values. Wenninger and colleagues found that individualistic participants were more likely to use self-enhancement behavior to manage their envy. Cultural values, however, did not affect how much participants used gossiping and discontinued attention in Facebook for envy management. Further, Ahn et al. (2021) measured benign and malicious envy among 152 US (56 percent male) and 145 Korean (44.8 percent male) college students in response to a desired object (an Apple watch) owned by a fellow student. They found a stronger positive association between the two types of envy among Korean than among US participants, which was interpreted as Korean culture being more tolerant of simultaneously feeling benign and malicious envy. Finally, my colleagues and I have examined the emotional experience of being envied in two cultures (Rodriguez Mosquera, Parrott, and Hurtado de Mendoza 2010). This work will be discussed next in more detail as it is closely related to Foster's envy axes and other anthropological work on fear of envy discussed in previous sections.

We grounded our studies in Foster's two axes model of envy (Foster 1972) and Exline and Lobel's sensitivity about being the target of a threatening upward comparison model (Exline and Lobel 1999), with both models suggesting that being envied by another should be a mixed emotional experience involving pleasure and *dis*pleasure. To examine the pleasure and displeasure dimensions of being envied, we conducted two studies among Spanish and US student adults. In a first study using the emotional narrative method, 48 US (36 women, 12 men) and 44 Spanish (23 women, 21 men) college students were asked to write about a recent situation in which they thought they may have been envied by another. The overwhelming majority of Spanish (91 percent) and US (98 percent) participants reported a situation in which the envious other was a close other, typically a friend. Several aspects of participants' emotional experience were measured, including the perceived implications of being envied. Interestingly, results showed that, whereas the Spanish participants more frequently mentioned being fearful of being disliked and excluded by the friend who envied them, the US participants more frequently mentioned that having what their friend wanted made them feel more self-confident (for details on the first study's measures, cross-cultural linguistic equivalence, and additional results, see Rodriguez Mosquera, Parrott, and Hurtado de Mendoza, Study 1, 2010). A second, experimental study among 174 Spanish (88 women, 86 men) and 205 US (106 women, 99 men) college students replicated and extended these findings.

Based on the most frequently reported antecedents in the first study, we presented participants with one of two scenarios that described them as having something that another person wanted. In the *Internship* condition, participants read about how they won a prestigious fellowship that a fellow student also wanted. In the *Better Life* condition, participants read about having a "better life" (e.g., having more friends) that a fellow student also wanted. Importantly, the scenarios did not include information about how the fellow student felt or responded. This study assessed several aspects of the participants' emotional experience of being envied, including cognitive appraisals, subjective experience, and coping responses (for details on the second study's measures and their cross-cultural linguistic equivalence, see Rodriguez Mosquera, Parrott, and Hurtado de Mendoza, Study 2, 2010).

Results showed that US participants had a more intensely *ambivalent* experience of having what another wants compared to Spanish participants. More specifically, the US participants appraised the fellow student's wanting of what they had as increasing their self-confidence and as being self-affirming. However, at the same time, US participants also reported being more concerned about the fellow student feeling inferior and hostile toward them. Furthermore, these participants also experienced ambivalent feelings. Compared to the Spanish, US participants reported feeling both prouder and guiltier for having something that another wanted. Moreover, US participants also reported more ambivalent coping responses as they were more likely to be nice (an approach behavior) and, at the same time, to distance themselves (an avoidance behavior) from the fellow student who wanted what they had.

Further, in order to examine the role of cultural values in the emotional experience of being envied, we created first a "fear of envy" index by averaging scores on the participants' ratings of the fellow student's (1) ill-will toward them; (2) feelings of inferiority; and (3) feelings of envy toward them. Regression analyses with several individual difference measures (including cultural values) as predictors yielded the cultural orientation of *vertical individualism* as the only significant predictor of the US participants' fear of envy. The more the participants valued success, ambition, and competition (the cultural values that define vertical individualism), the more they feared the fellow student's envy. A regression analysis with the same individual difference measures was also conducted for positive appraisal measures, with vertical individualism also emerging as the strongest significant predictor: the more US participants valued vertical individualism, the more they evaluated the fellow student's coveting as making them feel better about themselves and what they had. In contrast, *horizontal collectivism* (a cultural value orientation that emphasizes cooperation, connectedness, and conflict avoidance) predicted Spanish participants' primary response to the fellow student's coveting: the more the Spanish participants valued horizontal collectivism, the more they expected others to celebrate in their success (for other results from the second study, see Rodriguez Mosquera, Parrott, and Hurtado de Mendoza, Study 2, 2010).

Taken together, these two studies show that being the target of another person's envy is an ambivalent emotional experience characterized by both pleasure and displeasure. Furthermore, this research supports Foster's two axes of envy. Although cultural anthropological research has clearly documented the existence of the fear axis of envy across many cultures, the competitive axis of envy has not been systematically studied in cultural anthropology. Our studies confirm that being the target of other's envy also leads individuals to feel good about what they have, as expected by Foster. In addition, and also in line with Foster's expectations, we found that a cultural emphasis on success, ambition, and competition (or vertical individualism) intensifies the pleasure of being envied. Moreover, this research also expands on Foster's competitive axis of envy. In particular, our research demonstrated that the pleasure dimension of being envied is, in itself, a *complex* and *multifaceted* emotional experience because it is characterized by (1) positive cognitive appraisals centered on self-affirmation and increased self-confidence, (2) the experience of uplifting emotions like pride, and (3) an increased motivation for positive social engagement (e.g., being friendly to the envious other). Thus, from a psychological perspective, being the target of other's envy can be a quite empowering emotional experience, especially if one values ambition, success, and competition.

CONCLUSION

This chapter reviewed research on culture and envy in cultural anthropology and psychology, research that covered a wide variety of cultures situated in different historical, economic, ecological, and demographic contexts. The reviewed research revealed envy to be a deeply relational emotion, even when it is considered and studied as an individual emotional experience. Indeed, the elicitation of envy is rooted in social comparison processes and envy's affective signature is the covetous desire for what *others* have. Thus, envy would not exist without others as there would be nothing for us to covet. In this way, envy is intimately tied to sociability.

Relatedly, envy is always felt and expressed in a cultural context, and neither envy nor other emotions are ever separated from culture. Indeed, emotional life is grounded in culture and emotions cannot be fully understood without taking the cultural context in which they are experienced into account (Haidt and Keltner 1999; Rodriguez Mosquera 2018). Cultural values, norms, and practices therefore shape emotions at different levels of analyses: individual, dyadic, and group/community. This multilevel effect of culture on emotions is supported by the reviewed research on culture and envy in this chapter. Taken together, the following conclusions about the relationship between culture and envy can be drawn from this research (for additional ethnographic research on envy that supports these conclusions, see Ariel de Vidas 2007; Bunkbar 2014, 2017; Castellanos 2015; Dawson 2014; Dean 2013; Junge 2014; Taggart 2012; Tapias and Escandell 2011; and Van Vleet 2003).

First, common across all cultural anthropological work on envy is the *evil eye*, or the connection between seeing an object, the desire for that object, and the potential harm projected onto the owner of that object. Second, the economy and social structure of a community determines the objects or possessions that are culturally construed as the potential *objects of others' envy*. Third, envy in some cultures is culturally viewed as *empowering* and *aspirational*, as the emotion that motivates individuals and families to excel. Fourth, individuals who endorse *vertical individualism* (characterized by the cultural values of competition, ambition, and success) experience being the target of others' envy as an *ambivalent* emotional experience of fearing the other's envy and, at the same time, rejoicing in their coveting. Fifth, envy in some cultures is bounded by *social class*, with those who have more wealth being expected to engage more in social competition, feel more intense envy, and be more often the target of others' envy. Sixth, *concealment, denial, symbolic sharing*, and *demand sharing* emerge as core cultural practices in the management of others' envy. Sixth, a cultural concern with the fear of others' envy influences house *architecture* in some cultures, with houses being built to allow for the cultural practice of concealment.

Seventh, Foster's concept of the *limited good* to explain the fear of others' envy is not a pan-cultural ethos. The reviewed research showed other factors that explain the prevalence of a cultural concern with the fear of others' envy, in particular (1) some cultures simply do not share the limited good ethos and have an economy that allows for wealth accumulation; (2) economic changes such as the introduction into a market economy; (3) economic changes in the form of economic prosperity; (4) demographic, ecological, and health changes due to colonization processes; (5) cultural disruptions in the form of interference with cultural practices of concealment and symbolic sharing.

Finally, the reviewed research shows that envy, and especially a cultural concern with the fear of others' envy, plays a central role in the management of social relations and the maintenance of social structures. A cultural concern with the fear of other's envy targets what is considered *excessive* in a community, the wealth or resource accumulation in the hands of a few individuals or families that needs to be regulated, especially in communities that try to maintain *egalitarian* social structures and endorse *equality* and *cooperation* as core cultural values. Thus, envy is a complex emotion that operates in complex ways across cultures. It is an emotion situated at the heart of cultural networks of values, norms, and practices, deriving its power from the fact that it is both *feared* and, at the same time, *necessary* for the social regulation of wealth, status, and power.[3]

NOTES

1. For more information on how Unamuno viewed envy, see Ingrid Vendrell Ferran's contribution to this volume "'I Could Have Been You": Existential Envy and the Self" (chapter 4).

2. For a more detailed picture of this functional approach to envy, see Jens Lange and Jan Crusius's contribution to this volume "How Envy and Being Envied Shape Social Hierarchies" (chapter 2).

3. I thank Sara Protasi for their insightful and constructive comments on this chapter. Correspondence concerning this article should be sent to Patricia M. Rodriguez Mosquera, Psychology Department, Wesleyan University, 207 High Street, Middletown, CT 06459, USA.

REFERENCES

Ahn, Sowon, Young-Won Ha, Myung-Soo Jo, Juyoung Kim, and Emine Sarigolly. 2021. "A Cross-Cultural Study on Envy Premium: The Role of Mixed Emotions of Benign and Malicious Envies." *Current Psychology: A Journal for Diverse Perspectives on Diverse Psychological Issues.* http://dx.doi.org/10.1007/s12144-021-01679-7.

Ariel de Vidas, Anath. 2007. "The Symbolic and Ethnic Aspects of Envy among A Teenek Community (Mexico)." *Journal of Anthropological Research* 63: 215–37. https://www.jstor.org/stable/20371150.

Burbank, Victoria. 2014. "Envy and Egalitarianism in Aboriginal Australia: An Integrative Approach." *The Australian Journal of Anthropology* 25: 1–21. https://doi.org/10.1111/taja.12068.

Burbank, Victoria. 2017. "The Embodiment of Sorcery: Supernatural Aggression, Belief and Envy in a Remote Aboriginal Community." *The Australian Journal of Anthropology* 28: 286–300. https://doi.org/10.1111/taja.12228.

Castellanos, Daniela. 2015. "The Ordinary Envy of Aguabuena People: Revisiting Universalistic Ideas from Local Entanglements." *Anthropology and Humanism* 40: 20–34. https://doi.org/10.1111/anhu.12066.

Crusius, Jan and Jens Lange. 2021. "Counterfactual Thoughts Distinguish Benign and Malicious Envy." *Emotion* 21: 905–20. https://doi.org/10.1037/emo0000923.

Dawson, Hannah. 2014. "Youth Politics: Waiting and Envy in a South African Informal Settlement." *Journal of Southern African Studies* 40: 861–82. https://doi.org/10.1080/03057070.2014.932981.

Dean, Melanie. 2013. "From 'Evil Eye' Anxiety to The Desirability of Envy: Status, Consumption and the Politics of Visibility in Urban South India." *Contributions to Indian Sociology* 47: 185–216. https://doi.org/10.1177/0069966713482999.

Dundes, Alan. Ed. 1992. *The Evil Eye: A Casebook*. Madison, WI: University of Wisconsin Press.

Eves, Richard. 2000. "Sorcery's the Curse: Modernity, Envy and the Flow of Sociality in a Melanesian Society." *Journal of the Royal Anthropological Institute* 6: 453–68. https://doi.org/10.1111/1467-9655.00026.

Exline, Julie Juola, and Marci Lobel. 1999. "The Perils of Outperformance: Sensitivity about Being the Target of a Threatening Upward Comparison." *Psychological Bulletin* 125: 307–37. https://doi.org/10.1037/0033-2909.125.3.307.

Foster, George M. 1965a. "Cultural Responses to Expressions of Envy in Tzintzuntzan." *Southwestern Journal of Anthropology* 21: 24–35.

———. 1965b. "Peasant Society and The Image of Limited Good." *American Anthropologist* 67: 293–315.

———. 1967. *Tzintzuntzan: Mexican Peasants in a Changing World*. Boston: Little, Brown and Company.

———. "The Anatomy of Envy: A Study in Symbolic Behavior." *Current Anthropology* 13: 165–202.

Ghosh, Amitav. 1983. "The Relations of Envy in an Egyptian Village." *Ethnology* 22: 211–23.

Hupka, Ralph B., Otto Jürgen, Nadia V. Tarabrina, and Lucy Reidl. 1993. "Cross-Cultural Comparisons of Nouns Associated with Jealousy and the Related Emotions of Envy, Anger, and Fear." *Cross-Cultural Research* 27: 181–211. http://dx.doi.org/10.1177/106939719302700302.

Hupka, Ralph, B., Zbigniew Zaleski, Otto Jürgen, Lucy Reidl, and Nadia V. Tarabrina. 1997. "The Colors of Anger, Envy, Fear, and Jealousy." *Journal of Cross-Cultural Psychology* 28: 156–71. http://dx.doi.org/10.1177/0022022197282002.

Izquierdo, Carolina, and Allen Johnson. 2007. "Desire, Envy and Punishment: A Matsigenka Emotion Schema in Illness Narratives and Folk Stories." *Medicine and Psychiatry* 31: 419–44. https://doi.org/10.1007/s11013-007-9067-x.

Jensen de López, Kristin, Laura Quintanilla Cobian, Marta Giménez-Dasí, and Encarnacion Sarria Sánchez. 2012. "Young Children's Understanding of Envy: Precursors of Young Children's Understanding of Self-Conscious Emotions: Envy Across Cultures." *Psyke and Logos* 33: 27–49.

Junge, Benjamin. 2014. "'THE ENERGY OF OTHERS': Narratives of Envy and Purification among Former Grassroots Community Leaders in Porto Alegre, Brazil." *Latin American Research Review* 49: 81–98.

Keltner, Dacher, and Jonathan Haidt. 1999. "Social Functions of Emotions at Four Levels of Analysis." *Cognition & Emotion* 13: 505–21.

Khan, Abdul K., Chris M. Bell, and Samina Quratulain. 2016. "The Two Faces of Envy: Perceived Opportunity to Perform as a Moderator of Envy Manifestation." *Personnel Review* 46: 490–511. http://dx.doi.org/10.1108/PR-12-2014-0279.

Kim, Hyun-Jeung Joyce, and Ralph B. Hupka. 2002. "Comparison of Associative Meaning of the Concepts of Anger, Envy, Fear, Romantic Jealousy, and Sadness

Between English and Korean." *Cross-Cultural Research* 36: 229–55. http://dx.doi.org/10.1177/10697102036003003.

Lange, Jens, Delroy L. Paulhus, and Jan Crusius. 2018. "Elucidating the Dark Side of Envy: Distinctive Links of Benign and Malicious Envy with Dark Personalities." *Personality and Social Psychology Bulletin* 44: 601–14. http://dx.doi.org/10.1177/0146167217746340.

Lee, KiYoung, Michelle K. Duffy, Kristin L. Scott, and Michaéla C. Schippers. 2018. "The Experience of Being Envied at Work: How Being Envied Shapes Employee Feelings and Motivation." *Personnel Psychology* 71: 181–200. https://doi.org/10.1111/peps.12251.

Liu, Fang, Dege Liu, Juncheng Zhang, and Jingxing Ma. 2019. "The Relationship between Being Envied and Workplace Ostracism: The Moderating Role of Neuroticism and the Need to Belong." *Personality and Individual Differences* 147: 223–28. https://doi.org/10.1016/j.paid.2019.04.040.

Liu, Yan, Julie N.Y. Zhu, and Long W. Lam. 2020. "Obligations and Feeling Envied: A Study of Workplace Status and Knowledge Hiding." *Journal of Managerial Psychology* 35: 347–59. https://doi.org/10.1108/JMP-05-2019-0276.

Parrott, W. Gerrod, and Patricia M. Rodriguez Mosquera. 2008. "On the Pleasures and Displeasures of Being Envied." In *Envy*, edited by Richard Smith, 117–32. Cambridge: Cambridge University Press.

Parrott, W. Gerrod, and Richard H. Smith. 1993. "Distinguishing the Experiences of Envy and Jealousy." *Journal of Personality and Social Psychology* 64: 906–20. https://doi.org/10.1037/0022-3514.64.6.906.

Protasi, Sara. 2021. *The Philosophy of Envy*. New York: Cambridge University Press.

Scott, Kristin L., Stefan Tams, Michaéla C. Schippers, and KiYoung Lee. 2015. "Opening the Black Box: Why and When Workplace Exclusion Affects Social Reconnection Behaviour, Health, and Attitudes." *European Journal of Work and Organizational Psychology* 24: 239–55. https://doi.org/10.1080/1359432X.2014.894978.

Smith, Richard H., W. Gerrod Parrott, Ed F. Diener, Richard H. Hoyle, and Sung Hee Kim. 1999. "Dispositional Envy." *Personality and Social Psychology Bulletin* 25: 1007–21. http://dx.doi.org/10.1177/01461672992511008.

Smith, Richard H., and Sung Hee Kim. 2007. "Comprehending Envy." *Psychological Bulletin* 133: 46–64. http://dx.doi.org/10.1037/0033-2909.133.1.46.

Rodriguez Mosquera, Patricia M. 2018. "Cultural Concerns. How Valuing Social-Image Shapes Social Emotion." *European Review of Social Psychology* 29: 1–37. http://dx.doi.org/10.1080/10463283.2017.1412180.

Rodriguez Mosquera, Patricia M., W. Gerrod Parrott, and Alejandra Hurtado de Mendoza. 2010. "I Fear Your Envy, I Rejoice in Your Coveting. On The Ambivalent Experience of Being Envied by Others." *Journal of Personality and Social Psychology* 99: 842–54. http://dx.doi.org/10.1037/a0020965.

Romani, Simona, Silvia Grappi, and Richard P. Bagozzi. 2016. "The Bittersweet Experience of Being Envied in a Consumption Context." *European Journal of Marketing* 50: 1239–62. https://doi.org/10.1108/EJM-03-2015-0133.

Tapias, Maria, and Xavier Escandell. 2011. "Not in the Eyes of the Beholder: Envy Among Bolivian Migrants in Spain." *International Migration* 49: 74–94. https://doi.org/10.1111/j.1468-2435.2011.00705.x.

Taggart, James M. 2012. "Interpreting the Nahuat Dialogue on the Envious Dead with Jerome Bruner's Theory of Narrative." *Ethos* 40: 411–30. https://doi.org/10.1111/j.1548-1352.2012.01268.x.

Unamuno, Miguel de. 1998. *Obras Selectas.* Austral Summa.

van de Ven, Niels, Marcel Zeelenberg, and Rik Pieters. 2010. "Warding off the Evil Eye: When the Fear of Being Envied Increases Prosocial Behavior." *Psychological Science* 21: 1671–77. https://doi.org/10.1177/0956797610385352.

van de Ven, Niels, Marcel Zeelenberg, and Rik Pieters. 2009. "Leveling Up and Down: The Experiences of Benign and Malicious Envy." *Emotion* 9: 419–29. http://dx.doi.org/10.1037/a0015669.

Van Vleet, Krista. 2003. "Partial Theories: On Gossip, Envy and Ethnography in the Andes" *Ethnography* 4: 491–519. https://doi.org/10.1177/146613810344001.

Wenninger, H., Christy MK Cheung, and Hanna Krasnova. 2019. "College-Aged Users Behavioral Strategies to Reduce Envy on Social Networking Sites: A Cross-Cultural Investigation." *Computers in Human Behavior* 97: 10–23. https://doi.org/10.1016/j.chb.2019.02.025.

Wu, Sherry Jueyu, Xuechunzi Bai, and Susan T. Fiske. 2018. "Admired Rich or Resented Rich? How Two Cultures Vary in Envy." *Journal of Cross-Cultural Psychology* 49: 1114–43. http://dx.doi.org/10.1177/0022022118774943.

Yang, Shu-Yuan. 2013. "Envy, Desire, and Economic Engagement Among the Bugkalot (Ilongot) of Northern Luzon, Philippines." *Research in Economic Anthropology* 33: 199–225. http:/doi:10.1108/S0190-1281(2013)0000033010.

Chapter 2

How Envy and Being Envied Shape Social Hierarchies

Jens Lange and Jan Crusius

Humans have a strong tendency to form social hierarchies (Magee and Galinsky 2008). They do so quickly and spontaneously. Even when contextual factors minimize the potential for hierarchical structures, they are hardly ever completely absent. This preference for hierarchical organization partly stems from the fact that being at the top of a hierarchy has important advantages. For instance, higher-ranked persons have access to valuable resources, better health, or power over others (e.g., Fournier 2020; Sapolsky 2005; Von Rueden, Gurven, and Kaplan 2011).

Consequently, people are highly vigilant about their social rank. They continuously strive for higher social rank (Anderson, Hildreth, and Howland 2015) and even when they have a high position, their desire to stay at the top remains almost insatiable (Anderson, Hildreth, and Sharps 2020). If humans have a fundamental need for social rank, it follows that humans should be equipped with a set of strong psychological tools allowing them to deal with changes in their position in the hierarchy (Pettit et al. 2016; Sivanathan, Pillutla, and Murnighan 2008). Rising in the hierarchy elicits reactions aimed to reinforce the current course of action, whereas threats to one's position elicit reactions aimed to prevent losing one's rank. Among these strong reactions are emotions. That is, people react emotionally to rank improvements and rank threats, eliciting behaviors aimed to communicate rank improvements to others or averting potentially detrimental consequences of rank threats. Emotions therefore contribute to the regulation of social hierarchies (Steckler and Tracy 2014). One emotion that is at the center of these dynamics, we argue, is envy.

We propose that envy regulates social hierarchies in two ways. First, higher-ranked persons' successes elicit envy in lower-ranked persons. Second, lower-rank persons' envy in turn elicits reactions in higher-ranked persons. Envying and being envied thus occur in a dynamic relationship. To unravel the complexities of this dynamic, we argue in favor of considering the different ways in which social hierarchies form, and how emotions are multifaceted experiences. We review evidence for a broad framework that considers these points.

ENVY

Theoretical approaches agree that envy situations include three elements: two persons and an object (e.g., D'Arms 2018; Smith and Kim 2007). One person is advantaged by having the object. The other person is disadvantaged by lacking it. Envy objects include achievements, possessions, or characteristics. Importantly, in all situations, the object is highly self-relevant for the disadvantaged person (e.g., Salovey and Rodin 1984). Put differently, the disadvantaged person experiences envy to the extent that lacking the object reflects negatively on the person's self-evaluation.

Broad evidence indicates that the object's relevance often means higher social rank of the advantaged person (e.g., Crusius and Lange 2017; Fiske 2010; Leahy 2021; see also Rodriguez Mosquera in this volume; Romero in this volume). Specifically, the object may signal to observers that the person is highly ranked. Hence, envy may often not be elicited by lacking the object but by the advantages associated with it. People envy others primarily for socially valued characteristics such as wealth, attractiveness, status objects, academic success, popularity, or authority (DelPriore, Hill, and Buss 2012). Being advantaged on these dimensions leads to more respect and social influence. Put differently, it leads to a higher social rank. Being disadvantaged on these dimensions, in turn, leads to a lower social rank. Thus, the identity relevance of lacking envy objects may often signal that one's social rank is lower than expected. In line with this notion, changes in people's self-evaluation correspond to changes in their social rank (Mahadevan, Gregg, and Sedikides 2019).

In situations relevant for one's social rank, envy then constitutes a response to inferiority, dealing with this threat to a fundamental need. To do so, envy includes various affective, cognitive, and motivational reactions (e.g., Lange, Weidman, and Crusius 2018; Parrott and Smith 1993). Relatedly, people with a higher desire to attain social rank, such as people with higher greed, narcissism, or entitlement, tend to experience envy more intensely (Crusius, Thierhoff, and Lange 2021; Lange, Crusius, and Hagemeyer 2016; Lange,

Redford, and Crusius 2019). The goal of the diverse reactions included in envy might thus be to level the rank difference relative to the advantaged person (e.g., Sayers 1969; Van de Ven, Zeelenberg, and Pieters 2009).

According to this perspective, one of envy's social functions is to contribute to the regulation of social hierarchies. It helps persons overcome rank differentials, ensuring that they may eventually gain access to the advantages afforded to those who have higher rank than they have. Notably, this perspective challenges the common view on envy that depicts envy as an immoral emotion with maladaptive consequences for enviers and society. Envy may not be uniformly negative but may even have value such that some of the consequences of envy help enviers improve their outcomes (for a discussion, see Lange and Protasi 2021; see also Romero in this volume).

The social-functional approach to envy also has implications for persons who exceed another person's rank. If envy aims to level differences in rank, enviers are a threat to a higher-ranked person's position. Accordingly, this person must react to a lower-ranked person's envy to protect their standing and its ensuing advantages. Hence, higher-ranked persons and their enviers could engage in a self-reinforcing cycle of complex emotional interactions.

We propose to analyze this dynamic by dividing it into four steps (figure 2.1). First, if envy is a response to other persons' social rank, it will be elicited

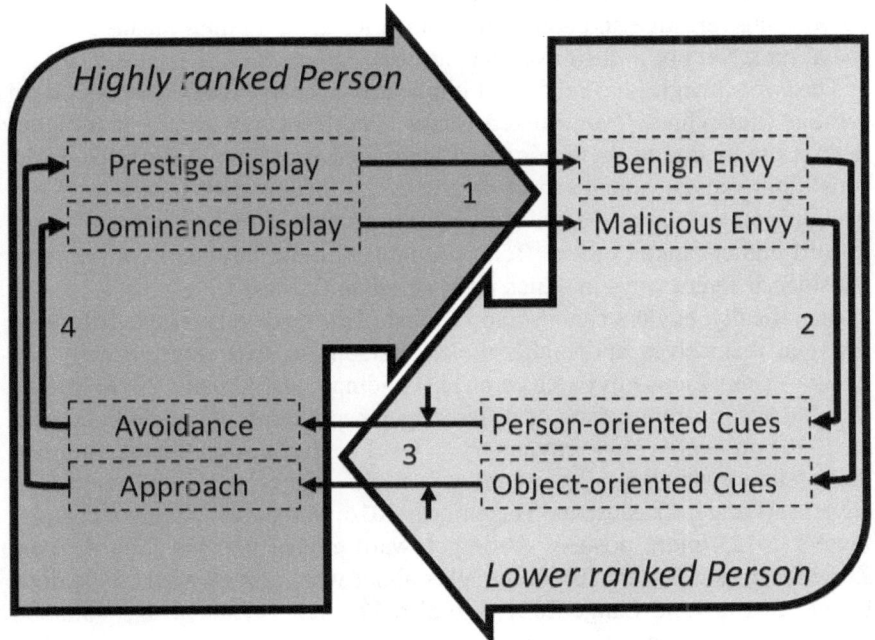

Figure 2.1 Four steps describing how envy and being envied shape social.

if a difference in ranks has been established and communicated to others. Second, envy may manifest itself in emotional expressions and behavioral cues communicating itself to others, allowing higher-ranked persons to infer the envy of others. Third, in response to being envied, higher-ranked persons react with either approach or avoidance behavior to deal with this situation. Fourth, these reactions can change the position of higher-ranked persons, starting the circle anew. Jointly, these four steps comprehensively outline key elements of the process in which envy and being envied shape social hierarchies.

STEP 1: RANK DISPLAYS AND ENVY

Anthropological and psychological evidence indicates that people attain social rank in at least two ways (e.g., Henrich and Gil-White 2001; Maner and Case 2016). When people pursue a *prestige* strategy, they gain respect by showing competence, sharing knowledge, and contributing to the group such that others have opportunities to advance. When people pursue a *dominance* strategy, instead, they intimidate others and elicit fear to secure their position, while they may even lack competence. Notably, despite their differences, both prestige and dominance strategies lead to higher social rank (Cheng et al. 2013). Thus, prestige and dominance strategies differ in their means to reach social rank, yet not in their eventual success.

The two strategies have different implications for lower-ranked persons. In prestige hierarchies, lower-ranked persons can learn how to obtain a higher rank in the long term. In dominance hierarchies, however, lower-ranked persons' future advancement can be obstructed by incompetent superiors. These two different situations have implications for lower-ranked persons' envy toward higher-ranked others. Before turning to these implications, we must consider different ways in which envy can manifest itself.

Specifically, enviers can also accomplish their goal to level the difference between themselves and higher-ranked persons in two ways, namely via benign or malicious envy (e.g., Lange, Weidman, and Crusius 2018; Van de Ven 2016; for a comparison of different perspectives on envy, see Crusius et al. 2020). In *benign envy*, enviers try to level themselves up, that is, improve their relative standing. Benign envy includes higher perceived control to advance (Lange, Crusius, and Hagemeyer 2016; Van de Ven, Zeelenberg, and Pieters 2012), more positive feelings toward envied persons (Van de Ven, Zeelenberg, and Pieters 2009), thoughts about what oneself could have done better (Crusius and Lange 2021; see also Vendrell Ferran in this volume), and a focus on means to improve (Crusius and Lange 2014; Protasi 2016). Moreover, benign envy fosters improvement behaviors, such as increased effort in achievement tasks (e.g., Lange and Crusius 2015; Van de Ven, Zeelenberg, and Pieters 2011), higher motivation to obtain a better grade (Khan, Bell, and Quratulain 2017), or a higher tendency to purchase products that facilitate productive work (Salerno, Laran, and Janiszewski 2019).

In *malicious envy*, enviers try to level the envied person down, that is, harm the envied person's social rank. Malicious envy includes higher subjectively perceived undeservingness of envied persons' position (Lange, Crusius, and Hagemeyer 2016; Van de Ven, Zeelenberg, and Pieters 2012), more negative feelings toward them (Van de Ven, Zeelenberg, and Pieters 2009), thoughts about how others should have acted differently (Crusius and Lange 2021), and a focus on envied persons (Crusius and Lange 2014; Protasi 2016). Moreover, malicious envy fosters harming behaviors such as choosing more difficult tasks for envied persons (Lange and Crusius 2015), deception in negotiations (Yusainy et al. 2019), or schadenfreude when envied persons fail (Lange, Weidman, and Crusius 2018; Van de Ven et al. 2015).

Therefore, we would expect that the two ways of attaining social rank affect lower-ranked persons' envy differently. When higher-ranked persons in prestige hierarchies share competencies and knowledge with lower-ranked persons, lower-ranked persons may experience control to change their situation. These perceptions of control should elicit benign envy. When lower-ranked persons in dominance hierarchies are obstructed by incompetent superiors, they should perceive higher-ranked person's position as undeserved. These subjective perceptions of undeservingness should elicit malicious envy. Prestige and dominance are neither fixed nor exclusive characteristics of social hierarchies. How people perceive them should thus be highly malleable. Hence, when higher-ranked persons display specific signals that lead lower-ranked persons to infer that higher-ranked persons pursue a prestige or dominance hierarchy, these displays should elicit benign and malicious envy, respectively.

Evidence is in line with these hypotheses. For instance, higher-ranked persons can signal their higher position by displaying different forms of pride in response to a success (Cheng, Tracy, and Henrich 2010) that, in turn, elicit different forms of envy in lower-ranked persons (Lange and Crusius 2015; see also Lange and Boecker 2019). Specifically, in these studies, participants were or imagined being outperformed by another person in a competition. After winning the competition, the person displayed different forms of pride signaling either prestige or dominance. When higher-ranked persons displayed authentic pride, communicating achievement, accomplishment, and self-worth, observers inferred that higher-ranked persons pursued a prestige strategy. Accordingly, authentic pride expressed by higher-ranked persons elicited benign envy in lower-ranked persons. When higher-ranked persons displayed hubristic pride, communicating that they are snobbish, stuck-up, and arrogant, observers inferred that higher-ranked persons pursued a dominance strategy. Accordingly, hubristic pride expressed by higher-ranked persons elicited malicious envy in lower-ranked persons. Thus, higher-ranked persons' displays of social rank shape lower-ranked persons' envy (Crusius and Lange 2017; see also Romero in this volume).

STEP 2: CUES TO ENVY

In competitive situations, lower-ranked persons' envy should become a threat to higher-ranked persons' social rank. Benign envy predicts improved effort in lower-ranked persons (Lange and Crusius 2015; Van de Ven, Zeelenberg, and Pieters 2011) that can eventually translate into higher social rank (Lange, Crusius, and Hagemeyer 2016). Malicious envy predicts harming behavior that can lower higher-ranked persons' standing in the eyes of others (Lange and Boecker 2019). Either way, higher-ranked persons may lose their relative advantage if enviers' behavioral strategies are successful. Given people's fundamental desire for social rank (Anderson, Hildreth, and Howland 2015), it is likely that they react to this threat.

Notably, before higher-ranked persons can react to this threat, they need to identify enviers in the first place. To do so, envy must manifest in expressive cues that higher-ranked persons can perceive. Envy could change lower-ranked persons' facial, vocal, or bodily expressions. Typically, emotions distinguish themselves in at least one of these cues (Keltner et al. 2019). Hence, also for envy it may be possible to identify distinct expressive cues.

However, theorizing on envy implies that looking for such expressive cues is a fruitless endeavor. A frequent notion is that enviers disguise their envy (Miceli and Castelfranchi 2007). In fact, they may disguise their envy to such an extent that they even deny it toward themselves (Smith and Kim 2007). Hence, if envy never manifests in expressive cues, it should be impossible to perceive lower-ranked persons' envy.

Recent evidence puts this earlier research into perspective (Lange et al. 2020). Dovetailing with the earlier arguments, when unacquainted persons engaged in a competition, successful persons were unable to accurately judge how envious their unsuccessful competitors were. However, when acquainted persons judged each other's inclination to be envious across situations, these judgments were accurate. That is, participants' judgments of acquainted persons' inclination to be envious across situations correlated positively with these persons' self-ratings of these inclinations. This was the case even when controlling for the similarity of the two partners and the possibility that they projected their own (similar) personality on the other person. Thus, with sufficient time or across repeated observations, it may be possible to perceive envy, even if direct evidence for this notion is not yet available.

One reason for the need of time or repeated observations may be that people have to integrate multiple pieces of information to accurately perceive others' envy (e.g., Puranik et al. 2019; Rodriguez Mosquera, Parrott, and Hurtado de Mendoza 2010). Sometimes, a single situation may provide all necessary cues. Often, the necessary cues to others' envy may leak only when the persons meet each other in different situations, however. In this respect, envy is different from other emotions that are observable from single, distinct cues.

Research started investigating cues to persons' benign and malicious envy. It suggests that observers infer the specific envy forms from three classes of cues (Lange, Fischer, and Van Kleef 2022; see also Puranik et al. 2019). First, a requirement common to benign and malicious envy is that a person is perceived as being worse off than someone else. Second, the situation has painful implications for the person as evidenced by a facial expression. These facial expressions should be different for benign and malicious envy. Specifically, observers should be more likely to infer that a relatively inferior person is benignly envious when a person displays disappointment (which shares a facial expression with sadness). In contrast, observers should be more likely to infer that a relatively inferior person is maliciously envious when this person displays anger. A third cue, specific for benign versus malicious may be whether the person directs attention to either the envied other or the object. An inference of benign envy should be more likely when an inferior person directs attention to the envy object. An inference of malicious envy should be more likely when an inferior person directs attention to the envied other. Lange et al. (2022) presented combinations of these cues in controlled experimental designs or via dedicated photographs. When all three cues were combined in a single situation, facilitating their integrated perception, observers inferred the respective envy form in line with the predictions. Notably, research suggests that enviers indeed display these cues (e.g., Crusius and Lange 2014; Van de Ven, Zeelenberg, and Pieters 2012). However, no research has yet investigated whether enviers display these cues and observers then use the displayed cues accurately to infer enviers' emotion.

STEP 3: REACTIONS TO BEING ENVIED

How higher-ranked persons react to the threat posed by lower-ranked persons is difficult to predict. Early research indicated that people dislike being the target of an upward comparison by another person (Exline and Lobel 1999). More recent research indicates that being envied is an ambivalent experience (Duffy, Lee, and Adair 2021; Fileva 2019; Parrott 2017). Specifically, higher-ranked persons react to being envied with both positive and negative feelings; sometimes they like it and sometimes they do not. These feelings may, in turn, spur motivation to approach or avoid enviers, respectively.

A variety of studies document this ambivalence. For instance, in situations in which they have been envied, people reported that they tried being nice in return, distanced themselves, or deflected attention from themselves (Rodriguez Mosquera, Parrott, and Hurtado de Mendoza 2010). In one study, people imagined that another person is envious and has no control to change the situation (Romani, Grappi, and Bagozzi 2016). Based on the appraisals that shape benign and malicious envy, low control implies that the other person was more likely perceived as maliciously envious. This situation elicited positive feelings when people disliked the envier and negative feelings when people liked the envier. In another study in a work context, being envied predicted both positive feelings as well as anxiety to lose the relationship with the envier (Lee et al. 2018). The positive feelings predicted higher work engagement, which in turn predicted higher job performance. In contrast, anxiety predicted lower work engagement, which in turn predicted lower job performance. In other studies in a work context, being envied predicted efforts to socially reconnect but also predicted higher experienced job tension and desire to leave the organization (Scott et al. 2015) as well as the tendency to hide knowledge from others (Y. Liu, Zhu, and Lam 2020). Finally, when people had an advantage over another person following a random draw, they were more likely to mitigate this person's envy by being more prosocial (Van de Ven, Zeelenberg, and Pieters 2010). This prosocial tendency was more likely to the extent that they perceived the person's envy as malicious.

Thus, being envied causes a variety of reactions in higher-ranked persons. It elicits positive and negative feelings and envied persons sometimes try to get closer to enviers and sometimes they distance themselves. Studies document this pattern in remembered situations, the work context, or in experimentally-induced comparison situations. This diversity of methodological approaches underlines that reacting ambivalently to being envied is a robust phenomenon. Until now, there is less theorizing or research predicting which reaction is more likely in a particular situation.

Taking the distinction between benign and malicious envy into account may partly clarify this complexity (see also Parrott 2017), even though no direct evidence supports this proposition. Specifically, we predict that higher-ranked persons who are benignly envied appreciate this situation more. Being benignly envied implies that lower-ranked persons consider higher-ranked persons as role models and try emulating their success. Being in such an exemplary role should bolster higher-ranked persons' confidence and hence elicit positive feelings. The higher appreciation for being benignly envied may subsequently foster approach tendencies, potentially to connect with enviers, to further reinforce self-confidence, or to appease enviers such that enviers cannot threaten the superior position of higher-ranked persons. In contrast, we predict that higher-ranked persons who are maliciously envied dislike this situation. Being maliciously envied implies that lower-ranked persons consider higher-ranked persons' success as subjectively undeserved and try undermining it. Depending on how effectively enviers can put the harmful intentions into practice, the more afraid higher-ranked persons will be. The higher dislike for being maliciously envied may subsequently foster avoidance tendencies, potentially to get out of the reach of enviers, isolate them, or to distract oneself from the threat.

One theoretical framework aligns with these ideas (Puranik et al. 2019). It proposes that approach is more likely when the involved parties are in interdependence relationships. Interdependence implies that a groups' success depends on close collaboration. According to the framework, in these contexts, being envied predicts appeasement behaviors. In contrast, when interdependence is low, being envied predicts self-protective behaviors. The framework aligns with our predictions because interdependence should be a hallmark of prestige hierarchies, whereas it is less likely to be characteristic for dominance hierarchies. In interdependent groups, given that prestige hierarchies foster benign envy, lower-ranked persons should be more likely to be benignly envious. Higher-ranked persons may then appease enviers, helping them to achieve greater collaborative success in the future and to mitigate enviers' efforts to improve. In contrast, in less interdependent groups, all members must fight for themselves because success is ascribed to individuals and not the team. Relationship-promoting initiatives could even backfire and harm individual success. In such an environment, people might tend to dislike higher-ranked others, eliciting malicious envy. Higher-ranked persons would then need to protect their rank, ideally by avoiding enviers such that they cannot interfere with higher-ranked persons' work.

Two studies further support our arguments. First, in one study, a cooperative as compared to a competitive context led to less feelings of being envied. In this study, according to our opinion, the measure of envy mapped more onto malicious than benign envy (Ye et al. 2021). Second, another study relied on people from Spain as participants and compared them to people from the US (Rodriguez Mosquera, Parrott, and Hurtado de Mendoza 2010; for a detailed discussion of the role of culture in envy see Rodriguez Mosquera in this volume). Culturally, Spain is characterized by horizontal collectivism that values higher connectedness and cooperation compared to more individualistic cultures such as the United States. In line with our reasoning, Spanish participants expected more benign envy in others than US participants. Thus, situations and cultural contexts that emphasize collaboration are more likely to foster perceptions of being benignly envied, while the same situations also foster approach. In contrast, situations that emphasize competitiveness are more likely to foster perceptions of being maliciously envied, while the same situations also foster avoidance.

However, our proposition cannot explain all findings. In particular, sometimes higher-ranked persons experience positive feelings when being maliciously envied (Romani, Grappi, and Bagozzi 2016). One interpretation for this finding may be that these positive feelings reflect increased psychological distance between envied persons and enviers. Positive feelings occurred only in situations in which higher-ranked persons disliked enviers. Hence, it may have been pleasurable to see these enviers suffer. This notion is further supported by the finding that higher-ranked persons reported negative feelings toward malicious enviers they liked. These negative feelings may signal empathy toward enviers, a reaction that can soothe the situation.

Another finding that may initially seem at odds with our proposition is that higher-ranked persons sometimes appease malicious enviers (Van de Ven, Zeelenberg, and Pieters 2010). However, we think this finding is nevertheless compatible with our reasoning. In the study, higher-ranked persons' success resulted from a random draw. Therefore, they may have felt uncomfortable with being advantaged as compared to other persons. Believing that the other persons consider higher-ranked persons' advantage as subjectively undeserved (i.e., is maliciously envious), the higher-ranked persons should be motivated to make it up to the other persons. Appeasement becomes, hence, more likely. Moreover, appeasement behaviors may help higher-ranked persons deal with their own negative feelings that result from being the target of an upward comparison (Exline and Lobel 1999). We expect that when higher-ranked persons' advantage stems from a competitive interaction, a different pattern will occur. Higher-ranked persons can infer from malicious envy that lower-ranked persons consider their advantage as subjectively undeserved (for a review of such inferences see Lange, Heerdink, and Van Kleef 2021). When higher-ranked persons instead think that they earned their advantage, they may think of lower-ranked persons as disrespectful. Such thoughts should render avoidance more likely.

Thus, higher-ranked persons who are maliciously envied may appease lower-ranked persons they want to keep close and avoid lower-ranked persons they perceive as distant to begin with. This reasoning implies that the path from being maliciously envied to avoidance is likely moderated. We propose two moderators that determine how the path will unfold: interpersonal closeness and competitiveness. Higher-ranked persons may feel bad for being maliciously envied and appease malicious enviers when they are close to these enviers and when they received non-competitive rewards. In contrast, higher-ranked persons may feel good for being maliciously envied and avoid malicious enviers when they are not close to them and when they received competitive rewards.

Moreover, we expect that also the path from being benignly envied to approach is moderated. When being benignly envied, higher-ranked persons may sometimes fear losing their position. Avoiding benign enviers then assures that these enviers cannot learn from higher-ranked persons or emulate their success. Potentially, the same moderators as for being maliciously envied are important for being benignly envied as well. Specifically, higher-ranked persons may approach benign enviers when they are close to these enviers and when they earned their success in a competitive context. In contrast, higher-ranked persons may avoid benign enviers when they are not close to these enviers and when they received their success without engaging in a competition.

Even though we argue that the paths from being benignly and maliciously envied to approach and avoidance behaviors, respectively, are moderated, we nevertheless think that they occur most frequently in their direct form. Specifically, we expect that higher-ranked persons react to being benignly envied most frequently with approach and to being maliciously envied with avoidance. This expectation is based on the idea that common situations eliciting benign and malicious envy will steer reactions by higher-ranked persons toward the respective behavior. In most contexts, benign and malicious envy result from competitive encounters, or at least the hierarchy is based on non-random achievements (DelPriore, Hill, and Buss 2012). Moreover, prestige hierarchies often foster mutual liking, whereas dominance hierarchies foster mutual disliking (for related arguments, see Cheng et al. 2013; Henrich and Gil-White 2001; Lange and Crusius 2015). In combination, these characteristics should foster approach toward benign enviers and avoidance of malicious enviers.

STEP 4: RANK IMPLICATIONS OF APPROACH AND AVOIDANCE

Finally, we argue that reactions to being envied further regulate social hierarchies. Approaching benign enviers may reinforce higher-ranked persons' prestige. Approach may include appeasing enviers, but may also increase higher-ranked persons' own effort and performance, as studies document (e.g., Lee et al. 2018). Hence, higher-ranked persons would strengthen their image of being a cooperative, knowledgeable, and successful person. In contrast, avoiding and ignoring malicious enviers may protect higher-ranked persons' dominance without much effort. By reducing contact to malicious enviers, higher-ranked persons lower the risk of becoming a victim of harming behaviors that will challenge or even diminish their intimidating image.

Research at least indirectly supports these predictions. First, previous theorizing predicts that approach fosters mutually supportive relationships between coworkers, whereas avoidance lowers it (Puranik et al. 2019). Hence, approaching benign enviers may further improve social relationships, potentially reinforcing the prestige hierarchy. In contrast, avoiding malicious enviers may further isolate lower-ranked persons, potentially protecting the dominance hierarchy. Second, envied persons were more likely to be ostracized when they were high on neuroticism and low on their need to belong, suggesting that they would not try to reconnect with enviers (F. Liu et al. 2019). From our perspective, trying to socially reconnect with benign enviers may keep relationships with them alive and consequentially reinforce a prestige hierarchy.

Additional findings also support our proposition. Specifically, expressing positivity as hubristic pride fosters perceptions of dominance (Cheng, Tracy, and Henrich 2010). Hence, expressing positivity towards disliked malicious enviers can reinforce the dominance hierarchy. Moreover, appeasing others by sharing one's failures next to one's successes mitigates their malicious envy and fosters their benign envy (Brooks et al. 2019). Hence, approach following being maliciously envied may protect the dominance hierarchy or even lead to perceptions of prestige when lower-ranked persons start experiencing benign envy. Thus, various studies indicate that reactions by envied persons could further strengthen or protect their social rank.

Interestingly, sustaining or increasing social rank could start the cycle with the four steps anew. Potentially, approach and avoidance initially decrease lower-ranked persons' envy. Nevertheless, the maintained superiority keeps higher-ranked persons in an exposed situation, potentially leading to more envy by others in the future. Thus, envy and being envied shape the social hierarchy continuously.

SUMMARY AND DISCUSSION

In sum, diverse evidence is in line with the conclusion that envy and being envied shape social hierarchies. We analyzed the entire process from rank displays via envy to being envied and corresponding reactions by dividing it into four intertwined steps. Moreover, we argue to consider the two different envy forms—benign and malicious envy—to unravel the dynamic complexities of this process.

Importantly, many of our conclusions are based only on indirect evidence. This point primarily applies to research on being envied, which is still in its infancy. The few studies on this topic rarely distinguished between benign and malicious envy. Accordingly, future research should investigate how higher-ranked persons react to being benignly and maliciously envied and which moderators affect their reactions. Furthermore, categorizing higher-ranked persons' reactions in terms of approach and avoidance may turn out to be too broad. Instead, it may be reasonable to develop a more fine-grained classification covering reactions such as appeasement, teasing, or ostracism. Moreover, we deem it important to investigate how these reactions eventually affect the existing hierarchy.

Research on being envied will further benefit from methodological advancement. So far, research on being envied is mostly based on self-report, almost uniformly relying on one particular three-item scale (Vecchio 2005). Two items of this scale measure resentment. Resentment is conceptually distinguishable from envy but, if anything, close to malicious envy (Crusius and Lange 2014; Van de Ven, Zeelenberg, and Pieters 2009, 2012). Therefore, one risk is that research on being envied focused on an emotion other than envy or focused primarily on being maliciously envied. Interestingly, potentially to take this confound into account, sometimes authors replaced the term *resentment* with *envy* when using the scale (Lee et al. 2018). The present reasoning implies that future research should develop and validate new scales to measure being benignly and maliciously envied.

Relatedly, it is not certain whether and when self-reports of being envied are valid. In all studies we are aware of, people reported that they are envied. However, the research did not ensure that this impression is accurate. Only in one case did authors complement their main studies with additional data to investigate this question. It suggested that perceptions of being envied may sometimes correlate with actual envy judgments (Lee et al. 2018). Given that, in other studies, people failed to perceive the envy of unacquainted competitors (Lange et al. 2020), we are hesitant to conclude that perceptions of being envied are always accurate. More research is needed on the chronic and situational determinants of people's motivation as well as their ability to show or to hide their envy. Such research should also provide insight into when observers' judgments are more likely to be accurate. At the same time, it is often not important that these perceptions are accurate given that any reaction will mostly depend on higher-ranked persons' subjective perception that they are envied and not necessarily on the accuracy of this perception. However, research on being envied has a different meaning when it is about attributions of envy to others as compared to actually being envied.

Ideally, future research would even investigate all four steps simultaneously. One context for such an investigation is a rivalry. A study could follow rivals over repeated interactions in which they establish a hierarchy, measuring lower-ranked rivals' envy and higher-ranked rivals' displays of rank as well as perceptions of being envied and ensuing reactions. For instance, the study could investigate fans of known rivals in team sports in which these teams repeatedly compete. Such a comprehensive study could advance our understanding of the regulatory role of envy in social hierarchies.

CONCLUSION

Given their fundamental desire for social rank, people constantly try to advance in social hierarchies or to protect their standing. We argue that one emotion contributing to these efforts is envy. Importantly, envy shapes social hierarchies not only by governing the behavior of those who are worse off. Envy also affects behavior in those who are its target. Specifically, not only do lower-ranked persons react with envy to higher-ranked persons rank displays to change the situation in their favor; higher-ranked persons also try to keep the hierarchy in check by mitigating or distancing themselves from the threat enviers pose. We hope that the present framework facilitates future research by structuring the existing literature and pointing out promising avenues to illuminate how envy and being envied shape social hierarchies.[1]

NOTE

1. We thank Sara Protasi, Felipe Romero, and the other contributors of this volume for valuable feedback. Correspondence should be addressed to Jens Lange, University of Hamburg, Differential Psychology and Psychological Assessment, Von-Melle-Park 5, 20146 Hamburg, Germany, lange.jens@outlook.com.

REFERENCES

Anderson, Cameron, John Angus D. Hildreth, and Laura Howland. 2015. "Is the Desire for Status a Fundamental Human Motive? A Review of the Empirical Literature." *Psychological Bulletin* 141 (3): 574–601. https://doi.org/10.1037/a0038781.

Anderson, Cameron, John Angus D. Hildreth, and Daron L. Sharps. 2020. "The Possession of High Status Strengthens the Status Motive." *Personality and Social Psychology Bulletin* 46 (12): 1712–23. https://doi.org/10.1177/0146167220937544.

Brooks, Alison Wood, Karen Huang, Nicole Abi-Esber, Ryan W. Buell, Laura Huang, and Brian Hall. 2019. "Mitigating Malicious Envy: Why Successful Individuals Should Reveal Their Failures." *Journal of Experimental Psychology: General* 148 (4): 667–87. https://doi.apa.org/doi/10.1037/xge0000538.

Cheng, Joey T., Jessica L. Tracy, Tom Foulsham, Alan Kingstone, and Joseph Henrich. 2013. "Two Ways to the Top: Evidence That Dominance and Prestige Are Distinct yet Viable Avenues to Social Rank and Influence." *Journal of Personality and Social Psychology* 104 (1): 103–25. https://doi.org/10.1037/a0030398.

Cheng, Joey T., Jessica L. Tracy, and Joseph Henrich. 2010. "Pride, Personality, and the Evolutionary Foundations of Human Social Status." *Evolution and Human Behavior* 31 (5): 334–47. https://doi.org/10.1016/j.evolhumbehav.2010.02.004.

Crusius, Jan, Manuel F. Gonzalez, Jens Lange, and Yochi Cohen-Charash. 2020. "Envy: An Adversarial Review and Comparison of Two Competing Views." *Emotion Review* 12 (1): 3–21. https://doi.org/10.1177/1754073919873131.

Crusius, Jan, and Jens Lange. 2014. "What Catches the Envious Eye? Attentional Biases within Malicious and Benign Envy." *Journal of Experimental Social Psychology* 55 (November): 1–11. https://doi.org/10.1016/j.jesp.2014.05.007.

———. 2017. "How Do People Respond to Threatened Social Status? Moderators of Benign versus Malicious Envy." In *Envy at Work and in Organizations: Research, Theory, and Applications*, edited by R. H. Smith, U. Merlone, and M. K. Duffy, 85–110. New York, NY: Oxford University Press.

———. 2021. "Counterfactual Thoughts Distinguish Benign and Malicious Envy." *Emotion* 21(5), 905–920. https://doi.org/10.1037/emo0000923.

Crusius, Jan, Josephine Thierhoff, and Jens Lange. 2021. "Dispositional Greed Predicts Benign and Malicious Envy." *Personality and Individual Differences* 168 (January): 110361. https://doi.org/10.1016/j.paid.2020.110361.

D'Arms, Justin. 2018. "Envy." In *Stanford Encyclopedia of Philosophy*, edited by E. N. Zalta. https://plato.stanford.edu/archives/spr2018/entries/envy/.

DelPriore, Danielle J., Sarah E. Hill, and David M. Buss. 2012. "Envy: Functional Specificity and Sex-Differentiated Design Features." *Personality and Individual Differences* 53 (3): 317–22. https://doi.org/10.1016/j.paid.2012.03.029.

Duffy, Michelle K., KiYoung Lee, and Elizabeth A. Adair. 2021. "Workplace Envy." *Annual Review of Organizational Psychology and Organizational Behavior* 8 (1): 19–44. https://doi.org/10.1146/annurev-orgpsych-012420-055746.

Exline, Julie Juola, and Marci Lobel. 1999. "The Perils of Outperformance: Sensitivity about Being the Target of a Threatening Upward Comparison." *Psychological Bulletin* 125 (3): 307–37. https://doi.org/10.1037/0033-2909.125.3.307.

Fileva, Iskra. 2019. "Envy's Non-Innocent Victims." *Journal of Philosophy of Emotion* 1 (1): 1–22. https://doi.org/10.33497/jpe.v1i1.25.

Fiske, Susan T. 2010. "Envy up, Scorn down: How Comparison Divides Us." *American Psychologist* 65 (8): 698–706. https://doi.org/10.1037/0003-066X.65.8.698.

Fournier, Marc A. 2020. "Dimensions of Human Hierarchy as Determinants of Health and Happiness." *Current Opinion in Psychology* 33: 110–14. https://doi.org/10.1016/j.copsyc.2019.07.014.

Henrich, Joseph, and Francisco J Gil-White. 2001. "The Evolution of Prestige: Freely Conferred Deference as a Mechanism for Enhancing the Benefits of Cultural Transmission." *Evolution and Human Behavior* 22 (3): 165–96. https://doi.org/10.1016/S1090-5138(00)00071-4.

Keltner, Dacher, Disa Sauter, Jessica Tracy, and Alan Cowen. 2019. "Emotional Expression: Advances in Basic Emotion Theory." *Journal of Nonverbal Behavior* 43 (2): 133–60. https://doi.org/10.1007/s10919-019-00293-3.

Khan, Abdul Karim, Chris M. Bell, and Samina Quratulain. 2017. "The Two Faces of Envy: Perceived Opportunity to Perform as a Moderator of Envy Manifestation." *Personnel Review* 46 (3): 490–511. https://doi.org/10.1108/PR-12-2014-0279.

Lange, Jens, Agneta H. Fischer, and Gerben A. Van Kleef. 2022. "'You're Just Envious': Inferring Benign and Malicious Envy from Facial Expressions and Contextual Information." *Emotion* 22(1), 64–80. https://doi.org/10.1037/emo0001047.

Lange, Jens, and Lea Boecker. 2019. "Schadenfreude as Social-Functional Dominance Regulator." *Emotion* 19 (3): 489–502. https://doi.org/10.1037/emo0000454.

Lange, Jens, and Jan Crusius. 2015. "The Tango of Two Deadly Sins: The Social-Functional Relation of Envy and Pride." *Journal of Personality and Social Psychology* 109 (3): 453–72. https://doi.org/10.1037/pspi0000026.

Lange, Jens, and Sara Protasi. 2021. "An Interdisciplinary Perspective on the Value of Envy." *Review of Philosophy and Psychology*, April. https://doi.org/10.1007/s13164-021-00548-3.

Lange, Jens, Aaron C. Weidman, and Jan Crusius. 2018. "The Painful Duality of Envy: Evidence for an Integrative Theory and a Meta-Analysis on the Relation of Envy and Schadenfreude." *Journal of Personality and Social Psychology* 114 (4): 572–98. https://doi.org/10.1037/pspi0000118.

Lange, Jens, Birk Hagemeyer, Thomas Lösch, and Katrin Rentzsch. 2020. "Accuracy and Bias in the Social Perception of Envy." *Emotion* 20 (8): 1399–410. https://doi.org/10.1037/emo0000652.

Lange, Jens, Jan Crusius, and Birk Hagemeyer. 2016. "The Evil Queen's Dilemma: Linking Narcissistic Admiration and Rivalry to Benign and Malicious Envy." *European Journal of Personality* 30 (2): 168–88. https://doi.org/10.1002/per.2047.

Lange, Jens, Liz Redford, and Jan Crusius. 2019. "A Status-Seeking Account of Psychological Entitlement." *Personality and Social Psychology Bulletin* 45 (7): 1113–28. https://doi.org/10.1177/0146167218808501.

Lange, Jens, Marc W. Heerdink, and Gerben A. Van Kleef. 2021. "Reading Emotions, Reading People: Emotion Perception and Inferences Drawn from Perceived Emotions." *Current Opinion in Psychology*, June. https://doi.org/10.1016/j.copsyc.2021.06.008.

Leahy, Robert L. 2021. "Cognitive-Behavioral Therapy for Envy." *Cognitive Therapy and Research* 45: 418–27. https://doi.org/10.1007/s10608-020-10135-y.

Lee, KiYoung, Michelle K. Duffy, Kristin L. Scott, and Michaéla C. Schippers. 2018. "The Experience of Being Envied at Work: How Being Envied Shapes Employee Feelings and Motivation." *Personnel Psychology* 71 (2): 181–200. https://doi.org/10.1111/peps.12251.

Liu, Fang, Dege Liu, Juncheng Zhang, and Jingxing Ma. 2019. "The Relationship between Being Envied and Workplace Ostracism: The Moderating Role of Neuroticism and the Need to Belong." *Personality and Individual Differences* 147 (September): 223–28. https://doi.org/10.1016/j.paid.2019.04.040.

Liu, Yan, Julie N.Y. Zhu, and Long W. Lam. 2020. "Obligations and Feeling Envied: A Study of Workplace Status and Knowledge Hiding." *Journal of Managerial Psychology* 35 (5): 347–59. https://doi.org/10.1108/JMP-05-2019-0276.

Magee, Joe C., and Adam D. Galinsky. 2008. "Social Hierarchy: The Self‑reinforcing Nature of Power and Status." *The Academy of Management Annals* 2 (1): 351–98. https://doi.org/10.1080/19416520802211628.

Mahadevan, Nikhila, Aiden P. Gregg, and Constantine Sedikides. 2019. "Is Self-Regard a Sociometer or a Hierometer? Self-Esteem Tracks Status and Inclusion, Narcissism Tracks Status." *Journal of Personality and Social Psychology* 116 (3): 444–66. https://doi.org/10.1037/pspp0000189.

Maner, Jon K., and Charleen R. Case. 2016. "Dominance and Prestige: Dual Strategies for Navigating Social Hierarchies." In *Advances in Experimental Social Psychology*, edited by James M. Olson and Mark P. Zanna, 54: 129–80. Elsevier. http://linkinghub.elsevier.com/retrieve/pii/S0065260116300144.

Miceli, Maria, and Cristiano Castelfranchi. 2007. "The Envious Mind." *Cognition & Emotion* 21 (3): 449–79. https://doi.org/10.1080/02699930600814735.

Parrott, W. G. 2017. "The Benefits and Threats from Being Envied in Organizations." In *Envy at Work and in Organizations*, edited by R. H. Smith, U. Merlone, and M. K. Duffy, 455–74. New York: Oxford University Press.

Parrott, W. G., and R. H. Smith. 1993. "Distinguishing the Experiences of Envy and Jealousy." *Journal of Personality and Social Psychology* 64 (6): 906–20. https://doi.org/10.1037/0022-3514.64.6.906.

Pettit, Nathan C., Sarah P. Doyle, Robert B. Lount, and Christopher To. 2016. "Cheating to Get Ahead or to Avoid Falling behind? The Effect of Potential Negative versus Positive Status Change on Unethical Behavior." *Organizational Behavior and Human Decision Processes* 137 (November): 172–83. https://doi.org/10.1016/j.obhdp.2016.09.005.

Protasi, Sara. 2016. "Varieties of Envy." *Philosophical Psychology* 29 (4): 535–49. https://doi.org/10.1080/09515089.2015.1115475.

Puranik, Harshad, Joel Koopman, Heather C. Vough, and Daniel L. Gamache. 2019. "They Want What I've Got (I Think): The Causes and Consequences of Attributing Coworker Behavior to Envy." *Academy of Management Review* 44 (2): 424–49. https://doi.org/10.5465/amr.2016.0191.

Rodriguez Mosquera, Patricia M. 2022. "A Sociocultural Perspective on Envy: On Covetous Desire, the Evil Eye, and the Social Regulation of Equality." In *The Moral Psychology of Envy* (in this volume), edited by Sara Protasi. Rowman & Littlefield.

Rodriguez Mosquera, Patricia M., W. Gerrod Parrott, and Alejandra Hurtado de Mendoza. 2010. "I Fear Your Envy, I Rejoice in Your Coveting: On the Ambivalent Experience of Being Envied by Others." *Journal of Personality and Social Psychology* 99 (5): 842–54. https://doi.org/10.1037/a0020965.

Romani, Simona, Silvia Grappi, and Richard P. Bagozzi. 2016. "The Bittersweet Experience of Being Envied in a Consumption Context." *European Journal of Marketing* 50 (7/8): 1239–62. https://doi.org/10.1108/EJM-03-2015-0133.

Romero, F. 2022. "On the Epistemic Effects of Envy in Academia." In *The Moral Psychology of Envy* (this volume), edited by Sara Protasi. Rowman & Littlefield.

Salerno, Anthony, Juliano Laran, and Chris Janiszewski. 2019. "The Bad Can Be Good: When Benign and Malicious Envy Motivate Goal Pursuit." *Journal of Consumer Research* 46 (2): 388–405. https://doi.org/10.1093/jcr/ucy077.

Salovey, Peter, and Judith Rodin. 1984. "Some Antecedents and Consequences of Social-Comparison Jealousy." *Journal of Personality and Social Psychology* 47 (4): 780–92. https://doi.org/10.1037/0022-3514.47.4.780.

Sapolsky, R. M. 2005. "The Influence of Social Hierarchy on Primate Health." *Science* 308 (5722): 648–52. https://doi.org/10.1126/science.1106477.

Sayers, D. L. 1969. *The Other Six Deadly Sins*. New York: Harcourt, Brace & World.

Scott, Kristin L., Stefan Tams, Michaéla C. Schippers, and KiYoung Lee. 2015. "Opening the Black Box: Why and When Workplace Exclusion Affects Social Reconnection Behaviour, Health, and Attitudes." *European Journal of Work and Organizational Psychology* 24 (2): 239–55. https://doi.org/10.1080/1359432X.2014.894978.

Sivanathan, Niro, Madan M. Pillutla, and J. Keith Murnighan. 2008. "Power Gained, Power Lost." *Organizational Behavior and Human Decision Processes* 105 (2): 135–46. https://doi.org/10.1016/j.obhdp.2007.10.003.

Smith, R. H., and Sung Hee Kim. 2007. "Comprehending Envy." *Psychological Bulletin* 133 (1): 46–64. https://doi.org/10.1037/0033-2909.133.1.46.

Steckler, Connor M., and Jessica L. Tracy. 2014. "The Emotional Underpinnings of Social Status." In *The Psychology of Social Status*, edited by Joey T. Cheng, Jessica L. Tracy, and Cameron Anderson, 201–24. New York: Springer.

van de Ven, Niels. 2016. "Envy and Its Consequences: Why It Is Useful to Distinguish between Benign and Malicious Envy." *Social and Personality Psychology Compass* 10 (6): 337–49. https://doi.org/10.1111/spc3.12253.

van de Ven, Niels, Charles E. Hoogland, Richard H. Smith, Wilco W. van Dijk, Seger M. Breugelmans, and Marcel Zeelenberg. 2015. "When Envy Leads to Schadenfreude." *Cognition and Emotion* 29 (6): 1007–25. https://doi.org/10.1080/02699931.2014.961903.

van de Ven, Niels, Marcel Zeelenberg, and Rik Pieters. 2011. "Why Envy Outperforms Admiration." *Personality and Social Psychology Bulletin* 37 (6): 784–95. https://doi.org/10.1177/0146167211400421.

———. 2009. "Leveling Up and Down: The Experiences of Benign and Malicious Envy." *Emotion* 9 (3): 419–29. https://doi.org/10.1037/a0015669.

———. 2010. "Warding off the Evil Eye: When the Fear of Being Envied Increases Prosocial Behavior." *Psychological Science* 21 (11): 1671–77. https://doi.org/10.1177/0956797610385352.

———. 2012. "Appraisal Patterns of Envy and Related Emotions." *Motivation and Emotion* 36 (2): 195–204. https://doi.org/10.1007/s11031-011-9235-8.

Vecchio, Robert. 2005. "Explorations in Employee Envy: Feeling Envious and Feeling Envied." *Cognition & Emotion* 19 (1): 69–81. https://doi.org/10.1080/02699930441000148.

Vendrell Ferran, I. 2022. "'I Could Have Been You': Existential Envy and the Self." In *The Moral Psychology of Envy* (this volume), edited by Sara Protasi. Rowman & Littlefield.

Von Rueden, C., M. Gurven, and H. Kaplan. 2011. "Why Do Men Seek Status? Fitness Payoffs to Dominance and Prestige." *Proceedings of the Royal Society B: Biological Sciences* 278 (1715): 2223–32. https://doi.org/10.1098/rspb.2010.2145.

Ye, Yijiao, Yijing Lyu, Ho Kwong Kwan, Xingwen Chen, and Xuan-Mei Cheng. 2021. "The Antecedents and Consequences of Being Envied by Coworkers: An Investigation from the Victim Perspective." *International Journal of Hospitality Management* 94 (April): 102751. https://doi.org/10.1016/j.ijhm.2020.102751.

Yusainy, Cleoputri, Ziadatul Hikmiah, Cathy Sofhieanty, and Muhammad Ibrahim. 2019. "Deception in Negotiation: The Predicting Roles of Envy and Individual Differences." *ANIMA Indonesian Psychological Journal* 33 (4): 203–12. https://doi.org/10.24123/aipj.v33i4.1794.

Chapter 3

On the Epistemic Effects of Envy in Academia

Felipe Romero

> Spending plenty of time on something can be the most sophisticated form of revenge.
>
> —Haruki Murakami, *The Wind-Up Bird Chronicle*

Do a quick Google search. Type "envy" and "academia." You will find many anecdotes of envious academics in opinion pieces, blog entries, forums, and social media posts. Some of these anecdotes are bitter, and some are heartbreaking. But they all reveal the same: academics often feel miserable because of their colleagues' success. They compete and compare themselves with others, envying positions, grants, research visits, paper acceptances, conference travels, awards, and the like. If you are an academic, the odds are that you have been in that situation at some point. If that doesn't sound familiar, you are an exemplar of equanimity. Or, perhaps, you don't experience much envy because you are one of those who inspire it.

Here I'm going to focus on envy that academics experience *qua contributors to the production of knowledge*. I will refer to this kind of envy as "academic envy." With this focus, I intend to explore the *epistemic effects* of academic envy. This approach is not the only possible one to explore envy in academia. From a general perspective, and contrary to a romantic ideal, academia since the twentieth century has increasingly become a work environment like many others. (Indeed, many universities increasingly resemble corporations.) As such, some of the insights from the vast psychological literature on envy in the workplace may apply. However, my approach here puts at the forefront one aspect distinctive of academia and less present in other work environments, namely, the centrality of epistemic work. My motivation is social epistemological. Work on the social epistemology of science reveals how various contextual factors govern academics' work and affect epistemic outcomes, factors such as communication protocols, institutional structures, and researchers' particular conditions. One contextual factor that deserves attention is that researchers are not dispassionate machines that produce knowledge but human beings with rich emotional lives. Given the pervasiveness of academic envy, I believe it is a helpful entry point to study how such emotional lives impact academics' work and, ultimately, epistemic progress.

I proceed as follows. First, I give a characterization of envy that captures prototypical cases of envy according to the philosophical literature. Second, I use this characterization to present a classic argument according to which envy is collectively disadvantageous and, therefore, an emotion that we should prevent from arising in society. Third, before evaluating whether this argument holds in the academic context, I discuss distinctive aspects of the academic environment based on work on the economics and social epistemology of science. These aspects concern the features of the groups within which academics compare themselves, the kind of goods that researchers envy, and the strategies that the envious academic employs to eliminate her envy. Fourth, based on these distinctive aspects, I argue that the argument from collective disadvantage doesn't apply to the academic context. On the contrary, I suggest that the best strategies available to the envious academic to reducing her envy typically lead to collective epistemic benefits. Finally, I briefly discuss whether we should restructure academic institutions to reduce envy. This question constitutes a challenge for the design of epistemic institutions as it reveals a tension between epistemic and social values. I argue that while it is desirable to modify the social structure of science to reduce the adverse psychological effects of social comparisons between academics, it is difficult to do so without severe epistemic drawbacks.

WHAT IS ENVY? THREE COMPONENTS

I will say that envy consists of three core components. But I do this with a methodological caveat. I am not proposing a definition of envy in terms of necessary and sufficient conditions by stating these components. In general, providing such definitions for emotions runs the risk of imposing more structure on our emotional life than it has. (Notice, however, that such clear-cut definitions can be helpful for modeling in some contexts despite their descriptive shortcomings, such as AI or economics.) In particular, envy often overlaps with other emotions triggered by unfavorable social comparisons. When you feel envy, you may also feel jealousy, resentment, schadenfreude, or selfishness. The boundaries are often unclear. To make matters harder, different languages carve the space of these emotions with words that are not easily inter-translatable (Protasi 2021, 28). Hence, I acknowledge from the outset that some cases of envy may escape my characterization, and for them, more refined analyses would be in order. Nonetheless, despite these difficulties, I extract some common aspects of envy that philosophers highlight, as they give us a good starting point to talk about appraisals and manifestations of the emotion in academia.

The first component is an *assessment of relative disadvantage*. Envy arises when the person compares herself to another with respect to specific goods (e.g., possessions, qualities, and status), and the comparison is unfavorable. This component is common in classic characterizations of the emotion (Aristotle 1967, 1386b; Hume [1757] 1898, sec. III, 4). The relativity aspect is crucial because envy arises even if the person's absolute position with respect to an envied good is favorable. Even in such cases, the unfavorable comparison leads to a state of distress. The envious person is in pain because she does not have the desired good and, importantly, because the other person has it.

The second component is an *assessment of proximity*. We certainly do not envy all of those who have something we desire. For instance, Mr. P does not envy everyone who has a Porsche, but it could be painful for him to see his coworker in one. In line with this familiar idea, several authors state that the comparisons that trigger envy are restricted to a specific group of others that we consider equals in relevant subjective ways, such as competitors, professional peers, and even friends. "Potter to potter and builder to builder," as Aristotle says (Aristotle 1967, 1381b; see also Hume [1757] 1898, sec. IV, 5; and Ben-Ze'ev 1992, 557). The intricacies of how proximity works are subtle, though. Being similar in terms of traits is not sufficient for us to experience someone as proximal if the traits are not part of our self-conception. For instance, you can be a lawyer to pay the bills but an artist at heart and hence not care about how similar other lawyers are to you. Also, how evident the other person's traits are to you (e.g., due to mere physical proximity) can increase the perception that the comparison is relevant to you even in the absence of more substantive similarity.

The third component is a *desire that the disadvantage be eliminated*. This component is one of the most intriguing aspects of envy. As D'Arms and Kerr say, "the function of envy is to benefit the envious agent's standing in some status hierarchies by motivating him to improve his comparative position" (D'Arms and Kerr 2008, 44).[1] Notice that this desire does not always arise when the previous two requirements—that is, disadvantage and proximity—are in place. The kind of relationship that people have can prevent this desire from arising. For instance, Mr. P may have this desire if one of his competitors gets a job, but he may not have this desire if his wife is also a competitor and she gets it. It's also worth noting that, thus stated, this component is relatively neutral. The desire alone does not entail a disposition to act to eliminate the disadvantage. In particular, the desire alone does not entail a malicious disposition, contrary to a possible perception of envy. Also, even when people have a malicious disposition, they often do not act against the people they envy. Several reasons operate as a brake: acting maliciously out of envy is socially condemned; envy involves a second-order emotion (i.e., the envious often feels terrible about feeling envious) that may prevent action; and other moral considerations may do the same.

Let's assume that the person wants to reduce her envy as my discussion focuses on these cases. How can she reduce her envy? Let's look at it in terms of the components. The first way is to try to reduce or block the weight of the assessment of relative disadvantage. The person can try to convince herself that the disadvantage is not so significant or that the envied good is unimportant to her. The second way is by trying to block or reduce the effects of the assessment of proximity. According to the literature on envy in the workplace, participants in psychological studies report adopting different mindsets to disengage from the people they envy (Vecchio 1997). These include, e.g., looking for support from other colleagues or discharging their feelings with friends. Thus, the person increases the psychological distance with respect to the envied and perceives that the disadvantage matters less.

The last way to reduce envy is to satisfy the desire by reducing or eliminating the relative disadvantage itself. An intuitive possibility is that the envious may engage in malicious behaviors. However, this need not be the case. Envious people have other strategies to improve their comparative position. Some authors regard these as different types, kinds, or varieties of envy (Crusius and Mussweiler 2012; Van den Ven 2016; Protasi 2021). Table 3.1 illustrates these strategies with an example. (The list may not be exhaustive but suffices for my purposes.) Suppose we have two agents, a and b. Agent a envies agent b. Let's say that we are considering just one particular good that they have. Let's say a has one unit of this good, b has two, and a feels very envious.

Table 3.1 Strategies to Eliminate Envy. Source: author-created

	a	b
Envy (initial state)	1	2
Self-destruction	0	0
Destruction	1	1
Emulation	2	2
Construction	3	2
	3	3

Starting at the initial state in the table (1, 2), *a* may adopt a *self-destruction* strategy that leaves everyone with no goods (0, 0). Imagine two kids playing. One damages all the toys in the game, including her own, just to make the other lose her toys too. The *destruction* strategy eliminates the advantage the other has (1, 1). *Emulation* involves closing the gap by obtaining what *b* has (2, 2). And the *construction* strategies involve resolving envy by surpassing the rival (3, 2) or lifting everyone (3, 3). With this characterization, we can now move to the arguments that regard envy as an emotion that we should prevent from arising.

ENVY AS COLLECTIVELY DISADVANTAGEOUS

We can identify two kinds of arguments suggesting that we should prevent envy from arising, given the *negative consequences* of situations in which people feel envy. (Importantly, these arguments are not against feeling the emotion itself since it is arguably apt to feel it in some situations.) First, some arguments concern the psychological well-being of the individual who feels envy. From this perspective, envy is an emotion that we should prevent from arising, given the distress and pain that it brings. Envy updates our self-conception; it tells us what our accomplishments mean and highlights what we haven't been able to obtain yet, which can be illuminating but also frustrating. Additionally, envy produces shame; that's why it is usually covert. And envy creates a painful second-order emotion, as mentioned before: we feel bad about feeling envy. I'm going to put this individual perspective aside for a moment, but we will revisit it in the final section on envy and the design of epistemic institutions.

The second kind of argument against envy concerns the effects of envy in collective life. The general idea of these arguments is that we should prevent envy because it is collectively disadvantageous. Such a collective disadvantage results from envious agents' preference for *suboptimal allocation of resources*. Let's look at it in terms of the example in Table 3.1. Suppose the agent has a strong desire to eliminate the relative disadvantage. The strategies that the agent has to satisfy the desire could lead to very different outcomes. For instance, on the one hand, construction makes everyone better off or, at least, improves the envious' situation without harming others. In other words, construction leads to improvements in which no agent loses. On the other hand, self-destruction makes everyone worse off. (In economic distribution terms, construction Pareto-dominates self-destruction.) When many agents apply a mixture of these strategies indistinctively (i.e., regardless of whether more efficient strategies are available), the overall outcome is suboptimal.

The fact that suboptimal allocations satisfy the envious' desire is arguably irrational when we consider that most inequalities don't affect the utilities of what we have (except positional goods that acquire their value given their uncommonness.) For instance, if a has one euro, her euro has the same value regardless of whether b has two or three. But as an envious agent, a would prefer a distribution in which she has, for instance, zero if that means that b loses the advantage as well.

Rawls ([1971] 1999) notoriously gave arguments against envy in the same vein (for discussion, see D'Arms 2016). His arguments rely on the observation that envy makes everyone worse off due to agents' disposition to level down even at a personal cost. (It's worth noting that not all authors share Rawls' observation.) The first argument is that envy should be excluded from his "original position" because it could lead us to adopt the wrong principles of justice Rawls ([1971] 1999, sec. 25). The second argument concerns the social conditions that produce envy. For him, envy is not likely to be strong in a well-ordered society. That is, if the principles of justice succeed in creating a well-ordered society, the circumstances that give rise to envy would be mitigated if not eliminated.

Now the question is, to what extent do these collective considerations against envy apply to the academic context?

ACADEMIC ENVY

To assess the argument against envy in the academic context, I will first explore how the general definitions discussed so far translate to such context. I will begin with the most straightforward one: the assessment of proximity. Who are the academics that we consider proximal? Similar to general cases of envy, you don't envy everyone who obtains what you want. (e.g., it would hurt more after you are denied a prestigious grant if the obnoxious show-off colleague with whom you share your office gets it.) Here it is helpful to think in terms of a *league*—that is, academics who share contexts with you and hence make comparisons of relative disadvantages salient. Here is a non-exhaustive list of such contexts: (1) graduate school classmates (as opposed to academics who went to graduate school at a different university), (2) colleagues at the same department, (3) colleagues at the same career stage, (4) other academics in your field, (5) close collaborators, and (6) academics of your gender and race. As an academic, you tend to envy more academics in your league and less those above or below your league. Now, notice that leagues are not "all or nothing" simply because, thankfully, nobody is too similar to you: while there could be substantial overlap in the contexts that you share with someone, there are contexts that you don't share. Notice also that the evaluation of who is in our leagues is very subjective. Some contexts may matter more to you than to other academics. The colleague down the hall might give a lot of weight to the fact that you two attended the same high school (he hasn't gotten over it), but you might give more weight to the fact that you are both at the same career stage now.

But what do we envy as academics? Recall that here I focus on envy that academics experience qua contributors to the production of knowledge. This focus leaves out other kinds of envy that academics experience, for example, as workers in an office environment or as members of a company. As producers of knowledge, understanding what academics envy requires looking at what we are rewarded for and how rewards work for epistemic work. Academics get rewarded for producing *epistemic goods*: scientific findings, theories, arguments, models, experimental designs, and so on. But not everyone who produces these goods is rewarded. Sociologists of science, and more recently social epistemologists, have studied the reward system of science, and one of their insights is that rewards in science are based on priority. (The literature talks about "science," but the essential insight applies to all research fields.) Their key observation is that only the first researcher that produces a novel epistemic good for the community is rewarded, while second runners get very little or nothing. This reward system is known as *the priority rule* (Merton 1957; Strevens 2003). Evidence for this rule comes from many episodes in the history of science in which researchers have fought viciously with others to establish priority over findings, from Newton and Leibniz and their disputes over calculus to the recent battles between scientists at MIT/Harvard and UC Berkeley over CRISPR/Cas9.

The primary reward that academics receive for their novel epistemic goods is *prestige*—that is, recognition from their colleagues about their priority. Since the twentieth century, scientists have established priority via peer-reviewed publications (this will be important later). Prestige comes in different forms: eponymy, prizes, academic positions, grants, invitations to speak, citations, teaching buyouts, a bigger office, and so on.

Notice that this reward system is imperfect in practice. First, priority ascriptions are primarily a function of what the community perceives, and these perceptions can be erroneous. Non-epistemic factors may lead the community to perceive a person as the producer of a novel finding when they are not. For instance, a researcher can be merely in the vicinity of a finding without being the actual producer but gain credit, for example, for doing a better job than the producer at popularizing the finding or for being the principal investigator in the laboratory that carried out the research without contributing to it. Hence, some priority ascriptions can be controversial.

Second, the prestige that academics acquire does not necessarily track the epistemic value of their contributions. This is understandable in light of the fallibility of science and the fact that assessing epistemic value is difficult and requires time (arguably years). Some goods seem very valuable right when they are published and make their producers famous at that time, but such assessment of high value might radically change decades later. Likewise, valuable goods can be largely ignored and rediscovered after years.

Many academics are aware of these imperfections in the reward system. Nonetheless, the community preserves and protects the practice of ascribing priority and prestige. They do so not by grounding prestige attributions on the value of epistemic goods per se (which, again, would be hard) but by focusing on tangible outputs, such as articles in selective journals, books published with prestigious presses, and the like. In practice, the community assumes that such outputs are reliable proxies of epistemic value and ascribes prestige accordingly. This is evidenced by how central such outputs are in hiring, promotion, and award decisions. Most researchers don't get those prizes only from having great ideas but from having them published in prestigious venues.

Notice also that even if prestige is the reward that academics want, the acquisition of prestige is intimately connected to the production of epistemic goods. If this weren't the case, academics would feel satisfied with acquiring prestige undeservedly—that is, with no epistemic grounds or tangible outputs. While this is an empirical matter, I'd say that this is not the case for most academics. For example, I'd conjecture that most academics wouldn't perceive it as a reward to be suddenly promoted to a higher position without meeting the requirements for promotion or winning an award that they clearly do not deserve. Furthermore, undeserved promotions or awards could arguably contribute to an academic's impostor syndrome.

With these ideas in mind, I suggest that *academic envy is triggered by an assessment of relative disadvantage with respect to the prestige that other academics in your league have*. Three clarifications are in order. First, some academics do not envy prestige, but other material resources and goods (e.g., research funds, reduced teaching loads, access to facilities, etc.) Nonetheless, envy in those cases is mediated by prestige because prestige allows academics to access these goods. Second, such described, academic envy leaves out kinds of envy experienced in academia qua workplace. For instance, you might envy your colleague because of some quality (e.g., their intelligence, their presentation skills, writing style, etc.). These qualities could lead to the production of knowledge, but they don't track differences in prestige. Third, this focus also leaves out envy that you may experience because of your colleagues' success in other academic activities, such as teaching and service.

I will now make other remarks about the nature of epistemic goods that will be helpful to evaluate the argument from collective disadvantage. Epistemic goods are taken to be *public goods* in the economics of science literature (Arrow 1962; Dasgupta and David 1994; Stephan 2012). As such, they have two special features that make them different from goods produced in other spheres in society. The first one is that they are not used up when consumed. This is referred to as *non-rivalry*. The second one is that once they are built, anyone can use them. This is referred to as *non-excludability*. The classic example that illustrates these two features is a lighthouse. First, once you construct a lighthouse, the light that it provides is not used up. Second, it doesn't matter whether there is one boat or one hundred boats on the coast. Any of them can use the light, and you can't prevent some in particular from using the light.

The non-excludability of epistemic goods implies that a researcher cannot appropriate the epistemic goods she produces. That is, once a finding is published in a peer-reviewed publication, anyone from the scientific community can (leaving publisher paywalls aside) benefit from it—that is, get inspired by it and use it. This is one of the reasons why the priority rule has become the reward system of science. The priority rule, the story goes, solves the problem of incentivizing research. The discoverer can't appropriate and sell the finding, but she can appropriate the right to priority, which results in other derived benefits. (While I focus here on academic research, it's worth noting that industry research since the twentieth century circumvents the public character of knowledge with the patent system.)

Another feature of epistemic goods that grounds the priority rule is that they have diminishing returns (Peirce 1967). When a researcher produces a novel epistemic good, further reports of the same discovery provide very little epistemically. For instance, a second person could make the same discovery independently, contributing to the confirmation that that finding is correct. (Recent discussions about replicability show that the contribution of second runners often is understated.) However, as we iterate in that process of repetition, the contributions become negligible. The hundredth person reporting the same good likely contributes very little.

The final feature that I will mention is that, unlike other public goods, *you can't destroy epistemic goods*. Once you produce and publish an epistemic good, you can't reverse its propagation. To make sense of this idea, contrast epistemic goods with public goods as the lighthouse. You can demolish a lighthouse, but once a paper reporting a new result is out there, it is virtually impossible to prevent it from reaching others. Maybe burning libraries and books could have achieved this at some point in the remote past, but this is no longer practically feasible.

REDUCING ACADEMIC ENVY AND COLLECTIVE DISADVANTAGE REVISITED

We can now discuss how we can reduce academic envy. I will do this, again, in terms of the general components of envy presented earlier—that is, an assessment of relative disadvantage, an assessment of proximity, and a desire that the disadvantage be eliminated. First, we can try to reduce the weight of the assessment of relative disadvantage. Your colleague has published two papers on your topic, and you have one. But thinking about it, the disadvantage is not so significant: his work has lower quality than yours, and it's not only quantity that matters to you, right? The second way to reduce envy is to reduce the weight of the assessment of proximity. Recall that one of the coping strategies for envy in the workplace is to distance ourselves psychologically from the envied. As academics, such disengagement could involve reevaluating whether the envied and you belong to the same league. She is a computer scientist, and you are a philosopher. The publication rules of her field are very different; hence the comparison does not make sense. Disengaging could also involve avoiding the envied, looking less at her CV online, and so on.

The last way is to try to satisfy the desire to eliminate the relative disadvantage. According to my analysis, we have four strategies to do this in general cases of envy (i.e., self-destruction, destruction, emulation, and construction.) The question is, do these strategies apply to the academic context? Answering requires evaluating whether the envious academic can employ them effectively. Recall that the production of epistemic goods and prestige are intimately related (with the caveat that, in practice, we rely on imperfect proxies to assess the value of epistemic goods). Hence, changes in prestige could eliminate envy when they track changes in epistemic goods. Having this in mind, I suggest that *the envious academic can only apply strategies in which she can eliminate the epistemic grounds of her relative disadvantage*. This poses a limitation for the applicability of the self-destructive and destructive strategies. Since we can't destroy epistemic goods, the self-destructive and destructive strategies are not a mechanism to change the envied academic's prestige and hence can't effectively reduce envy.

This point has crucial implications for the argument from collective disadvantage discussed earlier. Recall the argument: envious agents may adopt self-destructive and destructive strategies to get rid of their envy, and these strategies lead to suboptimal distributions of goods. However, if envious academics can't adopt these strategies, envy is not collectively disadvantageous in their context. Under the assumption that they want to reduce their envy, the remaining options are emulative and constructive strategies.

Emulation may reduce envy, but it depends on how you interpret it. Recall that epistemic goods have diminishing returns. Hence, simple imitation in epistemic terms is insufficient to help the envious academic match the prestige of her competitor.[2] That is, reporting goods that are the same or too similar to already existing ones will not grant her an equal amount of prestige. To emulate the competitor's prestige, the envious academic has to produce an epistemic good deemed novel by the community. So understood, the emulative strategy is collectively advantageous.

We can make similar remarks about the construction strategy. In epistemic terms, some forms of construction imply collaboration. For instance, collaboration involves building on top of the work of others, opening research avenues for others, or working together with those you envy towards a common goal (think of adversarial collaborations), all of which are collectively advantageous.

Notice, however, that my remarks do not imply that it is easy to get rid of academic envy. Emulating and constructing to the point that matches the envied person's prestige can be difficult. The low-hanging fruits have already been taken in many fields, making it less likely for researchers to develop equally valuable epistemic contributions in succession. Given these difficulties, emulation and construction may fall short, leading to what Protasi calls "inert envy" (Protasi 2021)—that is, a state of envy in which the person's incapability to act causes her further frustration. Nonetheless, we have to think specifically about what we envy. If you envy the prestige of a Nobel Prize, perhaps you are doomed to feel inert envy. If you envy prestige that results from less exclusive academic achievements, such as papers and grants, the motivation to emulate or construct can get you there. And even if you don't fully resolve your envy, your attempts to emulate and construct may still bring epistemic benefits for others.

You might still think that some behaviors inspired by envy can be destructive in academia. Hence, I will discuss in what sense they are harmful and their epistemic relevance.

Destructive but Epistemically Irrelevant Behaviors

One possible kind of destructive behavior is available to the envious academic: malicious behaviors with no direct or indirect epistemic consequences (e.g., burning your envied colleague's car.) For these, I'd say that their prevalence is low, not only because they also entail violations of other sorts of norms but also because they wouldn't reduce the relative disadvantage regarding prestige and hence wouldn't reduce or eliminate envy effectively.

Seemingly Destructive but Epistemically Beneficial Behaviors

You might think that there is something very close to destruction: you can *criticize* epistemic goods. The close competitor working on your same topic published a paper in *The Journal of the Best*. But his argument overlooks a crucial aspect that makes his argument fundamentally flawed. You have to respond. You have to criticize the paper, show the error. Destructive as it may seem, that kind of action is not destructive when interpreted in epistemic terms. In fact, from an epistemic perspective, *criticizing someone else's work is collectively advantageous*. When we criticize someone else's work correctly (i.e., without inducing errors ourselves), we contribute to what the community knows around the original finding.

Consider two specific examples. The first one is replication work in experimental science. When someone conducts a replication of someone else's experiment, even in the unwelcome scenario in which the finding does not replicate, the replicator contributes to the collective good of having adequately confirmed theories. The second is the case of articles that present objections to existing articles, as it is common in the humanities. Such articles benefit the community by providing a more subtle understanding of the domain in question.

There is one extreme case in which the envied researcher's prestige is the product of careless or even fraudulent work. Another researcher motivated by the underserved prestige may try to blow the whistle and take her down. This action could indeed damage the reputation of the first researcher but wouldn't be suboptimal or destructive epistemically.

Destructive Behaviors with Indirect Epistemic Effects

You might also think that envy could motivate destructive behaviors with indirect epistemic effects. Consider the following: recommending the rejection of a paper you are refereeing when you shouldn't; recommending rejection of a grant proposal you are reviewing when you shouldn't; voting against a person in a hiring or promotion committee when you shouldn't; not citing your colleague's work when you should; burdening your colleague unfairly with extra work; engaging in fraud to fail to replicate someone else's work intentionally.

These behaviors occur for sure in academia. But is envy primarily to blame when they happen? To some extent, this is an empirical question, but I conjecture that envy wouldn't be primarily to blame. These behaviors constitute severe violations of norms of academic integrity, and most academics subscribe to such norms. When the norms that prevent these behaviors are violated, the person must have an inclination to play outside of them. Envy could exacerbate such an inclination, but envy alone wouldn't lead to malicious action.

You may have another worry related to the potential indirect epistemic drawbacks of trying to disengage to reduce the assessment of proximity. You may worry that, in extreme cases, if people disengage too much, they may decide to quit academia altogether. This observation could seemingly explain why people quit. Nonetheless, it's necessary to identify the different causes of quitting and their connection to envy. I would say that the most likely culprit of people disengaging and quitting is the pressure from hyper-competition. Academics, in particular early-career academics, have to be very productive to stay afloat. This pressure is draining and likely enough reason for many to decide to leave, even when they don't feel particularly envious of their peers' accomplishments.

There is one reaction to envy in the academic context that you could think is epistemically harmful indirectly: *gossip*. Gossip, in general, can be very damaging (or convenient) for an academic career. However, the epistemic effects of gossip are less obvious. I'd conjecture that gossip is not very effective in damaging the epistemic goods that academics produce. The gossip that could have such an effect would have to be related to the epistemic import of the academic's work. It is true that some academics form impressions about others' work based on gossip. However, when ascribing prestige, the community as a whole evaluates the epistemic import of others' work directly by looking at it. Perhaps the content of gossip could cause epistemic damage when it is widely accepted. Still, in such cases, such content would be arguably grounded in actual epistemic aspects (e.g., problems or merits) of the person's work.

ENVY AND EPISTEMIC INSTITUTIONS DESIGN

Should we restructure academia to reduce envy? So far, my assessment of envy might seem optimistic. However, recall that this assessment concerns a collective and epistemic perspective. At this point, it is worth returning to the arguments against envy from the perspective of the individual's psychological well-being, which I mentioned in passing at the beginning of the paper. Importantly, envy correlates with depression, neuroticism, and hostility (Smith et al. 1999), and it is associated with low self-esteem (Vecchio 2000). These alone, I believe, give us reasons to want to restructure academia in a way that leads to more healthy mindsets.

One condition that reduces the possibility (and pain) of comparison is when inequalities are much larger. As Hume remarks, "a great disproportion cuts off the relation of the ideas, and either keeps us from comparing ourselves with what is remote from us, or diminishes the effects of the comparison" (Hume [1757] 1898, sec. IV, 5). Consider two options for intervention that take on board this idea. The first option is to *intervene to decrease the possibility of proximity assessments between academics*—that is, we might try to create conditions in which academics do not compare themselves to others, or at least not in a way that produces pain. While intuitively desirable, it is hard to achieve such a restructuring without worrisome drawbacks. In academia, such a restructuring would entail, for instance, making the academic hierarchy more stratified, introducing larger gaps between the different levels. This could reduce envy but lead to concentration of power in the hands of a few and less democratic decision-making within institutions.

A second option is to *intervene to decrease the relative epistemic disadvantages that lead to prestige differences*. In practice, this could mean reforming the publication system and funding allocation procedures in a way that reduces productivity gaps between academics. (E.g., imagine a scenario in which everyone is allowed to publish at most N number of articles per year.) Another possibility could be to separate academics' rewards from their epistemic contributions. Thus, differences in epistemic contributions would not lead to envy, but probably at the expense of removing part of academics' motivation to produce novel research.

While we could refine these intervention options, the general worry about them is straightforward. Interventions like these may introduce injustices while being collectively disadvantageous in epistemic terms.

CONCLUSION

I characterized academic envy as the envy of the prestige that results from the production of epistemic goods by academics in one's league. I have suggested that this type of envy, unlike envy in other spheres in society, is not collectively disadvantageous. From a collective perspective, the general arguments against envy do not apply to the academic context. The reason is that the strategies that would reduce envy by leading to collective disadvantages are not readily available to the envious academic, given the nature of epistemic goods. Furthermore, the remaining strategies are usually collectively advantageous in epistemic terms. This creates a tension between the individual and collective assessments of envy and constitutes a challenge for reforming academia to make it a space in which envy is not prevalent.[3]

NOTES

1. This functional account of envy is endorsed by Niels van de Ven in "The Envious Consumer" (chapter 12) and by Jens Lange and Jan Crusius in "How Envy and Being Envied Shape Social Hierarchies" (chapter 2), both contributions to this volume.
2. For a general argument that emulation is not mere imitation, see Maria Silvia Vaccarezza and Ariele Niccoli's contribution to this volume: "Let the Donkeys Be Donkeys: In Defense of Inspiring Envy" (chapter 6).
3. I am grateful to Sara Protasi, Chloé de Canson, and Daphne Brandenburg for their valuable comments on previous drafts. I also thank the audience at the Moral Psychology of Envy Workshop, May 2021, and audiences at Tilburg University and the University of Groningen for helpful discussion. Correspondence should be addressed to: Department of Theoretical Philosophy, Faculty of Philosophy, University of Groningen; c.f.romero@rug.nl.

REFERENCES

Aristotle. 1967. *Rhetoric*. Translated by W. Rhys Roberts. http://www.public.iastate.edu/~honeyl/Rhetoric/index.html.

Arrow, Kenneth J. 1962. "The Economic Implications of Learning by Doing." *The Review of Economic Studies* 29 (3): 155–73.

Ben-Ze'ev, Aaron. 1992. "Envy and Inequality." *The Journal of Philosophy* 89 (11): 551–81.

Crusius, Jan, and Thomas Mussweiler. 2012. "When People Want What Others Have: The Impulsive Side of Envious Desire." *Emotion (Washington, DC)* (United States) 12 (1): 142–53.

D'Arms, Justin. 2017. "Envy." In *The Stanford Encyclopedia of Philosophy*, Spring 2017, edited by Edward N. Zalta.

D'Arms, Justin, and Alison Duncan Kerr. 2008. "Envy in the Philosophical Tradition." In *Envy: Theory and Research*, edited by Richard H. Smith, 39–59. Series in Affective Science. New York: Oxford University Press.

Dasgupta, Partha, and Paul A. David. 1994. "Toward a New Economics of Science." *Research Policy* 23 (5): 487–521.

Hume, David. (1757) 1898. "Dissertation on the Passions." In *The Philosophical Works of David Hume*, edited by T. H. Green and T. H. Grose, II: 138–66. London and New York: Longmans, Green and Co.

Merton, Robert K. 1957. "Priorities in Scientific Discovery: A Chapter in the Sociology of Science." *American Sociological Review* 22 (6): 635–59.

Peirce, Charles S. 1967. "Note on the Theory of the Economy of Research." *Operations Research* 15 (4): 643–48.

Protasi, Sara. 2021. *The Philosophy of Envy*. New York: Cambridge University Press.

Rawls, John. (1971) 1999. *A Theory of Justice*, revised edition. Cambridge, MA: The Belknap Press of Harvard University Press.

Smith, Richard H., Gerrod Parrott, Edward F. Diener, Rick H. Hoyle, and Sung Hee Kim. 1999. "Dispositional Envy." *Personality and Social Psychology Bulletin* 25 (8): 1007–20.

Strevens, Michael. 2003. "The Role of the Priority Rule in Science." *Journal of Philosophy* 100 (2): 55–79.

van den Ven, Niels. 2016. "Envy and Its Consequences: Why It Is Useful to Distinguish between Benign and Malicious Envy." *Social and Personality Psychology Compass* 10 (6): 337–49.

Vecchio, Robert P. 1997. *It's Not Easy Being Green: Jealousy and Envy in the Workplace* 562. Leadership: Understanding the Dynamics of Power and Influence in Organizations. Notre Dame, IN: University of Notre Dame Press.

———. 2000. "Negative Emotion in the Workplace: Employee Jealousy and Envy." *International Journal of Stress Management* 7 (3): 161–79.

Chapter 4

"I Could Have Been You"
Existential Envy and the Self

Íngrid Vendrell Ferran

> Envy is a thousand times more terrible than hunger, for it is spiritual hunger.
>
> —Unamuno (1921, 55)

This chapter explores a scarcely investigated kind of envy in which the subject targets the rival's entire being rather than one of her possessions, achievements, or talents. In the sparse literature on the issue, this kind of envy has been labeled as "existential envy" (Fernández de la Mora 2000; Scheler 2010; Taylor 2006; Vendrell Ferran 2006), and less frequently as "ontological envy" (Olson 2003). As I shall argue, existential envy is characterized by a weakening of the distinction between the envied good and the envied rival and by a strong focus on the envious self. In this sort of envy, strong feelings of an insurmountable inferiority, powerlessness, and despair appear connected to the counterfactual thought: "I could have been you!" Indeed, the envier thinks that, though it is no longer possible, she could have had the other's life, coming to see in the rival the person that she could have been but never became and experiencing, in this way, the shortcomings of her own existence.

Attention will be paid in particular to three interrelated aspects of the self in this kind of envy.[1] First, as Taylor notes, in existential envy the good and the owner of the good wholly coincide (2006, 52). However, an analysis of the relation between the self and its intentional object in this kind of envy is required in order to explain how the envier comes to blur the distinction between good and rival. Second, drawing on Kristjánsson (2010) and in particular on Salice and Montes Sánchez (2019) for whom envy is a self-conscious emotion,[2] I will argue that it is by virtue of a set of feelings of diminution in the envier's own self-worth that in existential envy there is a strong focus on one's own envious self. Lastly, following this lead, I will explore the self-disclosive dimension of this emotion. As I shall demonstrate, the existential envier becomes aware that another person is closer to her ideal self than she is, such that the rival painfully reminds her of unfulfilled but now unrealizable possibilities inherent to her being. In other words, the envier discovers that, though she could have been the other, now it is the rival who embodies the kind of existence that she covets but has failed to obtain. By linking existential envy to the idea of ontological possibilities of a human being, I explore an intriguing idea previously noted by phenomenologists such as Biemel (1957) and Zambrano (1991) and which was a central concern of Unamuno's philosophical and literary works (1921, 1966, 2009) according to which the envious self wants to become a different person.

This chapter proceeds as follows. I begin with an analysis of the intentional object of existential envy, that is, of what it means that the envier targets the other's being. Next, I explore existential envy's focus on the self by examining in detail the series of feelings of diminution in the envier's own value. I then turn to analyze the set of comparisons between self and other and the counterfactual thought "I could have been you!" which I take to be definitory of this kind of envy. In the final part of the chapter, the relation between the envier's bad self-image, self-reproach, and self-deception is discussed, prior to summarizing the main findings in the concluding remarks.

WHAT DO WE ENVY IN EXISTENTIAL ENVY? ON THE OVERLAPPING OF GOOD AND RIVAL

Envy has a triangular structure comprising the coveted object (good), the envied other (rival), and the envious subject (self). As mentioned above, in existential envy, good and rival overlap, because here the envious subject targets not the other's possessions, social status, or talents, but her entire being. How does this blurring of the distinction between good and rival come to be? To answer this question, a detailed analysis of the relation between the existential envier and her intentional object is required.

To begin with, as in envy in general, the existential envier chooses the rival on the basis of three criteria: closeness, similarity, and relevance to oneself. The rival is usually a person who is *close* in terms of time, space, age, and reputation (Miceli and Castelfranchi 2007, 453). The subject does not tend to envy persons who are distant and with whom she almost never interacts.[3] The rival is perceived as being a member of the in-group of the envier. In existential envy, the rival is usually a sibling, a close relative, or a friend.

Second, the existential envier chooses the rival on the basis of a perceived *similarity*. The similarity enables the envier to identify with the rival. Yet, as noted in the literature, the rival is placed in a better position than the envier, allowing a comparison that is slightly "upward" (Miceli and Castelfranchi 2007, 453; Smith 2000). In existential envy, the envier and the rival might share similar backgrounds, social status, education, and the like. However, the envier regards the rival as being the kind of person that she would like to be.

Lastly, while in envy the rival is chosen on the basis of those features that are *relevant* to the envious self (Smith 2000, 174), in the particular case of existential envy, the envier chooses the rival on the basis of the kind of existence she would like to have. What is relevant here is the rival's being. This poses the following question: Is it that only certain aspects of the rival are being envied or her entire existence?

A look into the existing accounts of existential envy reveals that both interpretations are possible: existential envy has been described as targeting existentially relevant aspects of the other's being as well as targeting the other's entire existence.[4] According to the first option, the envier targets *aspects of the rival's existence which are relevant for the envious self*. The subject envies *being like the rival in some existentially relevant respect*. This view has been defended by Fernández de la Mora for whom existential envy is "caused by qualities that are not congenital; but they are so intimately embodied within the nature of the envious person that they become a part of his own makeup, like a habit—thus sanctity and some other capacities" (2000, 69–70). The envier wants to be like the rival in one or another respect—to have some or even many of her features—but she does not want to be the rival in her totality.

According to the second option, the existential envier targets *the rival's entire being*. Here, the subject does not envy being like the other in some or other respect, but she envies *being the other* in her totality. For Scheler, existential envy "is directed against the other person's very nature" (2010, 30): "It is as if it whispers continually: 'I can forgive everything, but not that you are—that you are what you are—that I am not what you are—indeed that I am not you.' This form of envy strips the opponent of his very existence, for this existence as such is felt to be a 'pressure,' a 'reproach,' and an unbearable humiliation" (ibid.). Taylor's (2006) understanding of existential envy as the type of envy in which the rival and the good coincide also has to be interpreted along these lines. The envier regards the rival as being the kind of person she would like to be. In this respect, existential envy does not target specific domains of the other, but her entire being. As a result, the triangular structure is transformed into a dyadic one, in which the envier targets the rival as such.

In this chapter, I adopt the second understanding of existential envy. I take existential envy to be global rather than domain-specific. In so doing, I regard existential envy as similar to globalist emotions such as contempt (Bell 2013, 64), in which we target the other as a whole rather than a specific feature. This globalizing tendency explains why, though the existential envier might not find all aspects of the rival desirable, those desirable aspects tend to be more salient to the envier and are taken to be representative of the envied other's being. The desire to be the rival, and not just to possess one of the other's traits, is what leads to a blurring of the distinction between good and rival in this kind of envy.[5]

The existence of such a globalizing tendency, which evolves progressively in this type of envy, makes the two options compatible. In fact, I regard the first option (in which existential envy is aspect-oriented) as one that well accounts for the initial stages of the formation of this emotion—that is, the first step of a process potentially culminating in a stronger form of envy in which we desire to be the other in her totality. This process involves a globalizing tendency according to which the attentional focus moves from particular features which are existentially relevant to the rival as such.

Since in the globalizing kind of envy, attention is absolutely and obsessively directed toward the rival, the envier's existence is centered on the other, as observed by Biemel (1957), Unamuno (2009), and Zambrano (1991), rather than on her true self. Knowing that one cannot become the other, the existential envier regards the rival not only as irreplaceable but also as unobtainable, and as such they become the target of her hostility and the motive for her feeling diminished in her own self-worth. In this respect, this kind of envy has been described as the "most terrible" (Scheler 2010, 30) and the "worst case of envy" (Taylor 2006, 52).

EXISTENTIAL ENVY AND FEELINGS OF DIMINUTION IN SELF-WORTH

According to Salice and Montes Sánchez (2019), hostile envy has a strong focus of concern on the self.[6] More precisely, they argue that it is by virtue of feelings of disempowerment that the envier experiences a negative self-assessment. Expanding on this idea, I will analyze how the existential envier focuses on her own self and comes to a negative evaluation of her own person. For this, I take into account a series of feelings in which the diminution in one's own worth is sensed. I refer to these feelings in which the subject senses fluctuations in one's own value as "feelings of self-worth." Though this expression was coined by Voigtländer (1910), my concept differs from hers. While she uses the phrase to refer to all affective experiences that involve an apprehension of one's own value such as pride or courage, I distinguish the apprehension of value in feelings of self-worth (e.g., feeling inferior, feeling powerless, etc.) from the emotions which might entail such feelings (e.g., pride) and from character traits that are responsible for making us prone to experience such feelings (e.g., courage).[7]

The feelings of self-worth involved in existential envy are not limited to the feelings of inferiority usually stated in the literature on this emotion and to feelings of disempowerment mentioned by Salice and Montes Sánchez; they also involve feelings of disadvantage, helplessness, and hopefulness.[8] As I shall argue, each of these feelings is responsible for making the envier focus on a different aspect of her own value.

In the first place, envy has been regarded as necessarily entailing *feelings of inferiority* (Ben-ze'ev 1992, 552 and 556; Miceli and Castelfranchi 2007, 252; Protasi 2016, 537). These feelings play an important role in the self-assessment involved in envy because they give the envier a sense of being in a lower position than the rival (Heider 1958; Scheler 2010). Feelings of inferiority have a focus on the other as possessor of the good, on the self as lacking the good, and on the superior position of the other. In existential envy, these feelings take on an extreme expression because the good is unobtainable. Feelings of inferiority are presented as "undeserved" (as noted by Ben-ze'ev 1992, 563). They might trigger strong anger, indignation, rivalry, and, on certain occasions, also shame.

Though feelings of inferiority and *feelings of disadvantage* have usually been regarded as synonymous (Miceli and Castelfranchi 2007, 452), a distinction can be traced between the envier's inferiority regarding the rival and the envier's perception of her chances to overcome this inferiority. One might feel inferior to another person and at the same time assess the possibilities to overcome the inferiority as good. Feelings of advantage and disadvantage are focused not on the superior other and the inferior self, but on the possibilities that the environment offers to the self to achieve the good. Envy is usually hostile when the envier perceives obtaining the good as unlikely. In existential envy, the envious self is aware of the absolutely disadvantageous position because she cannot become the same person as the rival.

Some authors have argued that envy also involves feelings of disempowerment (Salice and Montes Sánchez 2019), also called *feelings of powerlessness* (Scheler 2010; more recently Fussi 2019). While the expression "powerlessness" underscores the inability to overcome a situation of comparative inferiority, "disempowerment" suggests that the envier once had a power that she has now lost (this is, however, not always the case: perhaps the envier never had such power). Since the existential envier tells herself, "I could have been you," she must believe that at least to a certain degree obtaining the desired outcome was within the realms of possibility. Unlike the feelings of disadvantage, feelings of powerlessness do not concern the chances that the environment offers to the envier; rather, they relate to her own resources and capacities to overcome the inferiority and obtain the good. Feelings of powerlessness can be regarded as a form of feelings of incapacity—that is, feelings in which the sense of "I can" that usually underlies our daily activities and that involves the certainty that we will be able to realize something, breaks down, bringing a lack of confidence and insecurity (for feelings of insecurity in envy, see Miceli and Castelfranchi 2007, 452). Given that the existential envier is aware that she cannot have the rival's being, she experiences an absolute lack of control over the outcome. As a result, feelings of powerlessness are accompanied by extreme hostility.

Finally, existential envy involves *feelings of helplessness and hopefulness*. For Miceli and Castelfranchi (2007, 457), in envy these feelings differ from the typical feelings of helplessness and hopefulness experienced in depression because the envier still has some vision of obtaining the good. Though this might be true of some instances of envy, it is certainly not the case with existential envy. On the one hand, the existential envier experiences these feelings because she is aware that she cannot obtain the desired good: she cannot become the rival. On the other hand, these feelings foster despair and involve self-reproach for being unable to attain the coveted good. In existential envy, helplessness and hopefulness make the envier focus on her lack of expectations to overcome her powerlessness.

The *feelings of injustice*, often mentioned in the literature on envy, deserve a separate mention. Do feelings of injustice indicate a diminution in the envier's own value? While some authors have argued that envy entails a "tendency toward equalization" (Heider 1958, 287; Salice and Montes Sánchez 2019), functions as an indicator of inequalities (La Caze 2001, 37), and involves the perception of a subjective injustice (Smith 2000), my view here is that the proclaimed feelings of injustice in envy are not genuine. Indeed, as has been argued by Miceli and Castelfranchi (2007), even the envier sometimes knows that such feelings are illegitimate because there is no sufficient reason for them. More precisely, I regard such feelings to be part of a self-deceptive strategy and as such they involve bad faith (Ben-ze'ev 1992, 551 and 553). The existential envier uses them to disguise, even to herself, not only strong feelings of hostility but also her own inability to obtain the desired outcome. Though she presents herself as a victim of unfair circumstances (claiming that in more favorable conditions she would have obtained the good), the existential envier does not want a fairer world but a world in which she occupies the better position. Therefore, such feelings are non-genuine: in envy, feelings of injustice are not genuine feelings of self-worth. However, by virtue of presenting the envier as a victim of unfairness, rather than as a person who can be held accountable for being unable to obtain the good, they fulfill a protective function, shielding the envier from a devaluation in others' and her own eyes.

To recap, in existential envy, the envier genuinely experiences herself as inferior, as being in a disadvantageous position, as being powerless, helpless, and hopeless. Though in each of them a distinct aspect of the envier's self is assessed and presented as diminished in worth, in all of them the subject genuinely experiences a diminution in her own value and becomes in different respects the focus of her own concern. These feelings, which I described as "feelings of self-worth," should not be conflated with the corresponding judgments that go along with them. Indeed, while one might assess oneself by judging that one is inferior, at a disadvantage, powerless, helpless, and hopeful, the kind of assessment that I have in mind here, and that is responsible for making the envier apprehend an aspect of her own value as diminished, is not a judgment but an affective state.

Due to these feelings of diminution in self-worth, the existential envier experiences, senses, and suffers an attack on her self-esteem. Indeed, though all kinds of envy undermine the envier's own self-concept (Heider 1958, 286; Smith 2000, 193) and involve a loss of self-esteem (Miceli and Castelfranchi 2007, 457), in existential envy, the attack is much stronger due to the unobtainable nature of the envied good. It is worth noting that the kind of self-esteem referred to here is episodic or state self-esteem—that is, the occurrent experience of a diminution in self-worth. Episodic self-esteem has to be distinguished from dispositional or trait self-esteem as an enduring feature of a person's character (for this distinction, see Salice 2020; dispositional self-esteem will be analyzed in a later section). These forms of self-esteem can come apart. Indeed, one can have a high dispositional self-esteem and nonetheless experience a diminution in one's episodic self-esteem, when for instance one is insulted, degraded, or becomes aware of one's inferiority, powerlessness, and so on, as happens in instances of envy.

COMPARISONS AND COUNTERFACTUALS: EXISTENTIAL ENVY'S INTENSITY AND QUALITY

Counterfactual thoughts are involved in many emotions such as shame, guilt, regret, and envy (Van de Ven and Zeelenberg 2014). These emotions involve upward counterfactuals regarding how the current situation could have been better (by contrast, downward counterfactuals are thoughts in which the self is in a worse situation). Given that envy is an emotion of upward comparison, it involves also upward counterfactuals in which the envier has obtained the coveted good. As Smith notes, "upward comparisons" create an "imagined, better alternative to one's current situation" (2000, 179). There is extensive literature on this notion that envy depends on counterfactual thinking.[9] More specifically, as argued by Elster (1999), the envious subject tells herself a story that involves the counterfactual thought "It could have been me," in which it would be plausible that she obtains the good (see also Ben-ze'ev 1992; Crusius and Lange 2020; Van de Ven and Zeelenberg 2014; for different variations of this counterfactual in envy, see also Protasi 2021, 70–83). My thought here is that this counterfactual also grounds existential envy. Yet, as I shall argue, the existential envier thinks not just "It could have been me" but, more precisely, "I could have been you!" To develop my argument, I examine the structure of comparisons to others and to the self, and the corresponding counterfactual thoughts in existential envy.

The *first comparison-to-another* takes place between the *subject's and the rival's "empirical selves."* What I call here "empirical self" entails the biographical, social, psychological factual features of the envier's being. This empirical self is only one among different possibilities inherent to a person's being since a person could have become a different person from the person she is. For instance, it is part of my empirical self that I am a philosopher. Though there was a possibility that I could have become a psychologist, this possibility was not realized and is now closed off.[10] In the course of life, only some of the possibilities inherent to our being can come to realization in our empirical self. In each decision we take, in each step in our personal history, we cut ourselves off from possibilities originally open to us. Each person is somehow aware that what lies within her can only be partially realized in life. This empirical self is our ontological reality, which is only one among different ontological possibilities that we could have realized.

The counterfactual thought associated with this comparison is "It could have been me." The envier thinks that she could have become the kind of person that the rival is. Yet, since existential envy targets the other's entire being, the counterfactual thought for this kind of envy is better expressed in terms of "I could have been you." The envier imaginatively engages with the possibility of being a different person. She thinks that she could have had the rival's empirical self. Put otherwise: she thinks that she could have been the rival.

Given that in existential envy, the envier chooses the rival in virtue of the kind of being she also wanted to be, this kind of envy involves a *second comparison-to-another* between *the rival's empirical self and what can be called the envier's "ideal self."* The "ideal self" refers to those possibilities of the envier's being that she would like to see realized in her empirical self. In this respect, the ideal self is configured by ideals, desires, and imaginings about the kind of person she would like to be. As employed here, the ideal self is framed within what the subject senses as an ontological possibility inherent to her being (independently of the possibility being real or merely imagined). For instance, being a famous dancer is not part of my ideal self because dancing is outside the realm of my possibilities (I lack the talent). Since each person has different ontological possibilities inherent to her being, each of us can have different ideal selves. Each of these ideal selves underscores an aspect of our being over others. One might have an ideal self as a good philosopher, as a good friend, and so on. Moreover, a person might have different versions of her ideal self. If becoming a good philosopher is part of one's ideal self, then there are many ways in which one can imagine being a good thinker. In the particular case of existential envy, the envier comes to focus on the ideal self as embodied by the rival. Indeed, as we have seen, in existential envy there is a narrowing of attention on the rival's being, which makes the other irreplaceable and unique. As a result, the envier comes to think that the rival is the "living image" of her ideal self. In so doing, she ignores other possible ideal selves.

In this picture, the rival is almost a proxy standing in for one of the envier's ideal selves, the specific ideal self which becomes the envier's main focus. As Zambrano puts it: "the vision of the other is the mirror of one's own life: we see ourselves in seeing the other" (1991, 268–70). As a result, the envier realizes that the rival is closer to her ideal self than she is. The counterfactual thought at the basis of this comparison between the rival and the envier's ideal self is not merely "I could have been you" but "I could have been my ideal self." Given that the rival is someone who is close, similar, and relevant, the envier realizes that she could have become the kind of person that the rival is.

This comparison leads to *a self-comparison* in which *the envier's empirical self is compared with her ideal self* (the ideal self now instantiated by the rival).[11] As a consequence, she experiences a discrepancy between the person she factually is and the person she could have been and would like to be. As already argued by Unamuno (1966), the envier becomes aware of the distance between her ontological reality and a desired ontological possibility. It is in this sense that he describes envy as "spiritual hunger" (1921, 55). This idea can also be found in Zambrano (1991, 262) who, inspired by Unamuno, depicts envy as a self-destructive greed for the other.

The counterfactual thought involved in this self-comparison is entirely focused on the self. The existential envier thinks "If only the circumstances had been different" as well as "If I only had done this or that." Given that the good is unobtainable, these thoughts do not motivate self-improvement. Rather, they appear coupled with hostility toward the other and herself (for being unable to obtain the good) and alternate between victimhood and self-reproach.

In my view, this self-comparison entails a moment of self-disclosure. As noted by Biemel (1957), in envy the subject becomes aware of desirable possibilities inherent to her being. In this respect, the self-disclosure has a positive moment. In the specific case of existential envy, the subject realizes that desirable possibilities inherent to her being have remained unfulfilled. However, since in existential envy the good is unobtainable, the envier also realizes that these possibilities are now closed off: she cannot become the rival. Consequently, the rival reminds her that these ontological possibilities could have been realized. In brief, existential envy has to do with the subject becoming aware of what she thinks are desirable possibilities inherent to her being, but which have remained unfulfilled and for which it is now too late to realize, while another person—the rival—has succeeded in developing or realizing these possibilities.

This set of comparisons and the coupled counterfactual thoughts upon which existential envy is based explain the *intensity* with which this emotion is experienced. According to Van de Ven and Zeelenberg (2014, 957), a person is more prone to engage in counterfactual thought when she feels "close to the outcome." For envy, this means that when the margin to obtain the good is experienced as small, it is easier for the envier to imagine an alternative situation in which she obtained the good. Counterfactual thought is also increased when the subject has the impression of "controlling" the situation. If people do not think that the situation could be changed by oneself, then they do not engage in counterfactual thought (2014, 967). The more an individual engages in these counterfactual thoughts, the more intense envy will be. Existential envy is particularly intense because the envier thinks that she "could" have been the other and that it was in her power to obtain the desired outcome.

Interestingly, as argued by Crusius and Lange (forthcoming), counterfactual thoughts are relevant in determining not only the intensity of envy, but also its *quality*. In their view, patterns of counterfactual thought can be employed to distinguish between benign and hostile envy. They establish these patterns by focusing on three elements: (1) directedness (upward, downward); (2) structure (if it adds a successful antecedent, such as "If I had done this or that" or if it subtracts it, such as "If only I had not let myself be distracted"); (3) and focus (on the self or the other). They found that benign envy was associated with upward, additive, and self-focused counterfactuals about what the envier could have done to obtain the good. By contrast, hostile envy was associated with upward and other-focused counterfactuals. In other words, in hostile envy the counterfactuals are about actions done by other people which could or should have led to a better outcome for the self, rather than actions done by the self because in these cases the envious self has less control over the situation.[12]

Along these lines, we can determine existential envy's quality. Its *unique pattern of thought* involves: (1) upward directed counterfactuals; (2) its structure can be additive or subtractive; and (3) it can be other-and self-focused. Like instances of hostile envy as described by Crusius and Lange, existential envy involves counterfactuals about actions of others that could have led to obtaining the good. However, it also involves counterfactuals about what the envier could have done to become the kind of person now instantiated by the rival. Does this imply that existential envy has a benign dimension? I think not. As described above, the self-focused counterfactuals do not aim at self-improvement because the possibilities to become the rival's being are closed off. Rather, these counterfactuals about the self take the form of a self-reproach. These thoughts remind the envier that if she had acted differently, she could have obtained the desired outcome.

SELF-IMAGE, SELF-REPROACH, AND SELF-DECEPTION

In this section, my aim is to explore how the self-reproach characteristic of existential envy is linked to the bad image that the envier has of herself and how it motivates self-deception.[13] In my view, in existential envy not only does the subject experience an attack on their episodic self-esteem (as examined earlier in the section on envy and feelings of self-worth); it also tends to be experienced by persons with low dispositional self-esteem.

The link between existential envy and low dispositional self-esteem cannot be plainly explained by claiming—as Taylor (2006) has done—that hostile envy is always linked to low self-esteem. In fact, hostile envy might be experienced not just by subjects with low self-esteem, but also by subjects with high self-esteem who nonetheless undergo episodes in which a diminution in their own value is sensed (see Vrabel, Zeigler-Hill, and Southard 2018, 103). Moreover, people with high self-esteem such as grandiose narcissists are able to experience hostile envy when they are moved by fear of failure and rivalry (as argued by Lange, Crusius, and Hagemeyer 2016, 169), which contradicts the widespread view that grandiose narcissists do not usually engage in counterfactual thinking due to the positive image that they have of themselves (as maintained by Van de Ven and Zeelenberg 2014, 968).

Yet, though hostile envy is not always linked to low self-esteem, existential envy is. Given that in this type of envy the subject wants to change places with the other and have the other's existence, we can assume not only that she is deeply unsatisfied with her being, but also that she regards her whole being as less worthy than that of the rival. The existential envier has a *bad image of herself*.

In my view, this bad self-image is linked to the existential envier's *self-reproach*. The envier reproaches herself not only in virtue of experiencing a highly morally condemned emotion, but also because she has been unable to obtain the good. As noted by Biemel (1957, 47), in seeing that the other has obtained the desired good, the envier sees herself as having fallen behind her own possibilities. In this respect, she is reminded of her failure. As we have seen, the envier has counterfactual thoughts about what she could have done, to become the kind of person now instantiated by the rival.[14]

Within this frame, *self-deception* appears as a mechanism to protect the envious self from the pains associated with this emotion. Though the link between envy and self-deception has been noted in the literature (Biemel 1957, 52; Miceli and Castelfranchi 2007, 449; Taylor 2006, 49), the question about where exactly in existential envy the self-deceptive mechanism is at work remains open. The envier is not deceptive about the value of the good and of the rival. Indeed, the envier still acknowledges that the good is desirable and that the rival is superior to her regarding the good. Rather, the envier is deceptive about her own envious self. But which aspect of the self is affected by this deception?

For Taylor, since the envious self is not esteem-worthy but defective, what the envier wants to protect is *the appearance of an esteem-worthy self*, which she and others can then respect (2006, 49). While I agree that self-deception has a protective function here, I believe that what the envier attempts to protect is not the appearance of an esteem-worthy self, but the aforementioned *painful self-reproach inherent to this kind of envy*. To this end, she deceives herself about the emotion she is experiencing. As seen earlier in the section about the feelings of diminution in one's self-worth, she tries to disguise her envy as feelings of injustice. In so doing, she can hide from others and herself the fact that she does not want a world of equals, but a world in which she is in a privileged position. But, most importantly, in disguising her envy in terms of feelings of injustice, she avoids being held accountable for her existential failure. She protects herself from being held responsible for the discrepancy between her ontological reality and her desired but unrealized ontological possibilities.[15] As a result, she can flee into an inauthentic and imaginary self.[16] However, this flight is only momentary since the envier is not totally self-deceptive and is reminded again and again that she can be made accountable for not having realized those desired possibilities inherent to her being.

CONCLUSION

This chapter offered an analysis of existential envy as a scarcely investigated kind of envy. I argued for three main claims: (1) that in existential envy, the differences between good and rival are weakened due to the envier's desire to become the other; (2) that strong feelings of a diminution in one's self-worth are responsible for the envier focusing on the self and experiencing a negative assessment; and (3) that existential envy has a self-disclosive nature according to which the envier discovers that desired possibilities inherent to her being have remained unfulfilled. If my analysis is right, then existential envy is an emotion that, despite targeting the rival for being the kind of person one would also like to be, is in fact an emotion about the self. More precisely, it is an emotion about one of our ideal selves that we could have become but have failed to realize.[17]

NOTES

1. For a different approach to the self of envy in which this emotion is contrasted with compassion, see Christina Chuang's chapter, "Compassion, Envy and the Self," in this volume.

2. One of the virtues of these accounts is that they describe envy by focusing on the self rather than on the good or the rival. In contrast, traditional approaches to envy have focused mainly either on the good and the consequent feelings of sorrow or anger for not possessing it—this type of definition can be found in Aquinas (Perrine 2011) and Klein (1997)—and/or on the rival as possessor of the good and the consequent feelings of comparative inferiority (Ben-ze'ev 2001; Fussi 2019). The focus on the good and the rival has also been employed to elaborate taxonomies of this emotion (Taylor 2006; Protasi 2016).

3. It is possible that an element of the comparison acquires self-relevance *a posteriori*. Once envy arises, one compares oneself to the other and in the course of this comparison, one might discover other elements which then become relevant for the self (Miceli and Castelfranchi 2007, 455).

4. Both notions of existential envy are distinguished here in terms of the targeted object. For an analysis of other aspects, see Vendrell Ferran (2022).

5. For an analysis of the significance of covetous desire in envy from a sociocultural perspective, see Patricia M. Rodriguez Mosquera's contribution "A Sociocultural Perspective on Envy" (chapter 1) in this volume.

6. They employ the notion of "focus of concern" to denote how a specific evaluative property is attributed to an object—in this respect, theirs differs from the notion of focus of concern as developed by Protasi (2016; 2021, 32–33). Taking the idea of an oscillation between object and focus, Salice and Montes Sánchez (2019) distinguish two accents in envy: when focused on the rival, envy is predominantly experienced in terms of hostility; when focused on the self, it is experienced with an accent of disempowerment. A similar idea can be found in Smith (2000, 183) for whom envy has a dual focus. When directed toward oneself, it produces feelings of depression; when directed toward others, resentment.

7. I prefer the expression "feelings of self-worth" to the expression "self-esteem feelings" (e.g., Keshen 1996) because it underscores the subject's experiences of a diminution in her own worth (for the link between envy and self-worth, see, for instance, Perrine 2011; Scheler 2010; and Heider 1958).

8. I take such feelings here to be constitutive ingredients or moments of existential envy as emotional experience. I leave aside the question of whether such feelings might motivate envy or appear as a result of envy.

9. I work here with the idea that envy is based on such counterfactual thoughts—that is, counterfactual thought leads to envy. This does not exclude the possibility that when envy is present, it also leads us to generate counterfactual thoughts (Van de Ven and Zeelenberg 2014, 954 and 967).

10. This concept of ontological possibilities inherent to our being is described by Hartmann outside the context of envy (e.g., 2014, 193). The idea that envy entails a question about the kind of person we want to be seems to me already present in Schoeck (1987).

11. This idea of a gap between two aspects of the self poses the possibility of self-envy—which, to my knowledge, is only mentioned in the contemporary literature by Ben-ze'ev (2000, 302), in his discussion of Hume's position on this issue. In my view, there are two possible explanations of self-envy. First, it can be interpreted in terms of a splitting of the self in which one part envies the other. This possibility has been examined by psychoanalyst López-Corvo (1994) and by Unamuno in a short narration (1966). Second, self-envy can also take place when the actual empirical self envies a past empirical self who was in a better position to obtain the good (e.g., by virtue of being more beautiful, more vibrant, more energetic, having more possibilities to succeed, etc.). The current empirical self might feel nostalgic about the past self and might be full of reproach, contempt, hate, and shame toward it.

12. Though both authors employ these elements to distinguish benign from malicious envy, in my view, all envy is malicious, since it is marked by hostility and motivates destructive actions. I tend to interpret what is called benign envy as cases of admiration or covetousness. I will not argue here for this view since it is irrelevant for the purposes of this paper.

13. For an analysis of the link between envy and self-deception, see Vanessa Carbonell's contribution to this volume, "Malicious Moral Envy" (chapter 7).

14. As observed in the literature, the counterfactual thought in envy is similar to counterfactual thought in regret (Van de Ven and Zeelenberg 2014, 967).

15. Though I cannot develop an argument for it here, in my view, feelings of injustice might also hide the fact that the mere existence of the rival makes the envier experience a diminution in her own value as well as that her envy is an expression of bad character (that she is not only greedy and covetous, but she is someone who cannot suffer that other people are superior and better placed than her).

16. The idea of envy and inauthenticity has been explored by Biemel (1957), though he does not link it with the sense of responsibility.

17. Early versions of this chapter were presented in a workshop organized by Sara Protasi in May 2021 and in the annual meeting of the EPSSE in Graz in June 2021. I am indebted to the audiences at these conferences and in particular to Alfred Archer, Aaron Ben-ze'ev, Jan Crusius, Sara Protasi, and Niels van de Ven for valuable suggestions. I am also grateful to Christina Chuang and Sara Protasi for insightful comments on an earlier draft of this paper that helped to substantially improve it. My gratitude goes also to Simon Mussell for proofreading the chapter.

REFERENCES

Bell, Malacaster. 2013. *Hard Feelings: The Moral Psychology of Contempt.* Oxford: Oxford University Press.

Ben-ze'ev, Aaron. 1992. "Envy and Inequality." *Journal of Philosophy* 89 (11): 551–81.

———. 2000. *The Subtlety of Emotions.* Cambridge, MA: MIT Press.

Biemel, Walter. 1957. "Über den Neid." In *Rencontre/Encounter/Begegnung. Contributions à une psychologie humaine dédiées au professeur F. J .J. Buytendijk,* edited by M. J. Langeveld, 40–50. Utrecht: Spectrum.

Crusius, Jan, and Jens Lange. 2014. "What Catches the Envious Eye? Attentional Biases within Malicious and Benign Envy." *Journal of Experimental Social Psychology* 55: 1–11.

Crusius, Jan, and Jens Lange. Forthcoming. "Counterfactual Thoughts Distinguish Benign and Malicious Envy." *Emotion.*

Elster, Jon. 1999. *Alchemies of the Mind: Rationality and the Emotions.* New York: Cambridge University Press.

Fernández de la Mora, Gonzalo. 2000. *Egalitarian Envy: The Political Foundations of Social Justice.* New York: ToExcel.

Fussi, Alessandra. 2019. "Envy and Its Objects." *Humana.Mente: Journal of Philosophical Studies* 35: 124–49.

Hartmann, Nicolai. 2014. *Aesthetics.* Berlin: De Gruyter.

Heider, Fritz. 1958. *The Psychology of Interpersonal Relations.* New York: John Wiley & Sons.

Keshen, Richard. 1996. *Reasonable Self-Esteem: A Life of Meaning.* Montreal: McGill University Press.

Klein, Melanie. 1997. *Envy and Gratitude and Other Works 1946–1963.* London: Vintage Classics.

Kristjánsson, Kristján. 2010. *The Self and Its Emotions.* Cambridge: Cambridge University Press.

La Caze, Marguerite. 2001. "Envy and Resentment." *Philosophical Explorations* 1: 31–45.

Lange, Jens, Jan Crusius, and Birk Hagemeyer. 2016. "The Evil Queen's Dilemma: Linking Narcissistic Admiration and Rivalry to Benign and Malicious Envy." *European Journal of Personality* 30: 168–88.

López-Corvo, Rafael. 1994. *Self-Envy: Therapy and the Divided Inner World.* London: Jason Aronson Inc.

Miceli, Maria, and Cristiano Castelfranchi. 2007. "The Envious Mind." *Cognition and Emotion* 21 (3): 449–79.

Olson, Paul. 2003. *The Great Chiasmus: Word and Flesh in the Novels of Unamuno.* West Lafayette: Purdue University Press.

Perrine, Timothy. 2011. "Envy and Self-Worth: Amending Aquinas' Definition of Envy." *American Catholic Philosophical Quarterly* 85 (3): 433–46.

Protasi, Sara. 2016. "Varieties of Envy." *Philosophical Psychology* 29 (4): 535–49.

———. 2021. *The Philosophy of Envy.* New York: Cambridge University Press.

Salice, Alessandro. 2020. "Self-Esteem, Social Esteem, and Pride." *Emotion Review* 12 (3): 193–205.

Salice, Alessandro, and Alba Montes Sánchez. 2019. "Envy and Us." *European Journal of Philosophy* 27 (1): 227–42.

Scheler, Max. 2010. *Ressentiment*. Milwaukee: Marquette University Press.

Schoeck, Helmut. 1987. *Envy: A Theory of Social Behaviour.* Indianapolis: Liberty Fund.

Smith, Richard H. 2000. "Assimilative and Contrastive Emotional Reactions to Upward and Downward Social Comparison." In *Handbook of Social Comparison: The Springer Series in Social Clinical Psychology*, edited by Jerry Suls and Ladd Wheeler, 173–200. Boston: Springer.

Taylor, Gabriele. 2006. *Deadly Vices*. Oxford: Oxford University Press.

Unamuno, Miguel de. 1921. *The Tragic Sense of Life in Men and in Peoples*. London: Leopold.

———. 1966. *Obras Completas IX*. Madrid: Escelicer.

———. 2009. *Abel Sánchez*. Oxford: Aris & Phillips.

van de Ven, Niels, and Marcel Zeelenberg. 2014. "On the Counterfactual Nature of Envy: 'It Could Have Been Me.'" *Cognition and Emotion* 29 (6): 954–71.

Vendrell Ferran, Íngrid. 2006. "Über den Neid. Eine phänomenologische Untersuchung." *Deutsche Zeitschrift für Philosophie* 54 (1): 43–68.

———. 2022. "Envy, Powerlessness and Feelings of Self-Worth." In *Empathy, Intersubjectivity, and the Social World*, edited by Anna Bortolan and Elisa Magrí, 277–99. Berlin: De Gruyter.

Voigtländer, Else. 1910. *Vom Selbstgefühl*. Leipzig: Voigtländer Verlag.

Vrabel, Jennifer K., Virgil Zeigler-Hill, and Ashton C. Southard. 2018. "Self-Esteem and Envy: Is State Self-Esteem Instability Associated with the Benign and Malicious Forms of Envy?" *Personality and Individual Differences* 123: 100–104.

Zambrano, María. 1991. *El Hombre y lo divino*. Madrid: Siruela.

Chapter 5

Envy, Compassion, and the Buddhist (No)Self

Christina Chuang

According to Spinoza, envy and compassion are opposites: envy is hate that affects a man so that he is displeased by another person's happiness and rejoices at that person's misfortune, while compassion is love that affects a man so that he is glad at someone else's good fortune and gets displeasure from his misfortune (*Ethics* III "Definitions of the Affects," 23 and 24). This opposition of envy and compassion is also found in other prominent philosophers who wrote about emotions, such as Aristotle (*Rhetoric* II.9, 1386b16).

In this chapter, I argue that this dichotomy between envy and compassion is mistaken because it relies on a conception of the self as a distinct and independent entity. Western theories of emotion construct envy and compassion as triggered by social comparisons and an evaluation of the self in relation to those who are similar to us in values, beliefs, and circumstances. Envy and compassion are both emotional responses to another person's well-being in relation to the agent under an individualistic notion of the self. However, they oppose each other in hedonic value and behavioral terms. While envy often produces unpleasant feelings and tends to motivate antisocial behavior, compassion often produces pleasant feelings and tend to motivate prosocial behavior (Goetz, Keltner, and Simon-Thomas 2010; Crusius et al. 2020).

Against this Western perspective, I propose a Buddhist approach rooted in the no-self doctrine, which sees the self as impermanent and interconnected with all other beings in the world. Exercising compassion toward others would turn out to be the same as self-compassion, which is the first step toward envy management. When one practices extending compassion to all sentient things, including one's own self, one comes to the realization that being joyful for others means being joyful for oneself, since all our actions are intertwined in a web of cause and effect.

In the first section, I sketch out one dominant Western perspective on envy and compassion, bringing to light the emphasis on the self as a distinct and independent entity for the sake of social comparison. In the second section, I give a brief overview of the Buddhist no-self doctrine. In the third section, I explain my own construction of a compassionate desire from an interconnected self. In the last section, I offer a discussion on how we can incorporate the no-self doctrine into a behavioral cognitive therapy model of envy.

SELF AND OTHER IN COMPASSION AND ENVY

Compassion and envy have much in common. They are emotional reactions toward the fortunes (or misfortunes) of others, which arise from our interaction with them, and which imply that the other is not indifferent to us for one reason or another (e.g., because we care about the other, because the other is relevant for us, or because the other stands in a relation of proximity, etc.)

However, envy and compassion oppose each other in hedonic valence and behavioral consequents. This opposition seemingly presupposes a common crucial element: perceived *similarity* between the subject (the person feeling the emotion) and the target (the person toward whom the emotion is felt). Qua distinct entities (the subject and the target), this similarity presupposes *a strong sense of self* and self-identity, and a clear distinction between self and others. In Western theories of emotion, social comparison is a necessary component for these emotions to arise. Envy and compassion are considered self-conscious emotions because representation of the self is implicated in the activation of the emotions (Chada and Nichols 2019, 1). Other familiar examples of self-conscious emotions include pride, shame, and guilt. According to Tracy and Robins, "the primary distinctive characteristic of self-conscious emotions is that their elicitation requires the ability to form stable self-representations ('me'), to focus attention on those representations (i.e., to self-reflect; 'I'), and to put it all together to generate a self-evaluation" (Tracy and Robins 2007, 191). The ability to represent the self as a stable "I" seems to be a prerequisite for emotions such as compassion and envy to arise.

I should clarify that my discussion focuses on compassion as an emotion, not as a virtue. As such, compassion should be distinguished from benevolence and kindness. Benevolence is broader in scope and focused on the assisting of others and kindness is a general wishing and concern for the well-being of others (Crisp 2008, 244). Compassion, on the other hand, is the direct response to alleviate the *suffering* of others at the right time and toward other people. By focusing on compassion as an emotion, I take the evaluative component as a dominant feature and draw a clear distinction between compassion and empathy—the latter of which is better understood as an innate psychological capacity.[1] I therefore avoid those Western accounts of compassion where it's central to morality or is portrayed purely as an instinctual response.[2]

Here, I focus on *Aristotelean* accounts of compassion because they highlight the constitutive role of evaluations in emotions and the importance of practical wisdom in executing compassionate actions. For Aristotle, compassion as an emotion can be excessive and is not unconditionally desirable. This sets up my comparison with the Buddhist view of compassion in the next section, which argues that compassion must have a reflective component (i.e., must be practiced with wisdom, otherwise it would be reckless).

Aristotle postulates a *similarity* requirement, which states that we feel compassionate only toward those who are similar to us in beliefs, values, and circumstances. Aristotle defines compassion (*eleos*) as "a feeling of pain caused by the sight of some evil, destructive or painful, which befalls one who doesn't deserve it, and which one might expect to suffer oneself or one of one's own, and moreover when the suffering seems close to hand" (*Rhetoric* II.8, 1385b13–16). Aristotle's view of compassion has three "cognitive requirements" (Nussbaum 2001, 306):

1. *The seriousness requirement*: the evil in question must be seen as significant rather than trivial.
2. *The desert requirement*: the evil must be seen as undeserved.
3. *The similar possibilities requirement*: the suffering must be something that the person experiencing compassion might expect to befall on himself or someone close to him.

For Aristotle, there are two implications of the third requirement. Those who are completely ruined or those who are very well-off cannot feel compassion as they either believe they cannot suffer any further or they are invincible.[3] Martha Nussbaum accepts the first two and makes a modification to the third requirement—she calls it the eudemonistic judgment requirement, which states that the onlooker must consider the suffering as a significant part of her own scheme of goals and ends (Nussbaum 2001, 319). In other words, the onlooker must believe that the misfortune *could happen to oneself* (315). This suggests that, on Nussbaum's account, the onlooker must have a robust sense of who she is and what her values and circumstances are, in order to make an intelligible social comparison—from which compassion will arise. The Aristotle-Nussbaum account of compassion presupposes that compassion somehow requires the ability to make judgments about what is similar (or different) between the self and the other—which, in my interpretation, implies that the self must be a stable and distinct entity for the comparison to be intelligible and informative.

Envy, likewise, is a self-conscious emotion triggered by social comparison in relation to one's self-evaluation and identity. Envy is a three-place relation that involves (1) the envier, the subject who feels the emotion; (2) the envied, the target toward which the emotion is felt; and (3) the good, "the object with regard to which the envier is in a disadvantageous position vis-à-vis the envied" (Protasi 2016, 536). The similarity factor is present in envy in both historical and contemporary accounts. Aristotle states that we envy only those who are similar to ourselves: "We feel [envy] toward our equals . . . those who are near us in time, place, age, or reputation. . . . So too we compete with those who follow the same ends as ourselves" (*Rhetoric* II. 10). Spinoza also offers an argument for the idea that there must be some relevant similarity between the envier and the envied (D'Arms and Kerr 2008, 6–7). Spinoza thinks that the envier must be a relative equal to the envied in order for envy to take place, since the envier must imagine that it's possible for her to possess the good.

In contemporary literature, the two factors that describe the social comparison phenomenon are: the similarity factor and the self-relevance factor (Smith and Kim 2007). First, the similarity factor states that we are envious of only those who are similar to us in some relevant sense (Protasi 2016, 536). Similarity is crucial for social comparison because it allows the comparison to be informative and diagnostic. The similar factor is well-established in empirical finding although what "similar" means depends heavily on the context (537). Sometimes it means a general category such as gender, race, or age, but sometimes it means sharing the same level of skills and interests such as two academics who have the same areas of specialization in the same university.

Second, the self-relevance factor states that the good of which we are envious in the envied is relevant to our sense of identity (537). The self-relevance factor explains why we don't feel envy in all instances of upward social comparison. For example, sometimes we feel positively affected when others outperform us without feeling like our sense of identity is threatened. The reason for this is that the domain in question is not relevant to what we aspire to be and what we perceive ourselves to be.

Scholars have debated over whether hostility is a necessary feature of envy, and consequently whether there can be two distinct kinds of envy, one emulative and benign and the other hostile and malicious.[4] My analysis is based on the understanding of envy as malicious, but even if benign envy existed, it would presuppose an understanding of the self as distinct from the envied, so the Buddhist perspective would still give us a good reason to avoid it. Furthermore, empirical evidence shows that even benign envy is *unpleasant* (i.e., can cause distress and pain in the subject). I'll focus on the unpleasant aspect of envy later in the chapter.

As I have illustrated in this section, Western models of compassion and envy portray these emotions as involving a similarity requirement, which presupposes a strong sense of the self in order to make an informative and diagnostic social comparison between the self and others. Although the triggered behavior is different (i.e., compassion compels the subject to alleviate the other's suffering while (malicious) envy compels the subject to bestow suffering onto the other), compassion and envy don't arise unless the subject makes an evaluative judgment about how one's circumstance is similar to the target.

THE BUDDHIST NO-SELF DOCTRINE

It's not my intention to argue for a robust metaphysical conception of the self. Rather, my purpose is to illustrate that a shift in one's perspective of the self can have an impact on the intensity of negative emotions being triggered when one's self-esteem is threatened. My view is Buddhist-*inspired* because I set aside the interpretative question of whether this view is metaphysical or epistemological and I simply adopt the main idea that the self is a flexible, impermanent, and interdependent entity. This means that we understand the self as nothing but a series of events that we perceive. If the self is not a distinct and independent entity, but rather fluid and open, it's easier to perceive resemblance between others and oneself. When we understand the difference between one person and another as *relative* rather than absolute, it becomes effortless to exercise compassion and be kind to one another.

According to the Buddhists, *anatta* is the no-self doctrine that in humans there is no permanent unchanging underlying substance called the soul or self.[5] We understand a person as nothing but the sum of the five *khandas* (aggregates) of matter: physical form, perceptions, feelings, mental formations, and consciousness. As such, it would be a mistake to identify the soul (or the self) with any one or more of the five because all five are "impermanent, sorrowful, and liable to change" (Jayatilleke 1963, 38–39). The no-self doctrine is made explicit in the classic Buddhist text, *Milinda's Questions* where the king Milina asks the monk Nagasena if Nagasena is any of the five aggregates, or all five, or something apart from the five (Lesser 1979, 59). Each time Nagasena replied, "O no, sire." The king declares that there is no Nagasena and therefore the monk must be lying about who or what Nagasena is. The monk explains to the ing that it's correct to speak of Nagasena as a person by convention. For instance, it's correct to speak of a chariot as a real object when the parts of the chariot are put together, but there is nothing to the chariot over and above its parts. Similarly, we can speak of Nagasena as a person but there is nothing to Nagasena over and above his parts, which are the five aggregates. Expressions such as "I" or "self" are merely grammatical devices and don't refer to anything metaphysically real (Giles 1993, 188).

Clinging to the notion of a permanent and distinct "I" (ego) is strongly denounced in Buddhist thought because ego-consciousness is the root of all unhappiness and suffering. "According to the teaching of the Buddha, the idea of self . . . produces harmful thoughts of 'me' and 'mine,' selfish desire, attachment, craving, ill-will, conceit, pride, egoism and other defilements, impurities and problems. It's the source of all the troubles in the world from personal conflicts to wars between nations" (Rahula 1967, 151). On this picture, the root of pain in envy goes beyond the lack of the envied good. The pain that the envier experiences result from the belief she can own the good, or control who owns the good. The real suffering, accordingly, is not merely lacking a good, but the envier's *clinging* to all things in the material world. I'll say more about this in the next section.

COMPASSIONATE DESIRE WITHOUT THE SELF

In this section, I sketch out the motivational structure of the Buddhist compassionate person: her actions are motivated by a universal concern for mankind, which stems from the desire of another's well-being without any self-interest. A truly compassionate person is motivated to address other people's suffering because other people's welfare directly guides her moral thinking. Her actions are motivated *directly* by other people's motivational states rather than mediated through her own mental processes. My formulation of compassion is in direct contrast with Aristotle and Nussbaum, who heavily emphasize the cognitive component of social comparison as the trigger for compassion. Nonetheless, my account doesn't entail that the compassionate agent blindly fulfills the other person's desires. The compassionate agent also makes *evaluative* judgments of the other's desires in order to care about her well-being.

Let me begin by explaining the two most important elements in Bodhisattva practice: wisdom and compassion (Kawamura 1981, 8). We can define the role of compassion in relation to wisdom: wisdom leads to selfless action for the sake of others because, without wisdom, one's compassionate actions will be defective (Florida 1991, 40). A Bodhisattva's wisdom can be defined as follows: (i) to realize the suffering of all sentient beings and (ii) to apply her compassion to them (Yao 2006, 191). A Bodhisattva's wisdom includes both the realization of all sentient beings' suffering and the necessity of physical action to relieve suffering. On the other hand, a Bodhisattva's compassion is not as easy to analyze. *Karuna* is the Sanskrit word that means "compassion"—it literally means "a trembling or quivering of the heart in response to another being's pain" (Conway 2001, 8). In contrast to the cognitively loaded Aristotle-Nussbaum view, Buddhist compassion is better characterized as an instinctual response that "takes the primitive form of mere pain or distress in the presence of pain or distress of others, independently of any imaginative reconstruction" (Crisp 2008, 234). Nonetheless, a survey of Buddhist literature points to a problem in explaining a Bodhisattva's compassion.[6] For the purpose of my argument, I take the interpretation that connects the practical aspect of compassion with wisdom: *karuna* means to relieve suffering and to give joy (Yao 2006, 192). Suffering and joy refer to a Bodhisattva's compassion while to relieve suffering and give joy refer to its purposes. This interpretation highlights the necessity of physical actions that one takes to relieve suffering (in addition the realization of suffering in all sentient beings).

As such, one cannot explain a Bodhisattva's compassion without wisdom and vice versa. Buddhist compassion has both an evaluative component and a feeling component. But what exactly is the suffering that a Bodhisattva feels when she's compassionate? It's our primordial suffering, which is the pain that stems from our existence and goes beyond any circumstance and situation (Walsh-Frank 1996, 9). For instance, suppose that Belle has lost her partner due to a car accident. From the Western perspective, the actual loss of the partner is the cause of suffering, and the intentional content of the pain is about the loss. For a Bodhisattva, however, the loss of the partner is merely the symptom. The real suffering stems from our *clinging* to the partner and our thinking that we have control over things (and therefore we can claim the right to ownership of things). The compassion that a Bodhisattva has is a response to the real *cause* of why Belle is experiencing grief: attachment to the material world. In other words, a Bodhisattva feels compassion because she has the realization that all sentient beings (herself included) share one and the same primordial suffering—we suffer because we cling to impermanent things and lack insight into true reality of the world (12–13). As such, a Bodhisattva's compassion can be extended to all humans insofar as she feels the deeper pain underlying all our suffering. Thus, there are no degrees to a Bodhisattva's compassion.

Now I can characterize a Buddhist agent's compassionate action clearer: it necessarily aims at benefiting others because its goal is to alleviate suffering. Rather than looking inwardly to see if one has the desire to help someone, a Buddhist agent is *directly* motivated by the suffering itself, but her compassionate desire must have a reflective component, otherwise it can be reckless and defective. For example, suppose that Gaston is in pain because he is recovering from alcoholism. The withdrawal symptoms are so severe that

Gaston decides to ask his friend Belle if he could take a sip of her whisky. Belle sees that Gaston is suffering—and she wants to help and her reason for helping is that she perceives that he desires to end the painful withdrawal symptoms. Gaston's desire then becomes the *reason* behind Belle's motivation to help, because she perceives Gaston's desire for well-being as her own. Nonetheless, it's exactly because Belle undertakes Gaston's desire for well-being as her own, that she also understands that it's not truly good for Gaston to have a sip of whisky (and relapse). Acting compassionately requires Belle to judge that Gaston's desire for a sip of whisky won't benefit his well-being, and this temporary suffering (from alcohol withdrawal) will lead to long-term happiness. If we asked Belle why she's not letting Gaston have a sip, she'd probably say "because Gaston needs to get better!" or "Gaston wants to recover from alcoholism," instead of "because I want to be a good friend and I want to help him get better!" The key difference between the two types of answers is that the former response "cite[s] *other* people's pro-attitudes rather than the agent's own" in explaining the behavior in question (Schmid 2010, 229). Thus, Belle is not motivated by *her own* desire to address the other's suffering but is motivated *directly* by the other person's desire to be happy. She doesn't need to make a comparison between her and Gaston in order for compassion to arise. Her actions are not aimed at fulfilling a desire of hers. Rather, they are directed at benefiting the well-being of the other.[7]

Based on this distinction drawn between being motivated by others' and one's own desires, the Buddhist compassionate agent undertakes other people's desires as her own—that is, she is able to *represent the other's desire as one's own*.[8] If we think of the self as a series of changing perceptions, this doesn't entail that there is no agency and therefore unintelligible to speak of the self (or "I") as a doer behind a deed. Rather, the "I" becomes more flexible at adopting other people's perspectives—and therefore better at representing others' desires as one's own and bonding affectively with others. A less rigid "I" allows us to be more responsive to other people's suffering because we recognize that the differences between self and others are relative, not absolute.

ENVY MANAGEMENT VIA SELF-COMPASSION

In this last section, I offer some practical answer to envy management using the Buddhist perspective. In particular, I aim to show how the no-self doctrine could fit into an integrative cognitive behavioral therapy (CBT) model of envy.[9] CBT is a form of psychotherapy that helps one identify dysfunctional thinking patterns (thoughts, beliefs, and attitudes) that result in negative behavioral patterns. While my analysis so far assumed envy as malicious and hasn't addressed the possibility of emulative envy, I'll conclude by showing that Buddhists reject all forms of envy—even in instances where it seems benign and may be morally good, we have reasons to avoid such feelings.

According to Exline and Zell (2008), although envy is a negative emotion, envy has useful "signal values" as it tells us that "something is amiss in our environment and may need to be corrected" (316). In their view, envy signals to us at least three things about our surroundings: desire, deficit, and disconnection. First, envy signals to the envier what she sees as important in life. For instance, someone who is envious of rich people typically think of being wealthy as an important goal in life (317). Furthermore, typically desires are strongly related to core themes involving identity and achievement, security, being loved, or physical survival. So, an envious person may believe that owning expensive cars and jewelry will guarantee that one can attain love and security, but very often she has misguided beliefs about how personal happiness or self-worth is contingent on attainment of the goal (Crocker and Wolfe 2001). The purpose of CBT is thus to test and evaluate the envier's belief system and assumptions.

The Buddhist no-self doctrine can help the envier see the contingency between self-worth and goal attainment. Recall the claim that envy arises when one's identity is threated.[10] This entails that in the background of envy is a strong sense of equality—the envier feels like she deserves the good by appealing to the notion of distributive justice. From a psychological perspective, this sense of equality can be explained by the evolutionary adaptive value of envy: members of groups compete for higher status because higher status is associated with "greater access to food, mates, procreative success, nesting sites, less depression, less anxiety, better health, better life prospects, lower cortisol [and so on]" (Leahy 2020, 3). Under this perspective, individuals are motivated by *dominance hierarchy* and envy's function is to regulate social status (Crusius and Lange 2017).[11] Envy can therefore be seen as adaptive because it "alerts the individual to personal shortcoming in status-relevant domains and spurs corrective action" (86). Nonetheless, this competition for higher status often leads envious individuals to (falsely) idealize those with higher status in society, assuming that the way to be happier in life is to gain status (Leahy 2020, 4).[12]

Given this, clinicians in envy treatment focus on two main maladaptive assumptions underlying envy associated with higher status: (1) idealizing status and (2) perceived range of valued action. Regarding the former, the clinician can attempt to "deconstruct" status by showing how status domains are "local." Status doesn't have absolute value because it's always arbitrary and dependent on the views of others (Leahy 2020, 4). Status reflects different perceived domains of values, but within each domain there are segments of the hierarchy that disagree about the status of an individual. For instance, we may think of professors and academics as having some level of status and prestige society. While this may be true, it's also the case that within different academic disciplines, certain subfields are valued more than others depending on the individual you ask.[13] It's impossible for us to truly know how anyone's work is viewed. Status will therefore turn out to be merely a temporary position in a local hierarchy (Leahy 2020, 4).

We can inject the no-self doctrine into the deconstruction of status to illustrate the subjective and relative nature of status. First, recognizing that the self is an illusion helps us recognize that the obsession with status is an "exaggerated concern with self-preservation at all costs, in the manner of Hobbesian Man" (Lesser 1979, 63). If the self is not a permanent entity, then we cannot truly *own* or possess things, whether material or mental, so we would realize that our attempt to maintain and add to our present sources of pleasure (via higher status) is unattainable (63). We would come to the realization that goal attainment doesn't necessarily bring one peace and self-worth insofar as our possessions are fleeting and temporary. When we believe the self as a series of causal events, then what makes me who I am is closer to what makes you who you are than what we have previously imagined. In turn, we are less likely to idealize things such as status and wealth since we would recognize that what makes you "you" and what makes me "me" are a series of loosely connected perceptions. If none of us are permanent and distinct entities, then none of us truly own our social status. Status becomes an illusion since what is considered as "high status" can always be interpreted (and re-interpreted) from multiple perspective. There is no fixed or absolute perspective from which we judge social status.

Second, envy signals a sense of deficit and personal failure in us—that we see ourselves as lacking in some important dimensions (Smith, Combs, and Thielke 2010). Typically, those who experience feelings of envy also feel a strong sense of helplessness because they believe that their important goals are out of their reach (Miceli and Castelfranchi, 2007; Smith and Kim 2007). The key here is to help the envier transform their helplessness into positive emotions and constructive actions. As such, *accepting* one's limitation is the most important task to pull an envious person out of a deficit mindset. But how does one learn to accept one's limitation? Many scholars have referred to Buddhism and suggested the idea of a "quiet ego" and the cultivation of humility and self-compassion (Baurer and Wayment 2008; Exline et al. 2004; Tangney 2000; Neff 2003). Acceptance of one's limitation starts with the acceptance of the self as flexible, open and interdependent on others. If we can learn to accept our insecurity (and inferiority) as inevitable, then we remove the source of our frustration and unhappiness—and thereby removing the motivation to destroy the good from the envied.

Let me highlight examples of dysfunctional beliefs about social comparison that can lead to destructive rumination and behavior (Leahy 2020, 3):

1. Labeling ("He's a winner, I'm a loser.")
2. Fortune-telling ("She'll continue to advance, I'll fall behind.")
3. Dichotomous thinking ("You either win or lose.")
4. Discounting positives ("The only thing that counts is getting ahead.")
5. Catastrophizing ("It's awful not to be ahead of others.")

If we examine this list of maladaptive beliefs, it's hard not to notice that all of them assume a strong sense of the self as independent and distinct entity, and that there is a competition between the self and others. The envier's mind operates on a dichotomy between the self and other—for instance, the other is the winner and the self is the loser (and these are the only two options available). This perception of the other as a direct competition is a failure to see that all beings are interconnected and every action has far-reaching actions. While it may be true that acting on one's self-interests in the short-term benefits oneself, the long-term consequences will eventually have an impact on one's own well-being. The world is a complex network of cause and effect, so each one of our actions has an effect on others and the world as a whole (but the envious person often forgets that the self is also part of the world). Buddhist thinker Shantideva wrote, "Everything is dependent on something else. Even that thing upon which each is dependent is not independent (MacKenzie 2020, 52). The COVID-19 pandemic illustrates the interconnectedness in the world clearly. Wealthy country A withholds vaccine supply to poor country B in order to protect its own citizens, but the lower rate of vaccination in other nations mean that the virus has more room to mutate further, and thereby reducing the efficacy of the vaccine. And if country A's economy is heavily dependent on migrant workers from country B, then the policy to withhold vaccine supply comes back to hurt country A (and the rest of the world) because it only perpetuates the spread (and mutation) of the virus further.

One may argue that the list of maladaptive beliefs only applies to malicious and not emulative envy, the latter of which can be seen as non-malicious and a morally good thing. Emulative envy typically provides the agent the positive motivation to improve oneself without pulling the envied down— and thus is benign because the agent is focused on the good (instead of the envied). However, from the Buddhist perspective, all envy should be rejected. For the Buddhists, emulative envy is still problematic insofar as it presupposes independent selfhood. That is, if the agent sees the target and herself as distinct entities, then the strive to self-improvement is problematic because it assumes that the "I" is equated to some permanent entity (and can be *better* than others)—and this fuels the desire to "own" things and for things to be "mine." The desire for things to be "mine," in turn, leads to the desire to want to control things. It's inevitable that the envious agent is bound to experience disappointment at some point and therefore bestow suffering upon herself, even if she is not motivated to harm others. For this reason, the Buddhists would not encourage emulative envy because it perpetuates the belief in a strong selfhood, which is the root of all suffering in the world.

Conversely, under the no-self doctrine, self-compassion helps us adopt a balanced view of the self within a broader perspective: "each of us makes up only a small part of the whole, but we still have worth, value and dignity" (Exline and Zell, 321). As I explained in the previous section, when one is compassionate toward other people, one undertakes another person's desire for well-being as one's own. One can learn to be kind and gentle toward the other when one sees the other's painful experience as a common and connected aspect of humanity rather than as an isolating one (322). When one practices self-compassion, one's own welfare is treated the same as other people's welfare. One can separate the "self" into a present self and a future self: the former who feels envious under the given circumstance, and the other who won't. The envier is motivated to harm others for the sake of obtaining the good because the envier is only thinking about her own future welfare. When we are able to see ourselves as made of different series of perceptions, we can look at ourselves as an object of introspection. By becoming more reflective of our mental states, we can better manage our emotions and pick out the maladaptive beliefs that cause destructive behavior.

Lastly, envy signals a sense of alienation and disconnectedness from others. This is where the no-self doctrine can be literally understood and applied. Envy typically signals broken relationships in the envier's personal network in various ways, including inferiority, shame, rivalry, and the sense of injustice. I have already covered coping strategies involving the deconstruction of status in an earlier part of this section. Here, I'll focus mainly on the guilt and shame we feel in envy.

Exline and Zell propose that two additional strategies may be employed to reduce the interpersonal alienation associated with envy (325). First, the envier would draw the envied person closer in psychological terms. Second, the envier would make the envied person less comparable to the self. These two strategies operate on one emotion that is incompatible with envy: love (Schimmel 1992).[14] The strategy is to bring the envied closer through love and kindness, without triggering comparison. This is the compassion that the Buddhist agent advocates toward the self and the other via the realization that we all share the same primordial suffering. Recall again that the Buddhists believe that the pain we feel from being unable to obtain the good are superficial symptoms of a deeper and more profound suffering, which is the suffering that comes from our clinging to things we cannot control. The guilt and shame we feel from envy, therefore, comes from not recognizing our clinging (and craving).

To illustrate this point, I refer to Sara Protasi's notion of inert envy, which she alleges to be the most unproductive kind of envy, and the one that brings the most guilt and agony to the agent. According to Protasi (2016, 541–42), inert envy is the result of being focused on the good yet at the same time believing that one is not capable of getting the good for oneself. Thus, inert envy is self-defeating, and especially painful as the envier experiences despair, frustration, self-loathing, and often shame and guilt for feeling envy. Consider Protasi's example:

> Indrani is infertile. She envies her friend Priya, who just got pregnant. Indrani values having a biological child for its own sake, and she is motivated to have one. However, she is aware that this possibility is precluded to her. Priya is a litmus test of what Indrani sees as a flow of hers: it shows her what she cannot have. She congratulates Priya on her pregnancy, but whenever she has a chance—she sympathetically of course—remarks on Priya's weight gain and fatigued looks. The day that Priya has a miscarriage, she feels some relief, but her envy is not satisfied.[15]

Even after the envied lost the "good," although the envier feels some relief, her envy is not satisfied. According to the Buddhists, Indrani feel despair, frustration and guilt, not only because she cannot have a kid, but also because she clings to the idea that her (nonexisting) child is something she can possess and have. Even though Priya lost her baby, Indrani's frustration doesn't completely go away because she holds onto the fundamental belief that we can control how things happen. We cannot stop envy unless we have a shift in the way we think about how we relate to others. If there is no such thing as a permanent self, the difference between one person and another becomes relative, not absolute. If Indrani can see that both her and Priya are processes, or series of causally connected events, then she can see the difference between her and Priya as of the same type, except in degree (Lesser 1979, 63). The difference between her and Priya are the same kind of difference between the stages of herself at different stages of his life. That is to say, "the difference between 'me' and 'not-me' is really a difference between events which have a relatively close causal connection with the chain of events that is 'my present self' and those which have a relatively distant one" (63). It follows that being kind to one's future self and to others is the same.

Accordingly, for Indrani, being kind to herself translate into being kind to Priya (through physical action). When we treat other's welfare *as our own*, we are essentially also improving our own welfare. To be truly kind and loving (to herself and to others), Indrani would take action to help Priya cope with the loss, such as offering an ear to listen to her or accompany her to support groups when she needs a friend. By recognizing that Priya and her are not that different at all—that is, they are both women who love children and want to be caretakers, then perhaps she would feel free to open up to Priya about the pain she suffers from not being able to conceive. Out of everyone that Indrani knows, Priya probably would be able to understand her pain better than anyone else. Thus, through sharing her pain, guilt, and frustration with the target of her envy, Indrani would finally be able to alleviate the guilt and frustration that she has been hiding.

CONCLUSION

In this chapter I have presented an analysis of envy and compassion from the Buddhist no-self perspective. My purpose is not to make a strong metaphysical claim about the existence of the self per se, but to suggest that a more flexible and interconnected view of the self would allow us to better manage destructive emotion such as envy. Practicing compassion by representing others' desire as one's own and caring about others' welfare as one's own would turn out to be the same as self-compassion. When we understand ourselves as interdependent on one another and sharing the same humanity, it becomes easier to relate to others and alleviate the desire to compete for social recognition, which is often a trigger for envy.[16]

NOTES

1. Francis Hutcheson (*An Inquiry into the Original of Our Ideas of Beauty and Virtue*), David Hume (*A Treatise of Human Nature*), and Adam Smith (*The Theory of Moral Sentiments*) all posit that human beings have a psychological capacity for feeling others' pain—and morality is built on this natural empathy we have. Schopenhauer's (*On the Basis of Morality*) account of compassion has also been interpreted as close to the Buddhists according to Reilly (2020).

2. Nussbaum (1996) and Aristotle (*Rhetoric*) hold a cognitivist view of compassion where judgments are needed in the similarity requirement. Crisp (2008) holds a noncognitivist view of compassion where it's more like an instinctual response to another's suffering.

3. Crisp rejects the Aristotle-Nussbaum accounts of compassion as he criticizes their views as excessively grounded in cognitive components. Crisp himself argues for a non-cognitive conception of compassion where it takes the primitive form of mere pain or distress in the pain or distress of others (237).

4. D'Arms and Kerr (2008) and Salice and Sanchez (2018) argue that hostility is always a feature of envy. Protasi (2016) argues that there can exist envy without hostility.

5. Britannica Encyclopedia, s.v. "anatta" accessed December 1, 2021, https://www.britannica.com/topic/anatta

6. See Beane (1974), Inada (2000), Walsh-Frank (1996), and Mizuno (1999) for further discussions on the difficulty in defining a Bodhisattva's compassion.

7. My formulation here is similar in spirit to David Wong's (1991) reading of Mencius, which argues that the compassionate person's reason for his action is directly outwardly so he acts directly in the welfare of the recipient. The other's suffering is a direct reason for him to act.

8. The agent's point of view is not completely excluded—only the self-interested point of view is excluded. For a more detailed discussion on the structure of desire and intension, see Schmid (2010).

9. Exline and Zell (2008) and Leahy (2020).

10. Salice and Sanchez (2017) explain the hostility in envy from two factors (1) desert and (2) violation of equality principle. In their view, regardless of whether the envied obtained the good by merit or luck, the envier applies the principle of equality due to her relative inferiority (231).

11. See also Lange and Crusius's contribution to this volume: "How Envy and Being Envied Shape Social Hierarchies" (chapter 2).

12. Salice and Sanchez's (2017) account also characterizes envy as a group-based emotion where the "good" desired by the envier, at the deeper level, is in-group esteem recognition. Although the "good" may manifest in a variety of material forms, ultimately the envier is seeking social recognition from his in-group members in order to feel valued, which is crucial for self-preservation (237).

13. For a different take on academic envy, see Felipe Romero contribution to this volume: "On the Epistemic Effects of Envy in Academia" (chapter 3).

14. See Protasi (2021) for an opposing view that argues love and envy and compatible.

15. Note that Protasi's notion of inert envy has evolved, and Indrani's story has changed a bit (see Protasi 2021, 55–61). However, my analysis still applies to the plausible form of envy depicted here.

16. This chapter has greatly benefited from the comments and encouragement of the following individuals: Vanessa Wills, Vanessa Carbonell, Neal Tognazzini, and Miriam Bankovsky. I am especially grateful to Íngrid Vendrell Ferran for her valuable feedback and Sara Protasi for her expertise and constructive suggestions.

REFERENCES

Aristotle. 1984. *The Rhetoric and the Poetics of Aristotle*, trans. by W. Rhys Roberts. New York: The Modern Library.

Carr, Brian. 1999. "Pity and Compassion as Social Virtues." *Philosophy* 74 (289): 411–29.

Chadha, Monima, and Shaun Nichols. 2019. "Self-Conscious Emotions Without a Self." *Philosopher's Imprint* 19: 1–16.
Conway, Jeremiah. 2001. "A Buddhist Critique of Nussbaum's Account of Compassion." *Philosophy in the Contemporary World* 8 (1): 7–12.
Crisp, Roger. 2008. "Compassion and Beyond." *Ethical Theory and Moral Practice* 11 (3), 233–46.
Crocker, Jan, and C. T. Wolfe. 2001. Contingencies of Self-Worth. *Psychological Review* 108: 593–623.
Crusius, Jan, and Jens Lange. 2017. "How Do People Respond to Threatened Social Status? Moderators of Benign versus Malicious Envy." In *Envy and work and in organizations*, edited by R. H. Smith, U. Merlone, and M. K. Duffy, 85–110, New York, NY: Oxford University Press.
Crusius, Jan, Manuel F. Gonzalez, Jens Lange, and Yochi Cohen-Charash. 2020. "Envy: An Adversarial Review and Comparison of Two Competing Views." *Emotion Review* 12 (1): 3–21.
D'Arms, Justin, and Alison Duncan Kerr. 2008. "Envy in the Philosophical Tradition." In *Envy: Theory and research*, edited by R. H. Smith, 39–59, New York: Oxford University Press.
Exline, Julia Juola, and Anne L. Zell. 2010. "Antidotes to Envy: A Conceptual Framework." In *Envy: Theory and research*, edited by R. H. Smith (chapter 17), New York: Oxford University Press.
Florida, R. E. 1991. "Buddhist Approaches to Abortion." *Asian Philosophy* 1 (1): 39–50.
Giles, James. 1993. "The No-Self Theory: Hume, Buddhism, and Personal Identity." *Philosophy East and West* 43 (2): 175–200.
Goetz, Jennifer L, Dacher Keltner, and Emiliana Simon-Thomas.. 2010. "Compassion: An Evolutionary Analysis and Empirical Review." *Psychological Bulletin* 136 (3): 351–74.
Jayatilleke, K. N. 1963. *Early Buddhist Theory of Knowledge*. London: Allen and Unwin.
Leahy, Robert L. 2020. "Cognitive-Behavioral Therapy for Envy." *Cognitive Therapy and Research*. Doi.org/10.1007/s10608-020-101355-y.
Lesser, A. H. 1979. "Eastern and Western Empiricism and the 'No-Self' Theory." *Religious Studies* 15 (1): 55–64.
MacKenzie, Matthew. 2020. "Indian Philosophy Helps Us See Clearly, Act Wisely in an Interconnected World." *The Conversation*, June 10. https://theconversation.com/indian-philosophy-helps-us-see-clearly-act-wisely-in-an-interconnected-world-135412.
Miceli, Maria, and Cristiano Castelfranchi. 2007. "The Envious Mind." *Cognition and Emotion* 21 (3): 449–79.
Neff, Kristin D. 2003a. "Self-Compassion: An Alternative Conceptualization of a Healthy Attitude toward Oneself." *Self & Identity* 2: 85–101.
———. 2003b. "The Development and Validation of a Scale to Measure Self-Compassion." *Self & Identity* 2: 223–50.

Nussbaum, Martha. 1996. "Compassion: The Basic Social Emotion." *Social Philosophy and Policy* 13 (1): 27–58.
———. 2001. *Upheavals of thought*. Cambridge: Cambridge University Press.
Protasi, Sara. 2016. "Varieties of Envy." *Philosophical Psychology* 29 (4): 535–49.
———. 2021. *The Philosophy of Envy. Cambridge*: Cambridge University Press.
Reilly, Richard. 2020. "Schopenhauer, Buddhism and Compassion." In *The Oxford Handbook of Schopenhauer*, edited by Robert L. Wicks. Oxford: Oxford University Press.
Salice, Alessandro, and Alba Montes Sanchez. 2018. "Envy and Us." *European Journal of Philosophy* 27: 227–42.
Schimmel, Solomon. 1992. *Seven Deadly Sins*. New York: Free Press.
Schmid, Hans Bernard. 2010. "Philosophical Egoism: Its Nature and Limitations." *Economics and Philosophy* 26: 217–40.
Smith, Richard H., and Sung Hee Kim. 2007. "Comprehending Envy." *Psychological Bulletin* 133: 46–64.
Smith, Richard H., Combs, David J. Y., and Stephen M. Thielke. 2010. "Envy and the Challenges to Good Health." In *Envy: Theory and Research*, edited by Richard H. Smith, chapter 16. New York: Oxford University Press.
Tangney, June Price. 2000. "Humility: Theoretical Perspectives, Empirical Findings and Directions for Future Research." *Journal of Social and Clinical Psychology* 19: 70–82.
Tangney, June P., and Ronda L. Rearing. 2002. *Shame and Guilt*. New York: Guilford.
Tracy, Jessica L., and Richard W. Robins. 2007. "The Self-Conscious Emotions: A Cognitive Appraisal Approach." In *The Self-Conscious Emotions: Theory and Research*, edited by Jessica L. Tracy, Richard W. Robins, and J. P. Tangney, 3–20, New York: Guilford Press.
Walsh-Frank, Patricia. 1996. "Compassion: A East-West Comparison." *Asian Philosophy* 6 (1): 5–16.
Wong, David. 1991. "Is There a Distinction between Reason and Emotion in Mencius?" *Philosophy East and West* 41 (1): 31–45.
Yao, Fuchuan. 2006. "There are no Degrees in a Bodhisattva's Compassion." *Asian Philosophy* 16 (3): 189–98.

Chapter 6

Let the Donkeys Be Donkeys

In Defense of Inspiring Envy

Maria Silvia Vaccarezza and Ariele Niccoli

Once upon a time, Aesop says, there was a donkey who wanted to be a pet dog. The pet dog was given many treats by the master and the household servants, and the donkey was envious of him. Hence, the donkey began emulating the pet dog. What happened next? The story ends up with the donkey beaten senseless, chased off to the stables, exhausted and barely alive. Who is to blame for the poor donkey's unfortunate fate? Well, there could be disagreement upon this, but we think emulation is to blame. And it is on the kinds of envy-related emulation that we focus in this chapter.

More analytically, we aim at vindicating the role of envy for moral exemplars within an exemplarist character educational framework. In the first section, we recall the central tenets of an exemplarist account of moral progress, and highlight how negative emotions, in general, have suffered a bad press within character education, with exemplarism being no exception. Then we provide a brief outline of standard strategies of defending envy by appealing to useful taxonomies of envy (e.g., Taylor 1988; Protasi 2016; Fussi 2018). After that, we put forward our "Donkey Objection" by recalling Aesop's fable on "foolish imitation," so as to show that when envy triggers mere emulation, it can bear devastating effects such as conformism and a lack of self-worth and personal integrity.

In response to this objection, we bring into play a distinction between two rival forms of imitation—emulation and inspiration—and we coin the label of "inspired envy" for those forms of imitation by inspiration triggered by envy that lead to self-improvement avoiding morally detrimental consequences.[1]

THE CENTRAL TENETS OF AN EXEMPLARIST ACCOUNT OF MORAL PROGRESS

Exemplarism is a recent moral theory first advanced by Linda Zagzebski (2010, 2015, 2017), where the emotion of admiration plays a significant role. In Zagzebski's view, admiration for exemplars enables agents and communities to identify role models that set the reference of all main moral concepts, such as virtue, right action, duty, and so on. One of the most promising developments of exemplarism, which will be our background in this chapter, is its application to moral education: given its intrinsic developmental potentialities, exemplarism has rapidly given rise to a distinct approach within Aristotelian character education, namely, exemplarist character education. The core assumptions of this approach are, roughly, that: (i) admiring and emulating role models or exemplars is the most effective way to shape a virtuous character (Kristjánsson 2015; Croce and Vaccarezza, 2017), and (ii) exemplar-related positive emotions such as admiration play a major role within this process (Engelen et al. 2018; Vaccarezza and Niccoli 2018). This can be seen as a further development of standard Aristotelian character education. Indeed, within the Aristotelian tradition (Sherman 1997; Steutel and Carr 1999), "[c]haracter is caught through role-modeling and emotional contagion" much more than being learned by studying lists of abstract values (Kristjánsson 2015, 21; see also Croce and Vaccarezza 2017).

The main merits of exemplarist character education can be summarized as follows: (i) it assigns theoretical legitimacy to the phenomenological evidence of the primacy of role models in shaping character; (ii) it makes a strong case for emotional development as central to character education, and in particular, it accommodates within the theory the central moral emotion of admiration. However, these important theoretical gains come at a cost: namely, an almost exclusive focus on admiration. One might wonder, at this point, which emotions besides admiration should be regarded as a relevant source in this process for role modeling to be successful and morally valuable. One might think of other positive exemplarity-related emotions, such as adoration (Schindler 2013), elevation (Haidt 2003; Kristjánsson 2017), gratitude (Haidt 2003), moral awe (Keltner and Haidt 2003; Kristjánsson 2017), and inspiration (Thrash and Elliot 2003, 2004). However, such exclusive focus on positive emotions looks far from granted: the encounter with moral exemplars, besides eliciting admiration, can trigger a wide range of negative emotions. For instance, the exemplar, insofar as she displays a higher moral status, can be seen as embodying a moral standard one feels inadequate to attain and therefore elicit shame; or, as possessing a (moral) good one lacks and is therefore envious of; or, finally, can make one feel guilty of not being able to meet as adequately as she does the moral requirements of a situation. In turn, these scenarios can be worsened if the exemplar in question is not a distant public or historical figure, such as a renowned moral hero or a saint, but a close-by morally excellent agent, with whom one can compare and compete. Provided that we can't help experiencing such emotions, nor can we prevent them from arising, what should we do with them?

Zagzebski's answer is that negative emotions are unfortunate obstacles and threats to moral development we should try to avoid (2017, 58–59). In a previous paper, we have already noted that this approach toward exemplarity-related negative emotions is at best unfair, at worst harmful, for both instrumental and intrinsic reasons (Vaccarezza and Niccoli 2019).

In what follows, we develop that argument further and discuss how a paradigmatically negative emotion like envy should be taken into serious account within exemplarist character education. First, because—as said— moral exemplars, insofar as they are seen as bearers of virtue, can easily become the object of such emotion, a fact whose underestimation or neglect could lead to a diminished impact of an exemplarist educational program. Second, because—under certain conditions—envy can fuel a positive effort of genuine moral growth and prove a source of moral striving that should not be wasted. It is this second point that we focus on primarily here. To defend it, we draw on existing defenses of a benign form of envy and argue that a further clarification of its possible lines of development is in order.[2]

ENVY, EMULATION, AND THE "DONKEY OBJECTION"

Some essential characteristics of envy are widely accepted (D'Arms 2017; Protasi 2016, 2021). First, envy obtains within a three-place relationship: the person who feels the emotion of envy (the envious), the person to whom the emotion is directed (the envied, or rival), and the good possessed by the latter (in our case, a morally valuable quality). Second, envy implies a comparative assessment according to which the envious person perceives herself—in some respect—in a position of inferiority to the envied person. Finally, feeling envious is an unpleasant and even painful experience, so envy is an emotion with a negative valence.

As a result of these three characteristics, the prototypical reaction of the envious person is to try to bridge the gap with the envied person by damaging or depriving them of the envied good, which is why envy is traditionally portrayed as a morally reprehensible emotion. As if that were not enough, experiencing envy also harms the envious person who, feeling humiliated and miserable because of their own inferiority, further reinforces their disadvantage.

Despite its bad reputation, some philosophers and psychologists have recently attempted to rehabilitate the emotion of envy from a tout-court condemnation and argue that it can have a positive value under certain conditions.[3] To do so, they appeal to a distinction between two main kinds of envy: a "benign," "emulative," or even "admiring" envy on the one hand, and "malicious" or "destructive" envy on the other. Such distinction resembles very closely Aristotle's discussion of envy (*phtonos*) and emulation (*zēlos*) in the *Rhetoric* (Aristotle 2007, 146, 1388a29–38),[4] and has been recently re-elaborated by several scholars in order to defend a positive moral role for envy. Let us now consider the two most prominent analyses that identify types of envy, which are argued to be not only morally acceptable but even desirable, because of the transformative motivation they would induce in the envious subject. We will then analyze the consequences of these defenses in the case of envy for moral exemplars, and move from the moral acceptability of envy to the more specific issue of the moral acceptability of envy for moral traits. It is important to note that, although we are considering the case of envy for moral traits, we do not aim at taking a stance over the moral versus nonmoral nature of some kinds of envy (see, e.g., La Caze 2001, 32). We do not claim, in other words, that the "core evaluative concern" (Ben-Ze'ev 2002, 148) of the forms of envy we consider is moral; rather, that moral qualities can be an object of envy and that the moral acceptability of envying them can be assessed.

Gabriele Taylor makes a fundamental distinction between state-envy and object-envy. In state-envy, the envious is not focused on the good the other has (e.g., an indomitable yet humble intellectual honesty) but on "the other's having that good" (Taylor 1988, 234).[5] State envy, in turn, admits a further distinction between "destructive" or "malicious" envy on the one hand and "emulative" envy on the other. While in the case of malicious envy, the gap between the envious and the envied is bridged by harming the envied, in the case of emulative envy, the envious person strives to raise their status in response to the perception of their own inferiority. In object-envy, however, the envious person is focused on the good that the envied person possesses and whose lack the envious realizes through envy. In this case, the envied has the function of showing the envious which types of goods they most desire:[6] this form of envy fades into admiration and helps to set the ideal standards to which the envious person aspires. That is why object envy can also be called ideal or admiring envy. Both emulative-state-envy and admiring-object-envy lead to emulative behavior in the broad sense of striving to become akin to the envied, in our case, akin to the envied moral exemplar.

Another influential analysis of envy is the one recently proposed by Sara Protasi (2016, 2021), according to which envy is differentiated into four varieties, identified by combining certain variables: the focus of the emotion

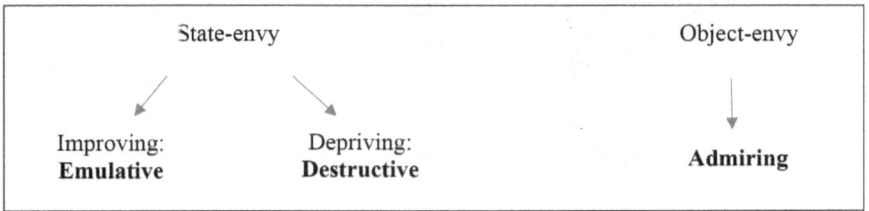

Figure 6.1 State-envy, object-envy, and their emulative forms. Source: (Taylor 1988, 2008)

(which can be directed at the good or the rival, as in Taylor's analysis) and the accessibility of the good (which can be perceived as obtainable or unobtainable).

In both cases, the only type of envy that is considered morally acceptable *and* not harmful for the envious is emulative envy. Leaving aside the more destructive and morally objectionable forms of envy (i.e., aggressive and spiteful envy), let us consider inert envy. Given that the good is perceived as unobtainable, this species of envy does not prompt any motivation to improve one's status but equally does not promote markedly malicious behavior toward the envied. On the other hand, in the grip of inert envy, "the envier experiences despair, frustration, self-loathing, and, often, shame and guilt for feeling envy" (Protasi 2016, 7; see also Protasi 2021, 55–61). Emulative envy, instead, would seem to have no negative consequences for either the envied or the envious. This variety of envy "is the result of being focused on the good and believing oneself to be capable of getting the good for oneself" (2016, 6).

To sum up, according to its advocates, benign envy can foster a process of emulation that is not only morally decent toward the envied (insofar as it does not imply malevolence) but also clearly positive for the envier (insofar as it implies the effort to improve one's own situation). However, we will argue, even benign envy may bring about substantial threats, related precisely to its emulative nature.

A caveat is in order before proceeding. We do not mean to take a stance over which one is the right taxonomy of envy. Rather, our point is that whenever an emulative kind of envy is at stake, a further distinction has to be made as to the kind of emulation triggered. This, in the case of envy for moral exemplars, is of crucial importance to draw a fruitful exemplarist charactereducational path. Therefore, we do not think we need to argue here for the existence of benign envy.[7]

To illustrate a potential objection against the view that emulative desire is a necessary and sufficient condition for benign forms of envy, let us make it more vivid with the aid of Aesop's fable, *The Donkey and the Pet Dog*:

Table 6.1 The four kinds of envy, including emulative envy. *Source*: Protasi (2016, 2021).

	Obtainable	*Unobtainable*
Focus on the good	Emulative	Inert
Focus on the rival	Aggressive	Spiteful

A donkey used to see the master's pet puppy dog fawning on him day in and day out. The puppy ate his fill of food from the master's table and was also given many treats by the household servants. The Donkey said to himself, "If my master and all the servants are so fond of that nasty little dog, then imagine what will happen if I do as the dog does." . . . As the Donkey was reflecting on his situation, he saw the master coming in. He let out a great "hee-haw" and quickly ran to meet him, leaping up and putting his two front feet on his master's shoulders, licking the master with his tongue and tearing the master's clothes with his hooves. The master collapsed under the Donkey's weight and at the sound of the master's shout all the servants came running. They grabbed sticks and stones and attacked the Donkey, beating him senseless and breaking his back and his legs. Then they chased him off to the stables, exhausted and barely alive. (Gibbs 2002, 294)

The emotion portrayed in this fable looks like a paradigmatic case of emulative envy: the two animals are peers who live in the same household, which means the goods enjoyed by the puppy are perceived as within the Donkey's reach; furthermore, the action tendency elicited is precisely emulation, for he tries to improve his situation by emulating a set of behavior displayed by the envied dog. However, as we can see, the Donkey ends up much worse off than he was at the beginning. Aesop's moral of the story is that "unworthy people should not try to usurp the position of their superiors." Ours, however, is rather different and points to the risks of *literal* imitation. This risk is reflected in a difference between envy and admiration at the motivational level. Although benign envy and admiration both promote an effort to elevate one's own situation (Van de Ven 2015), they seem to differ in some respects. Blatz et al. (2016) found that benign envy motivates people to copy the envied person and achieve short-term and specific goals, whereas admiration motivates people to achieve more long-term and abstract goals. Admiration thus tends to motivate people to emulate the achievements of the admired person or moral exemplar in less direct ways. (Engelen et al. 2018). It is precisely on this point that our objection and proposal are based. On the one hand, we intend to make explicit the dangers of literal imitation and, on the other, to identify under what conditions envy can fuel a process of affective and motivational transformation. Even though the Donkey example concerns a case of envy for nonmoral goods, we think the same pattern applies when moral goods are envied, and the behavior of moral exemplars is emulated. In such cases, consequences are even worse, for what is at stake is, more than the envier's chances to acquire some good, her chances of moral improvement.

We think that two main scenarios arise when a moral exemplar becomes the object of literal imitation, both leading to morally unwelcome consequences:

- *Failure scenario*: the envier tries to emulate the envied exemplar, but she fails. She feels powerless having failed to successfully replicate the envied exemplar's behavior and/or attitudes and develops a sense of a lack of self-worth and self-efficacy.
- *Success scenario*: the envier successfully replicates behavior and/or attitudes of the envied exemplar and develops moral conformism.[8]

Lack of self-worth has recently been highlighted as a major risk connected with experiencing envy (Perrine 2011; Vendrell Ferran 2021). According to several scholars, the structure of envy entails, besides a focus on the good and a focus on the rival, a focus on the self (see Kristjánsson 2010; Fussi 2019; Salice and Montes Sánchez 2019). In this respect, envy is an emotion of self-assessment that traces our own comparative inferiority about relevant values and goods that define the sense of identity of the self. Along these lines, Perrine claims that the feeling of inferiority involved in envy is conceptually connected with perceived diminished self-worth. On a more pessimistic account of envy, Vendrell Ferran (forthcoming) claims that genuine envy necessarily includes a focus on the self that reveals our own perceived powerlessness, which is more specific than perceived inferiority. In turn, feeling powerless leads to a diminished sense of self-worth.[9]

In our view, benign or emulative envy can also lead to experiencing a devaluation of the self, due to the failure of the emulative effort. Roughly, the idea is that a failure to become alike to the envied pushes back the envious person to a more intrusive—and morally questionable—kind of envy, in which the feeling of inferiority is associated with the feeling of powerlessness. As a result, a failed emulative process (i.e., literal emulation) promoted by envy (as well as others emulative desires) exposes the envious to the risk of diminished self-worth.

While lack of self-worth is objectionable for its psychological damage to the envier's self-perception and evaluation, conformism is widely regarded as posing a specifically moral threat to the agents who fall prey of it, besides jeopardizing the very possibility of attaining the envied good. From a virtue-ethical perspective, the reason why conformism is morally worrisome is that it implies mistaking moral guidance for technical advice (Annas 2004, 64). In other words, it makes it appear as if moral guidance merely meant being told what to do, rather than developing a virtuous character out of which becoming capable of making one's own choices. This, in turn, amounts to missing the target of moral development—that is, becoming virtuous agents and good practical reasoners. In Kantian terms, conformism entails a loss of autonomy since it shifts the source of agency outside the self's practical reason. As Kant would put it (*G* IV 408; see also Louden 1992, 2009), subjecting oneself to an exemplar equals endorsing a heteronomous principle of action, which means bypassing one's own practical authority. From this perspective, conformism implies therefore a loss of integrity:[10] not only do criteria of action come from outside of the self's practical reasoning; they also bypass one's personal commitments and practical identities. Seen this way, emulative envy for moral exemplars turns out to be self-defeating: the whole point of envying a moral exemplar is leveling up to the exemplar by becoming morally better, but the result seemingly ends up being a loss of practical authority and moral integrity. All the envier is left with is a merely superficial adherence to morality, which is well below what is required to be morally mature, let alone exemplarily good.[11]

Our exemplarist character educational account suggests that emulative envy for moral exemplars can only be morally acceptable—therefore channeled, rather than educated away—once the risk of emulation becoming literal, Donkey-like, imitation, is ruled out. To do so, it is necessary to carve out a morally valuable instance of emulative envy by means of two moves. These amount to a clarification (i) of the kind of emulation that can be morally acceptable; (ii) of the exemplars that are worthy of being envied, and of how we should construe them.

COMPLICATING EMULATION

To reiterate, the first move to carve out a morally and educationally valuable form of emulative envy consists in clarifying what a morally acceptable form of emulation amounts to. In this section, we claim that emulation need not be literal imitation but can take a different form, namely, that of inspiration.

To defend this claim, we bring into play a distinction (already advanced in Vaccarezza 2020) between two rival forms of emulation, namely, *imitation* and *inspiration*. While the former consists in literal replication of a model's behavior, which in the best-case scenario can only lead to conformism, the latter refers to being inspired by a model to develop one's own reflective and deliberative skills, so as to attain the good one aspires to in a personal, unique fashion. Along these lines, we coin the label of "inspired envy" for those forms of emulation that are triggered by envy and lead to self-improvement without a loss of integrity and autonomy in the subject.

The source of the distinction between imitation and inspiration can be traced back to an old disagreement upon the role of models in ethics. Historically speaking, such disagreement is rooted in a broader divergence upon the relation between exemplary models and their copies.[12] Three ancient paths to flourishing via reference to exemplary individuals can be identified in the Western philosophical tradition: (i) the Platonic mimesis of ideal models, (ii) the Stoic legacy focused on imitation of the Socratic sage, and (ii) the Aristotelian portrait of the *phronimos* as a source of inspiration. These three paths, originally intended to channel positive admiring reactions to the morally exceptional, seem to fit emulative envy as well, since they have different implications for whether, how, and to what extent one should emulate an (admired or envied) role model. The Platonic and Neoplatonic tradition, both in its pagan and Christian versions, conceives of the model as a universal norm to which one should literally—albeit imperfectly—conform (see, e.g., Plato, *Timaeus* 28A–50; *Republic* 484CD, 592b; Augustine, *De Civitate Dei* 8.6; *De Genesi ad litteram liber imperfectus* 16.57). The Stoic sage, embodied by Socrates, is the prime example of a saint—that is, a particular model who can be literally imitated to "become like him" (Seneca, *Moral Epistles* 95.1; *On Tranquility of Spirit* 5.2; *On Kindness* V 6.1–7). Finally, the Aristotelian *phronimos* represents a non-generalizable living standard that can be imitated only by analogy (*Nicomachean Ethics* VI).

These three ancient models present us with two more general ways of conceiving emulation. Socratic sanctity and Platonic ideal models call for *conformity* with an embodied or universal ideal, a standard the approximation to which indicates the trajectory of moral life. There may well be degrees in which this conformity obtains, yet the exemplar embodies a noninterpretable moral standard to which to conform. Be it a universal norm, such as in the Platonic tradition, or a particular saintly person, as in the case of the Stoic sage embodied by Socrates, emulation of the exemplar consists in an adaptation to the life of a particular person. If the model requires conformation, emulation can only take the form of an imitation, which means that literal imitation—common to Platonic and Socratic exemplarity—tends to realize the same type of action to the same degree as the model.

Unlike Socratic and Platonic exemplarity, the Aristotelian exemplarity of the *phronimos inspires* an analogical emulation—that is, an attempt to "do morally good" without prescribing any literal imitation of a specific course of action. Thus, it offers a formal, non-codifiable, kind of action-guidance, which avoids potentials allegations of heteronomy and conformism. Practical wisdom is equated by Aristotle with having an eye on the particular requirements of a situation (*NE* III.5, 1114b6), one which comes with time and moral training, and which enables one to find the right mean in each situation. The right mean, in turn, varies depending on the agent *and* the context (*NE* V.11,

1137b30–32): it would be pointless, therefore, to imitate what a sage does literally, for it may well be that what is wise and right for someone is excessive or defective for another (*NE* 1106b 1–5).

Along these lines, we propose to label *imitative* the envy triggered by moral exemplarity that results in literal imitation, and *inspired* the envy which is triggered by moral exemplarity, but elicits emulation by inspiration rather than a literal imitation of the role model. Inspired envy takes the envied moral exemplar as action-guiding in the formal way of inspiration to deliberate well, improving moral perception, consider the requirements posed by the various virtues, rather than construing the exemplar as a standard from which to deduce particular actions. The *phronetic* emulation that we label inspiration operates by analogy and calls for a revision of one's priorities based on an attempt to deliberate better and with more attention to a situation's moral features.[13]

It seems uncontroversial that, if we conceive of emulation as a form of inspiration, rather than literal imitation, charges of conformism and lack of self-worth fade away; however, one might wonder whether letting the envied model inspire one's conduct still amounts to an instance of envy rather than resulting in admiration.

To provide an answer to this objection, let us think about a case like the following:

> **S1.** Elisa thinks that her friend Laura is much more morally admirable than she is. Elisa envies Laura and, at times, finds herself resenting her as well. At first, her negative feelings prevent her from asking Laura for advice, or even trying to emulate her; however, with time, Elisa realizes that she really cares about becoming as good as Laura.
>
> In order to catch up, she begins to do the same things Laura does, with the unfortunate result of feeling frustrated, diminished or disempowered in her moral autonomy. However, if she is motivated enough, the persistent pain of witnessing Laura's moral superiority can eventually lead her to take a different route. She can start paying close attention to how Laura behaves, especially to how her moral reasoning works; she can look at how Laura always strives to do well, is open to criticism, is attentive to situations, and reflects on how to respond adequately. If Elisa succeeds in letting Laura inspire her, and so developing her own moral skills, envy can eventually make room for other emotions, since the gap which had triggered it has been filled.

What the vignette suggests is that emulation can be triggered by envy but need not remain anchored to it: when an inspired kind of emulation begins to take place, the envier enters a process of self-transformation. Inspiration, so to speak, despite being promoted by envy in the first place, acts as an intermediate step toward the overcoming of envy itself, which can make room to admiration or to other positive emotions. What was originally a painful feeling becomes a valuable starting point for a virtuous developmental path.

UNDERSTANDING EXEMPLARS

So far, we've claimed that different kinds of emulation lead to opposite moral consequences. Now that we tackled the issue from the envier's standpoint, it is time to have a look at the envied, to see whether a different choice—or a different construal—of exemplars can foster a tendency to develop one kind of emulation over the other.

To put it more bluntly: Who is a genuine exemplar, worthy of being envied in a morally acceptable and constructive way?

Our thesis is that, in order to pick a good instance of exemplary behavior that can foster the transformative process seen above, two kinds of alleged exemplars should be avoided. On the one hand, we should avoid seeing as moral exemplars agents who excel in some traits but are severely defective in other moral domains; a substantial lack of integration in their character may show lack of a more general responsiveness to reasons. On the other hand, we do not propose that a moral exemplar needs to be perfect or possess all the virtues to an exceptional degree at once, which is highly unlikely with real people. But does a third option even exist?

We believe it does, but identifying it implies, somehow, challenging the question itself: exemplarity, that is, is not at all a matter of possessing one or more traits but a whole different moral skill, as the centrality of phronesis in Aristotelian exemplarity suggests.

An exemplar genuinely worthy of being envied or admired, in our account, is someone who displays *phronesis*, conceived as overall ethical expertise, which manifests in several domains and reveals high responsiveness to moral reasons. This does not exclude that an exemplar has flaws; rather, due to her ethical expertise, she acknowledges her shortcomings and strives toward progress. What makes one morally exemplary is *striving to respond to reasons* rather than possessing one, more, or even all moral traits. What triggers imitative, rather than inspired, emulation is, in part, the tendency to focus on a trait or set of traits, instead of striving to be reason-responsive.

Such striving and expertise manifest themselves via virtuous actions; and yet, we should refrain from attributing to exemplars some static, automatic, and easily replicable moral trait. Our claim, in short, is that genuine exemplarity is rooted in practical wisdom, of which specific virtues are manifestations in each different moral field.[14] And practical wisdom, in turn, can be better understood as overall ethical expertise—that is, as a unified skill, which, although being general in scope, improves gradually. In other words, we can deem as wise not only the agents who display an utterly virtuous character but also those who (i) are affectively and cognitively oriented to an overall good life and *fare well* in at least some moral domains, but also (ii) acknowledge their shortcomings in other domains and try to improve there (De Caro, Vaccarezza, and Niccoli 2018).

To sum up, two opposite views of the proper object of moral emulation are at play here: on the one hand, the object of emulation is supposed to be a well-definable set of moral characteristics; on the other hand, the object of emulation is conceived as an open-ended, dynamic, and not entirely or directly replicable moral strive and orientation. And the moral status of the envy that is triggered depends as much on picking the suitable object of emulation as it does on working directly on transforming emulation.

However, "picking the wrong object" can obtain in two ways: first, it is the result of a *poor choice*, that is, the envier envies an unworthy target; second, it depends on a *poor construal* of an actually worthy target. Either way, an improper or improperly understood moral exemplar is more likely to let the wrong kind of envious emulation thrive, as we will show in a moment.

As an example of the first way in which the envier picks the wrong object, think about a case where an envied exemplar behaves insensitively or arrogantly toward the envier without expressing a sincere will to improve her non-exemplary traits:

> **S2.** Stefano thinks that his friend Marco is much more morally admirable than he is. Stefano envies Marco and, at times, finds himself resenting him as well. Marco makes no effort to alleviate Stefano's sense of frustration: either he simply fails to realize it, for he lacks humility and empathy, or he fosters Stefano's frustration by patronizing him and indicating him what to do to follow in his footsteps.
>
> In this case, Stefano has reasons to divert his attention from Marco to more suitable exemplars as objects of envy.

Here, the envied lacks phronetic expertise and exhibits only isolated moral traits. His arrogance and lack of thoughtfulness are likely to elicit frustration or, in the best-case scenario, an attempt to literal imitation. An arrogant agent is likely, among other things, to enjoy being emulated literally, or to patronize their envier. It will hardly be the case that they realize the envier's pain with genuine empathetic concern and encourage autonomy in the envier. In this case, the envier should avoid focusing attention on such persons, and instead pick genuine exemplars. There's nothing to envy, so to speak, nor to emulate in any ways.[15]

As an example of the second way in which the envier picks the wrong object, think about a case where the envier lacks relevant moral education or maturity, and isn't yet capable of responding appropriately to the exemplar. In this case, the envier may bear responsibility in nurturing inspiring envy rather than rival forms. The object of envy is not wrong in itself; rather, the envier is incapable of construing it adequately:

> S3. Filippo thinks that his friend Roberta is much more morally admirable than he is. Filippo envies Roberta and, at times, finds himself resenting her as well. However, Roberta is sufficiently ethically competent to be attentive, humble, and generous, so she perceptively realizes Filippo's envy and makes every effort to alleviate her sense of frustration. In particular, she always encourages Filippo to find his unique way of being virtuous and supports his attempts to do well.
>
> Despite Roberta's supportive and attentive attitude, Filippo still fails to construe Roberta properly. He can keep feeling bad about her accomplishments; he either spoils her qualities by gossiping behind her back or tries to imitate her literally to catch up with her. In this latter case, Filippo can try to imitate something Roberta does or one or more traits she displays. Such an attempt implies that Filippo misrepresents Roberta's role and nature as a moral exemplar by conceiving her as the possessor of some static, perfectly identifiable, and distinct trait that he could possess in the same way as Roberta does. This, besides implying a lack of autonomy, also fails to hit the target: what the envier would gain from such literal imitation of a trait or behavior is different from what makes the exemplar morally superior. If this is the case, it is time for Filippo to change his attitude. Roberta is an ideal model for whom Filippo can try to foster and nurture a different emulation.

To summarize, even if the envious person experiences a benign form of envy, there remains ample scope for becoming entangled in a type of emulation that is sterile and harmful. On the other hand, under certain conditions, emulative envy is an excellent opportunity to trigger a process of (self-)education and moral progress.

CONCLUSION: MORAL PROGRESS AND EDUCATIONAL IMPLICATIONS

We conclude with some brief remarks on real-life interactions with exemplars. It appears that the different kinds of emulation, both in the case of admiration and envy, are sometimes ways in which the very same exemplary individuals may be admired/envied and emulated rather than categories under which be subsumed. This means that it is perfectly possible that an exemplar is imitated by someone and is a source of inspiration for another, or that the same person learns through time how to develop a more mature form of emulation out of an initial attempt to imitate the exemplar literally. In the specific case of envy, a genuinely exemplary person can be the object of both destructive envy and emulative envy, and the latter can obtain in either an imitative or an inspired form.

What conclusion can we draw concerning exemplarist character education? From an educational perspective, the possibility of a transition from imitation to inspiration appears necessary to avoid frustration and a diminished sense of the self in those who are particularly fragile in this respect, namely the young. Also, particularly in the case of the young, we should refrain from letting education via role models become disrespectful of their autonomy.

We have already claimed that inspiration can promote moral progress and a transition away from envy. In these concluding remarks, we want to highlight that, in educational settings, this should not be conceived of as an abrupt change. Rather, the transition from a form of literal emulative envy to an inspiring one is to be seen as a slow educational path that moves from imitation to inspiration (see also Vaccarezza 2020).[16]

This intuition is tentative and would require empirical evidence to be supported; this is why we do not even attempt to make more specific recommendations concerning different ages and developmental stages. All we do here is to propose a developmental trajectory for envy to become a morally fruitful starting point, and suggest that such trajectory, if empirically confirmed, should become the backbone of an exemplary character educational program with respect to envy. In conclusion, exemplarist character education should be *pluralistic* and *developmental*: it should accommodate and organize within an organic and feasible educational path different positive and negative emotions, exploit their potentialities and the diverse kinds of imitation they inspire, and foster the transformation of morally questionable forms into morally commendable ones.

NOTES

1. We are most grateful to Sara Protasi and all participants in the "Moral Psychology of Envy Workshop" for their comments on the talk version of this chapter. We are also very much indebted to Vanessa Carbonell and to Julien Deonna, Fabrice Teroni and all members of the Thumos Group in Geneva for their helpful comments on a previous version of this chapter.

2. Vanessa Carbonell discusses what happens when envy for morally superior agents turns sour in her contribution to this volume: "Malicious Moral Envy" (chapter 7).

3. Among them, La Caze (2001) and Thomason (2015); Van de Ven, Zeelenberg, and Pieters (2011) even argue that benign envy fares even better than both admiration and malign envy in motivating the subject to improve.

4. However, Kristjánsson rejects the link between envy and emulation, claiming that while envy implies "pain at another's deserved good fortune . . . through emulation . . . we simply express, with admiration, the desirability of being like B in some respect, or having the same thing as B, without wanting to take anything away from B" (2006, 42).

5. It is likely that the object-state dichotomy breaks down when what is envied is someone's moral character. Thanks to Vanessa Carbonell for this remark.

6. It could also be the case that the envied shows the envier what goods he most thinks others desire, or will tend to judge him by. Thanks to Vanessa Carbonell for pointing this out to us.

7. Elsewhere we defend the claim that "benign" or even "virtuous" envy obtains (Vaccarezza and Niccoli 2018), but our point here applies to all the affective states that D'Arms groups under the label "emulative desire" (2017).

8. By talking of single instances, we are simplifying a bit: a more realistic picture would involve analyzing the developmental process that occurs over multiple iterations, where individual attempts may be failures and yet there may be progressive growth.

9. The conceptual link between envy and self-worth is captured, in the psychological literature, by the empirical evidence of robust connections between envy and self-esteem. For an in-depth analysis of associations among self-esteem and both malicious and benign envy, see Vrabel et al. (2018).

10. Despite our use of Korsgaard's (1996) label "practical identity," what we endorse here is a very general meaning of integrity, even though we are aware that many rival accounts could take different stances over the threats of conformism. We think that all of them, however, agree in rejecting it.

11. Kristjánsson rightly points out that "merely with learning experientially to imitate a charismatic leader, we risk ending up with blind hero-worship: unenlightened conformity" (2006, 41).

12. A broader defense of this point can be found in Vaccarezza (2020).

13. This distinction is, admittedly, speculative and requires empirical validation. Nevertheless, it is well-supported by ancient and contemporary philosophical discussion and is a research hypothesis worth testing.

14. We defend this non-standard interpretation of phronesis elsewhere (De Caro, Vaccarezza, and Niccoli, 2018; De Caro and Vaccarezza 2020).

15. The scenario discussed here would be categorized as one of social dominance by Jens Lange and Jan Crusius; see their discussion in their contribution to this volume, "How Envy and Being Envied Shape Social Hierarchies" (chapter 2).

16. On a similar note, Archer and Matheson (2020) provide a diachronic account of admiration.

REFERENCES

Annas, Julia. 2004. "Being Virtuous and Doing the Right Thing." *Proceedings and Addresses of the American Philosophical Association* 78 (2): 61–75.

Archer, Alfred, and Benjamin Matheson. 2020. "Admiration Over Time." *Pacific Philosophical Quarterly* 101 (4): 669–89.

Aristotle. 2007. *On Rhetoric: A Theory of Civic Discourse*. Translated with introduction, notes, and appendices by George A. Kennedy. New York: Oxford University Press.

Blatz, Lisa, Jens Lange, and Jan Crusius. 2016. "Gain with and without Pain? Upward Motivation in Admiration and Envy Differs in Abstractness and Long-Term Focus." Poster presented at the EASP Medium Size Meeting "Promoting a Social Approach to Emotions." Cologne.

D'Arms, Justin. 2017. "Envy." The Stanford Encyclopedia of Philosophy (Spring 2017 edition), edited by Edward N. Zalta. https://plato.stanford.edu/archives/spr2017/entries/envy/.

Ferran, Ingrid Vendrell. 2021. "Envy, Powerlessness and the Feeling of Self-Worth." In *Empathy, Intersubjectivity, and the Social World: The Continued Relevance of Phenomenology. Essays in Honour of Dermot Moran*, edited by Elisa Magrì and Anna Bortolan, 279–302. Berlin: De Gruyter.

Fussi, Alessandra. 2018. *Per una teoria della vergogna*. Pisa: ETS.

Gibbs, Laura. 2002. *Aesop's Fables*. Oxford: Oxford University Press.

Hacker-Wright, John. 2010. "Virtue Ethics without Right Action: Anscombe, Foot, and Contemporary Virtue Ethics." *Journal of Value Inquiry* 44: 209–24.

Hursthouse, Rosalind. 1999. *On Virtue Ethics*. Oxford: Oxford University Press.

Kawall, Jason. 2014. "Qualified Agent and Agent-Based Virtue Ethics and the Problems of Right Action." In *The Handbook of Virtue Ethics*, edited by Stan van Hooft, 130–40. Durham: Acumen.

Kristjánsson, Kristján. 2015. *Aristotelian Character Education*. London: Routledge.

La Caze, Marguerite. 2001. "Envy and Resentment." *Philosophical Explorations: An International Journal for the Philosophy of Mind and Action* 4 (1): 31–45.

Louden, Robert B. 1992. "Go-Carts of Judgement: Exemplars in Kantian Moral Education." *Archiv für Geschichte der Philosophie* 74 (3): 303–22.

———. 2009. "Making the Law Visible: The Role of Examples in Kant's Ethics." In *Kant's Groundwork of the Metaphysics of Morals. A Critical Guide*, edited by Jens Timmermann, 63–81. New York: Cambridge University Press.

Protasi, Sara. 2016. "Varieties of Envy." *Philosophical Psychology* 29 (4): 535–49.

———. 2021. *The Philosophy of Envy*. Cambridge: Cambridge University Press.

Taylor, Gabriele. 1988. "Envy and Jealousy: Emotions and Vices." *Midwest Studies in Philosophy* 13: 233–49.

Thomason, Krista K. 2015. "The Moral Value of Envy." *The Southern Journal of Philosophy* 53 (1): 36–53.

Tiberius, Valerie. 2006. "How to Think About Virtue and Right." *Philosophical Papers* 35 (2): 247–65.

Vaccarezza, Maria Silvia. 2020. "Paths to flourishing: ancient models of the exemplary life." *Ethics and Education* 15 (2): 144–57. DOI: 10.1080/17449642.2

Vaccarezza, Maria Silvia, and Ariele Niccoli. 2019. "The Dark Side of the Exceptional: On Moral Exemplars, Character Education, and Negative Emotions." *Journal of Moral Education* 48 (3): 332–45.

van de Ven, Niels. 2016. "Envy and Its Consequences: Why It Is Useful to Distinguish Between Benign and Malicious Envy." *Social and Personality Psychology Compass* 106: 337–49.

Vrabel, Jennifer K., Virgil Zeigler-Hill, and Ashton C. Southard. 2018. "Self-Esteem and Envy: Is State Self-Esteem Instability Associated with the Benign and Malicious Forms of Envy?" *Personality and Individual Differences* 123: 100–104.

Young, Robert. 1987. "Egalitarianism and Envy." *Philosophical Studies* 52: 261–76.

Chapter 7

Malicious Moral Envy

Vanessa Carbonell

Former United States president Donald Trump would like to win the Nobel Peace Prize. His predecessor, Barack Obama, won the prize early in his presidency. Trump managed to get nominated for the prize—as did Mussolini, Stalin, and Hitler—but a win has been elusive. Unable to secure the honor for himself, Trump resorted to denigrating the prize and its winners—calling the process "unfair" and saying Obama "did nothing" to deserve it (Wagner 2019; Farley 2020).

Famously insecure and competitive, Trump seems especially fixated on people widely regarded as admirable. As the coronavirus pandemic unfolded in 2020, Trump's fixation shifted from Obama to Dr. Anthony Fauci, the government's top infectious disease expert and a career public servant with a reputation for integrity, honesty, and selflessness (Specter 2020; Blow 2020; Bruni 2021). As Dr. Fauci's public profile rose, so too did Trump's ire. With Fauci's net approval rating at 71 percent and Trump's at negative 5 percent, the White House sidelined Fauci, curtailed his public appearances, and allowed an advisor to release a list of times Fauci's advice had been wrong (Abutaleb, Dawsey, and McGinley 2020). With Trump's encouragement, Fauci's public health advice became politicized and #fireFauci appeared on social media. Fauci received death threats (Stein 2020). At a press briefing in July 2020, Trump said, "[Fauci's] got this high approval rating, so why don't I have a high approval rating?" Referring to Fauci and his colleague Dr. Deborah Birx, Trump went on: "They're highly thought of, but nobody likes me" (C-SPAN 2020). By October, Trump's advisor Stephen Bannon was calling for Fauci to be subjected to medieval execution: "heads on spikes" (Peiser 2020). By November, Trump was saying he planned to fire Fauci after election day. He didn't, but his allies continued their efforts to discredit Fauci well beyond the end of Trump's presidency. In spring 2021, former Trump advisor Peter Navarro was calling Fauci "a sociopath" and "the father of the actual virus" (Baker 2021) while Senator Rand Paul was calling Dr. Fauci "a little dictator" and an "ignoramus" (Chamberlain 2021). The Fauci drama seemed to reach its apotheosis in the fall of 2021 when the tabloid media ran misleading stories claiming Fauci was personally responsible for scientific studies in which dogs were tortured (Millbank 2021). Donald Trump Jr. began selling t-shirts that said "Fauci Kills Puppies" (Dasgupta 2021). Still, it got worse: as the Omicron variant emerged in late November 2021, Fox News guest Lara Logan compared Dr. Fauci to Nazi doctor and war criminal Josef Mengele (Barr 2021).

Behind the name-calling lies a general pattern: a subject fixates on a rival's accomplishments or public esteem; seek the same for himself; and failing to get it, sets out to tarnish, denigrate, or sabotage the person, or the honor itself. These are the marks of envy, and it's no surprise that headlines from the Trump era often reference envy, or its cousin, jealousy, by name. What is especially interesting about these cases is that the people targeted are not merely famous but *admired* and morally so—Obama, beacon of hope, Nobel Peace Prize winner; Fauci, *mensch*, savior to the sick, trusted truth-teller. I propose that these are cases of *malicious moral envy*.

In this chapter, I briefly sketch what malicious moral envy is, and then argue that it is puzzling. The puzzlement is due, partly, to the fact that this emotion is self-defeating. The person who displays malicious moral envy betrays a set of attitudes that are in tension with one another: they value moral virtue or moral accomplishment and regard it as important to their identity; yet, they are moved to engage in harmful and morally vicious leveling-down behaviors like tarnishing and sabotaging. If they act on their malicious moral envy—as Trump and his followers did—they make themselves morally worse. But in addition to being self-defeating in this way, I argue that malicious moral envy reveals a deeper ambivalence and complexity in our relationship to moral standards and expectations. We are both attracted to and repelled by our moral betters. We admire them, but do not necessarily want to hold ourselves to their high standards. Leveling-down behavior is an expression of this ambivalence, and in its gentler forms, can even be an important way that a social community negotiates and navigates their shared moral expectations.

WHAT MALICIOUS MORAL ENVY IS

Malicious moral envy is a subtype of envy more generally. To map its contours, I make use of Sara Protasi's account and typology of the varieties of envy (Protasi 2016, 2021). Protasi defines envy as "an aversive response to a perceived inferiority or disadvantage vis-à-vis a similar other, with regard to a good that is relevant to the sense of identity of the envier" (2021, 25). Envy is thus intimately bound up in our practices of social comparison. It is crucial, according to Protasi, that the target (envied) be sufficiently similar to the subject (envier) so that the social comparison is coherent. It is also crucial that the envied good matters to the subject's sense of self, otherwise faring poorly in comparison would be of no consequence to the subject's self-esteem.

It is tempting to think of envy as being essentially a negatively valenced, even antisocial emotion, but Protasi and others suggest there are in fact multiple subtypes of envy, not all of which are necessarily antisocial. Envy can motivate you to level down your rival, and this has been called invidious, destructive, or malicious envy (D'Arms 2017). Envy can also motivate you to level yourself up, and this has been called benign envy. In Protasi's taxonomy there are even further discriminations to be made: when our focus is mainly trained on the valued good itself, our envy is "emulative" if we regard the good as obtainable, or "inert" if we do not.[1] When our focus is mainly trained on the envied person, our envy is "aggressive" if we think we can take it from them, or "spiteful" if we cannot (Protasi 2021, 43). Protasi acknowledges that real-life cases will be messy and vague. Still, her shorthand for the behavioral tendencies associated with each species is helpful: on aggressive envy we are moved to *steal* that valued good, and on spiteful envy we are moved to *spoil* it (43).

Robert Roberts also focuses on this negative side of envy and gives the following helpful schema:

> The defining proposition for envy, then, would appear to be something like this: *It is important for me to have the personal worth that would be established by my being or appearing to be equal or superior to R in respect X; however, I am or appear to be inferior to R in respect X; may R be or appear to be degraded in respect X.* (Roberts 2003, 262)

The last part is crucial: "may R be or appear to be degraded" expresses a desire, or perhaps an instruction, for leveling-down. The drive to *degrade* is what makes the envy malicious or destructive. Stealing the good is the best solution, as that would lower the rival while raising oneself in equal measure. Where stealing is not possible, spoiling is second-best: if I can't have what the rival does, my consolation is that at least they can't have it either. Or so the twisted logic goes.

What, then, would make malicious envy count as moral?[2] By "moral" here I just mean *regarding morality* or *about moral properties*, in the sense where moral is contrasted with nonmoral; I don't mean "moral" in the sense of "morally good," where moral is contrasted with immoral.[3] Malicious moral envy is thus malicious envy over someone's moral properties rather than their nonmoral properties. In principle, you could envy someone for their exquisite moral badness, their superiority as a scoundrel. But let's set that case aside and focus on the more common case. Malicious moral envy can be defined as follows:

Malicious moral envy: an aversive reaction to a perceived moral inferiority relative to a similar rival, with regard to a moral property (virtue, accomplishment, esteem, etc.)[4] relevant to one's identity, that provokes malicious leveling-down attitudes or behaviors.

This definition incorporates Protasi's *similarity condition* and *self-relevance condition*, as well as Roberts' *degradation* condition. It also makes clear that the valued good is the rival's *moral* properties, whether that be their virtuous character, their tangible moral accomplishments, or the warranted moral esteem in which others hold them. The inferiority the subject detects in themself is a *moral* inferiority, and the rival must be similar in whatever aspects of similarity are necessary for *moral* social comparison—perhaps reared in a similar culture, operating within a similar set of personal or financial constraints, developmentally and psychologically similar, and so on.

Recall *Trump v. Obama* and *Trump v. Fauci*. What makes these cases of malicious moral envy? Trump had an aversive reaction to his perceived (moral) inferiority relative to Obama, with regard to a valued good, namely the winning of a (moral) award, the Nobel Peace Prize. Obama meets the similarity condition because he, too, was a US President, a public figure, a person whose accomplishments will be tallied in history books. Indeed, he was the prior occupant of Trump's office, living quarters, airplane, and so on, so the rivalry was salient to Trump. Trump attempted to level himself up, by getting himself nominated for the prize. That effort failed (so far?), so the next pathway is to level down Obama (deeming his prize undeserved) and level down the prize itself (deeming the process unfair).[5]

This is spiteful envy—spoiling the valued good. The only remaining component is that the valued good must be relevant to the envier's identity. I won't examine Donald Trump's psychology at length. Suffice it to say that notwithstanding his narcissism (Conway 2019)—or perhaps because of it—it is plausible that Trump sees himself as a morally admirable and accomplished person, indeed a peacemaker who eschewed war (it is supposed to be a *peace* prize, after all). It is plausible, therefore, that the goal of faring well in *moral* comparison with other presidents would meet Protasi's *self-relevance* condition for him. Granted, there is a more superficial reading where he simply wants praise and merely values *winning*, and what he needs for his self-esteem is not to be a moral paragon but simply to be a winner.

But even on that reading, it is plausible that he values the Nobel Peace Prize more than most other prizes, precisely because it is considered a *moral* honor and he wants to be considered a winner in the moral domain just as much as in business, politics, entertainment, and so on.

The case of *Trump v. Fauci* is messier but no less striking. Many of Dr. Fauci's admirable qualities are in domains that would not meet the similarity or self-relevance conditions in a comparison with Trump. Dr. Fauci is known as: an accomplished scientist—not something Trump aspires to be; a selfless caretaker and advocate for HIV/AIDS patients—Trump is a germaphobe known for his lack of empathy; and a nonpartisan, devoted bureaucrat whose main allegiances are to science and public health—whereas Trump decries the federal government "swamp." For these reasons, it is only under specific conditions that Fauci would be similar enough to Trump to generate a *self-relevant* rivalry. Fauci only became a target of Trump's envy when he rose to a level of public prominence sufficient to generate a coherent social comparison.

In spring 2020, both men were central to the government's response to the pandemic. Both were high-ranking government officials. (Indeed, Fauci is the highest paid US federal employee, earning more than the president.) Both were on TV nearly every day. Both are New Yorkers of a certain age. With these similarities in place, what seemed to trigger Trump's malicious moral envy was that it became clear that the public *trusted* Dr. Fauci and did *not* trust him. This was not just a matter of fame, popularity, or approval.[6] Polls showed that Americans regarded Dr. Fauci as a reliable source of information about the pandemic—that is, information relevant to their well-being and even survival. Sixty-seven percent trusted Fauci, while only 26 percent trusted Trump (Sanger-Katz 2020). This, I argue, is a *moral* comparison: trustworthiness and honesty are moral properties, especially in a pandemic. Moreover, even epistemic properties that are not normally regarded as moral—such as credibility or expertise—can become moralized (not to mention politicized) in the right context. We should thus take into consideration that Trump has a documented history of deception and lying, while Fauci has a documented history of scrupulous truth-telling, nonpartisanship, scientific integrity, and caring for others. In this context, to regard Trump as not credible about the pandemic is not merely to regard him as factually uninformed but to regard him as untrustworthy in a moralized sense: not apt to save us, not having our best interests at heart. The poll was a moral rebuke.

Trump's malicious reaction was to level Fauci down: take away his microphone, question his judgment, threaten his job, spread rumors about his motives, and the like. The efforts were successful in that many Americans who had not heard of Dr. Fauci before the pandemic now regarded him as a suspect character. Meanwhile, Fauci won several new "moral courage" prizes to add to his collection.

PUZZLEMENT AND SELF-DEFEAT

Thus far I've tried to show that malicious moral envy is a recognizable subtype of envy. Because of his unusual psychology and the political partisanship surrounding him, examples involving Donald Trump are fraught. But he gives voice to thoughts and feelings that many others may be socially inhibited from expressing or acting upon. Indeed, I suspect that lesser forms of malicious moral envy are common in psychologically "healthy" people whose self-esteem is bound up with their moral identity. If you want to be morally good and you regard someone as similar to yourself but morally better, it makes sense that you would regard your moral inferiority as a problem to be solved—a mark of shame, a flaw, a source of angst, an opportunity for self-improvement. But self-improvement is hard and costly. If you cannot solve your problem by leveling yourself up, a remaining option is to level the person down. The motivation to tarnish moral standouts, to cut down the "tall poppy," is probably more common than we like to admit.

Broadly speaking, you have two methods for leveling down your moral rival: *spoiling* and *stealing*. It's hard to steal someone's moral properties or achievements, but you can try: take credit for their moral accomplishments, adopt or co-opt their moral projects, mimic or fake their moral virtues, claim they were only emulating you or stealing your idea, you were the *original* good person, and so on. If stealing is not feasible, spoiling is easier: expose their flaws, ruin their reputation, associate them with scandal, render them powerless, sabotage their projects, exile them from the social community, and so on.[7] Some of these vicious behaviors are familiar from professional contexts or petty rivalries between neighbors or family members. Morality is a social phenomenon, so the mechanics of moral leveling-down are not much different than any other form of social leveling-down.

The problem: a *good* person would not do these things. (Sabotage, fraud, co-optation, etc., are at least *prima facie* morally prohibited regardless of one's moral theory.) Spite and aggression are not morally neutral. These are vicious traits. If envy is an aversive reaction to one's own perceived (moral) inferiority relative to a similar other in a self-relevant domain, and if moral properties are a self-relevant domain, how can the envier coherently feel or act on malicious moral envy? How can they reconcile the vices of *spite* and *aggression* with valuing moral virtue in a way that is tied to their sense of identity? By engaging in the leveling-down behavior, the subject *makes themself morally worse*. Put another way, the existence of malicious moral envy seems both to *presuppose* that the envier values moral virtue, character, standards, and achievements, and also to reveal a lack of respect for these valued goods. Does the envier want to be morally good, or not?

My claim is not that there is any deep contradiction here, nor that the malicious moral envier is confused. But I do think there is a tension, a muddle, an ambivalence, a degree of irrationality, and that the morally best people would tend not to feel this way and certainly not to act on it. After all, to act on this attitude—to engage in leveling-down behavior and not just fantasize about it—is to level *oneself* down, morally. The emotion is thus self-defeating, in the sense that if you carry out its distinctive action tendencies, you undermine its defining aim, which was to reduce the distance between yourself and your rival in a moral comparison.[8]

EXPLAINING AWAY THE PUZZLE

Briefly, let's consider some "easy" ways to resolve the puzzlement associated with malicious moral envy. Ultimately, we will find that enough puzzle residue remains to ground a deeper examination.

First is simply to claim that I have not identified any real cases of malicious moral envy in the world. Cases involving Donald Trump are not genuine cases of malicious moral envy, one might complain. Trump does not envy Obama or Fauci's *moral* qualities, in this reading. He is simply in a competition with them for attention, love, media coverage, and so on. I concede that these other forms of envy are present in this case, but I have tried to show that there is, in addition, a moral dimension to the envy in these cases, including to the leveling-down behavior, where the goal appears not simply to make Obama and Fauci less loved, but less morally esteemed. Furthermore, other players were recruited into the envious game here, players without Trump's outsized reputation for narcissism.

A second route to explaining away the problem is to say that while these are genuine cases of malicious moral envy, they are not puzzling. There is no tension or inconsistency in wanting to be virtuous while engaging in non-virtuous behavior. This is, instead, a case of *akrasia*, or weakness of will: the envier wants to be as virtuous as the envied target but, try as they might, they simply cannot resist the temptation to be a jerk. Or perhaps they aren't even trying to be virtuous: they are not an akratic jerk but merely a jerk. After all, humans are messy, conflicted, flawed lumps of flesh, not consistent, efficient, logical, virtue-pursuing machines. There's no rule that says jerks cannot *want* to be morally good. Fair enough: it's less puzzling when the agent is severely akratic or severely a jerk. But not all cases will be like this. And moreover, I think this pushes the puzzle back one level, for we can then ask: What does it reveal about us that in moments of weakness, some of us react to another's moral virtue by enacting moral vice, and likewise, that even jerks are envious of their moral betters?

Finally, even after we set aside cases where all we have is a narcissist looking for love, a weak-willed dreamer, or a jerk behaving badly, a hidden ambiguity remains. Even in a case where it seems we have a moral envier who really does have an aversive reaction to a rival's moral virtue or goodness, we can ask: Does he value the moral goodness and accomplishment *as such*, or rather the appearance and social recognition of having (achieved) these things, and the relative position in a hierarchy of esteem that comes with it? Trump may not envy Obama's moral virtue, per se, but rather the fact that others give Obama highly moral marks. Indeed, he may not even believe that Obama and Fauci are morally superior to himself, or morally good at all. He may simply realize that other people regard them as such. He may regard their moral reputations as undeserved and, thus, view leveling-down as a warranted correction. This would not be a genuine case of malicious moral envy, but merely a case of envying someone's moral reputation.[9] To distinguish cases of genuine malicious moral envy from these other cases, we should simply specify that the object of envy must be a trait that the envier regards as moral. How can we tell? We cannot be certain, but it is telling that Trump's leveling-down behaviors are directed at people (like Dr. Fauci) whose moral reputations are validated by multiple independent pieces of evidence and underwritten by institutions with nonpartisan epistemic and moral authority, such as prestigious medical schools. This does not guarantee that Trump genuinely believes Fauci is his moral better, but it means Trump is targeting someone with a documented moral record and not *merely* an aura of esteem.

We've considered three debunking explanations of the cases of malicious moral envy we began with. I concede that it is impossible to tease apart whether any of these stories is the true tale of *Trump v. Obama* and *Trump v. Fauci*. Most likely, a little of each is mixed in with some genuine malicious moral envy. After all, moral motivations are usually inaccessible to observers, and sometimes to agents themselves.

In what remains, let's assume for the sake of argument that non-debunkable, genuine cases of *malicious moral envy* exist and are puzzling. Further probing the puzzlement will shed light on our moral lives more generally.

RESIDUAL PUZZLEMENT AND MORAL AMBIVALENCE

Recall the puzzle: the malicious moral envier has an aversive reaction to a target who fares better than him in a moral comparison, but instead of endeavoring to improve himself, he endeavors to tarnish the target. What is most puzzling is that our envier, by hypothesis, really does *value* or *admire* whatever grounds the target's high moral standing. Suppose it's their honesty, compassion, self-sacrifice, and moral courage, as demonstrated via a track record of tangible moral accomplishments and the testimony of reliable third-party observers. To tarnish or sabotage this person would be not only spiteful but dishonest, cruel, selfish, and cowardly. It would display the vicious counterparts to the target's virtues. Thus our envier's remedy for the problem of faring poorly relative to his competitor is a remedy that renders himself *even worse off* in this comparison. In the moral rat race, you can't lap your honest competitor by being dishonest, nor can you get ahead on compassion by being cruel. These leveling-down tendencies are not just counterproductive, they are almost *incoherent*.

What to make of this incoherence? I want to suggest that what we are seeing is a symptom of a broader ambivalence about morality, moral requirements, moral objectivity, and morality's general intrusion in our lives. This allows us to make some connections between the literature on envy's role in moral education (which often takes a virtue-ethical approach), and the literature on saints and heroes, supererogation, morality's demandingness, and moral motivation (which are just as often couched in deontological or consequentialist terms).

Moral exemplars and the admiration they elicit are thought to be a powerful tool for moral education, especially with respect to inculcating moral virtue (Zagzebski 2017). Vaccarezza and Niccoli (2019) have argued that even when exemplars elicit "negative" emotions like envy, they can still be a powerful tool. Envy and other negative exemplarity-related emotions, they argue, are instrumental to producing good outcomes but are also intrinsically valuable insofar as they provide epistemic access to sources of knowledge about value, and insofar as they represent a virtuous intermediate state between excess and defect. This is true of emulative envy, which counts as a negative emotion in their picture. But they are less sanguine about malicious ("destructive") envy. They recommend beginning moral education with distant exemplars—saints and heroes—precisely because these exemplars would be less likely to induce destructive envy than exemplars drawn from a peer group (2019, 340–41).

I agree with Vaccarezza and Niccoli that saints and heroes provide epistemic access to important moral knowledge. Whereas they focus on the fact that the emotions we feel about exemplars can provide direct awareness of moral properties, I've argued that learning about the lives of moral saints provides us with evidence about well-being and sacrifice, evidence that bears on what can be deemed obligatory rather than supererogatory (Carbonell 2012). The epistemology of sacrifice can actually influence the metaphysics of what morality demands, resulting in a ratcheting-up of moral requirements, with the outliers in the moral community serving as standard-bearers for others. This process begins when observers encounter saintly or heroic behaviors in others and begin to interrogate how demanding or costly those behaviors really are.

This all makes sense when what we feel toward exemplars is *emulative* envy. But what should we say about malicious envy? Acting out of malicious envy—slandering, sabotaging, exiling, or otherwise leveling-down a rival— is not only self-defeating but surely a net detriment to the moral community. It's neither instrumentally nor intrinsically valuable. But what about simply *entertaining* malicious envy as a feeling or appraisal, that is, talking about it with others, turning it over in your head, exploring its implications? Could this be less problematic? At the very least, to entertain the leveling-down of others, including subjecting their putatively valid moral accomplishments and motivations to scrutiny and skepticism, is consistent with a long and rich history of ambivalence toward moral exemplars and even toward moral goodness itself.

This ambivalence was famously explored by Susan Wolf in "Moral Saints" (1982), where she argues that moral theories and even our common-sense moral commitments put forward ideals that we don't *actually* want to emulate. It's telling, Wolf claims, that the protagonists we are drawn to in literature are flawed rather than morally perfect; perfect moral saints are repulsive in their humorless, single-minded devotion to morality.[10] We don't want to be them, to be like them, or to be around them. She claims there is "a limit to how much morality we can stand" (Wolf 1982, 423) and that it's possible for someone to be "too good" (421)—that is, it can be bad to be (too) good.

Granted, we can disambiguate this thought and re-write it to remove the air of paradox—*it is (non-morally) bad to be too (morally) good*. Wolf's thought, then, is that perfect adherence to the demands thrown up by our moral theories sometimes generates conflict with other ways of living an excellent life. But even this uncontroversial point sheds helpful light on our exploration of malicious moral envy. I am not claiming that Wolf's take-down of moral saints is an instance of moral envy, much less *malicious* moral envy, nor that she is merely giving voice to our envious thoughts. Rather, I want to suggest that malicious moral envy and the critical, skeptical examination of moral outliers have a common cause: our ambivalence about morality and our defensive stance toward any intrusions it should make into the other, non-moral sources of value and meaning in our lives. And this ambivalence might not be a bad thing.

We see an even stronger expression of this ambivalence in the literature on "admirable immorality." This idea has its intellectual roots in Nietzsche, but here I'll focus on more recent discussions. Just as Wolf (1982) suggests that it is not always better to be morally better, Bernard Williams (1981) suggests the world might be better without universal moral compliance, and Michael Slote (1986) argues that some *intrinsically* immoral character traits are nonetheless admirable. The underlying point of contention here is the "Overridingness Thesis," which is the view that "morality overrides all opposing considerations" (Slote 1986, 84).[11] Williams considers the example of Churchill's ruthless fire-bombing of German cities (preventing further bloodshed); Slote considers the example of a father who lies to the police about his son's whereabouts (manifesting unconditional love). Setting aside how we should best think about these particular examples, they serve as good illustrations of *moral ambivalence*.

Moral ambivalence, I propose, plays an important role in how moral communities negotiate shared standards and reconcile disagreements. If this is right, malicious moral envy and the *admiration of immorality* are two sides of the same coin. The malicious moral envier sees someone's moral goodness, feels negatively about it, and is moved to behave viciously toward that person. The admirer of immorality sees someone's moral badness or moral error, and nevertheless sees something praiseworthy in it. Granted, some cases in the literature on "admirable immorality" may not reflect ambivalence per se but, rather, a sensitivity to nonmoral considerations, or considerations beyond a particular normative theory, such as virtue considerations seen against the backdrop of a duty-based theory.[12] That is, what we're ambivalent about may be our theories, rather than the substantive moral qualities of an act or agent. However, admirable immorality involves—by stipulation—deeming an action both immoral *and* admirable. So it's certainly a more ambivalent position than simply claiming an action cannot be immoral because it is, say, what the virtuous person would do.

We also display moral ambivalence when we question and speculate about people's moral motivations. When someone we care about acts wrongly, it is tempting to find a narrative according to which they had good intentions and merely lost their way; this reduces the dissonance caused by the thought that someone *like me* has done something *like that*. Conversely, when someone does something morally extraordinary, a peanut gallery of critics will appear with debunking explanations—ulterior motives, hidden agendas, and even psychiatric diagnoses.

In her book about real-life moral heroes, Larissa MacFarquhar (2015) argues that this moral unease and disorientation is a reaction to the sublime:

> The life of a zealous do-gooder is a kind of human sublime—by which I mean that, although there is a hard beauty in it, the word "beautiful" doesn't capture the ambivalence it stirs up.... A sublime object, such as a mountain or a rough sea, inspires awe, but also dread. Confronting it, you see its formidable nobility, and at the same time you sense uncomfortably that you would not survive

in it for long. It is this sense of sublime that I mean to apply to do-gooders: to confront such a life is to feel awe mixed with unease—a sense that you wouldn't survive in that life for long, and might not want to. (MacFarquhar 2015: 3–4)

MacFarquhar traces the history of this unease, from Freud-inspired theories of "moral narcissism" and "psychotic altruism" (2015, 111–12) to the backlash against international humanitarian aid workers (164–65) to the way early altruistic kidney donors were assumed mentally ill (199–202). She sees a similar theme in the development of the organization *Al-Anon*, which succeeded in leveling down family members who enable alcoholics—they aren't selfless and devoted, they are "co-dependent" and as disordered as the person struggling with the addiction (155–58). Viewed through *Al-Anon's* pessimistic lens, "the logic of codependency suggests that helping is often a disease, because the one who helps is not free" (168).

The pathologizing of moral exemplars is a kind of leveling-down, and we've seen it in the way some world leaders have denigrated young climate activist Greta Thunberg.[13] A related phenomenon can be found in the philosophical literature on moral motivation, where some argue that the desire to do the right thing, when interpreted in a certain way, amounts to *fetishizing* morality (Carbonell 2013). Even where there is no suggestion of mental illness or deviance, the discovery of weaknesses or flaws in moral exemplars is often met with relief. In his book about the global health leader and (arguably) moral saint Dr. Paul Farmer, author Tracy Kidder (2003) sees traces of moral envy in Farmer's social circle:

Lately, he received a fair amount of criticism from friends for not spending more time with his family, and there were some who, when they spoke about this matter out of his earshot, seemed oddly animated. Their voices would rise, or they would smile conspiratorially. "Can you imagine what it's like being married to him?" I wonder if this was a species of moral envy. Jim Kim said, "Paul has a gift for making people feel guilty." Farmer counseled others to take vacations while taking none himself. He didn't disapprove of others having luxuries, so long as they gave something to the causes of the poor. He demanded a great deal from proteges and colleagues, and he always forgave them when they didn't measure up. And so I think it was a relief, for some, to find what looked like a chink in his moral armor. (Kidder 2003, 212)

Whereas *Trump v. Obama* and *Trump v. Fauci* are cases of genuinely *malicious* moral envy, what we see here is a more harmless analogue. These conspiratorial friends are not trying to ruin Farmer's reputation, sabotage his projects, or harm him in any way; nor do they seem spiteful. But they are engaging in a kind of leveling-down, motivated by a kind of envy. Their ambivalence—admiration mixed with guilt, awe mixed with skepticism, solidarity mixed with distancing, praise mixed with criticism—is a healthy social dynamic in a moral community that is deliberating, together, about what they can morally expect from one another. Like envy itself, this ambivalence may have important epistemic value (Exline and Zell 2008; Vaccarezza and Niccoli 2019).

CONCLUSION

Malicious moral envy is a subtype of envy more generally, and a paradigm case would involve genuinely destructive, antisocial behaviors toward someone deemed a moral rival. Such cases will be rare, because in all human interactions, destructive behavior is the exception, not the norm. And we would expect it to be even more exceptional among people who value and admire others for their moral properties or accomplishments. Indeed, malicious moral envy is self-defeating. Some purported cases of malicious moral envy can be explained away, or are hopelessly entangled with confounding variables. But some cases remain, and they are a species of a moral general genus of moral ambivalence. Ambivalence is sometimes a fitting attitude to have toward the messy and complicated moral landscape we are confronted with. In particular, the scope and limits of our duties to one another, along with the range of ways our character can be appraised for how we live up to those duties (or fail to), are essentially social matters. As we navigate and negotiate them together, we find that they are plastic, shifting and stretching in response to changing conditions. Expressions of moral ambivalence, up to and including malicious moral envy, are both a consequence of morality's social nature, and a tool for finding our way through it.[14]

NOTES

1. This chapter focuses on *malicious* moral envy. There is a fascinating literature on its *benign* counterpart. See Engelen et al. (2018), Kristjánsson (2006, 2017), Protasi (2021), Vaccarezza (2019), and Zagzebski (2015, 2017). See also Maria Silvia Vaccarezza and Ariele Niccoli's contribution to this volume: "Let the Donkeys Be Donkeys: In Defense of Inspiring Envy" (chapter 6).

2. There isn't space to situate my view historically, but Protasi (2021) provides an overview in the appendix. Protasi locates passages in Catherine of Siena, Aquinas, and Al-Ghazálí that plausibly are discussions of *moral envy*. However, it is harder to find any discussion of *malicious* moral envy.

3. I take no position on whether envy, in general, should count as a "moral emotion," either on the basis of its central evaluative concern or its typical consequences.

I am only suggesting that some cases of envy are moral. See Ben-Ze'ev (2002) on what makes an emotion moral, immoral, or morally neutral.

4. I am mixing types of moral evaluation here, intending to remain neutral with respect to moral theory. Thus, malicious moral envy should be an intelligible concept regardless of whether virtue theory, consequentialism, deontology, and so on, is the correct moral theory, and regardless of the envier's preferred theory (if any). Still, there will be complications that arise for each theory, and we might need theory to determine whether a particular case of moral envy is fitting—that is, whether the target is *enviable*.

5. Trump had a long history of racist behavior toward President Obama predating his own presidency. I bracket that here, but racist hierarchies complicate both the social comparison and the available options for leveling-down behavior. See chapter 5 of Protasi (2021) for more on political envy and racial prejudice.

6. Multiple types of envy are at play here. Trump mentioned Fauci's *approval rating*. This could be regarded as a (moral) assessment of someone's job performance, but also as a mere proxy for being liked or loved. As Sara Protasi has suggested to me, an alternative reading is that Trump simply needs love and envies Fauci for how much people love him. Reportedly, Trump's antipathy toward Fauci peaked when Brad Pitt portrayed Fauci on *Saturday Night Live*. This is malicious envy, but not malicious *moral* envy. According to the source: "Trump really can't stand it when you get bigger and more popular than him. Getting you off TV is the way he brings you down" (Costa et al. 2020).

7. *Blame* may count as a leveling-down behavior that manifests moral envy. Trump's allies Rand Paul and Peter Navarro have leveled-down Dr. Fauci by blaming him for the pandemic. See Neal Tognazzini's contribution to this volume: "'You're Just Jealous!': On Envious Blame" (chapter 8).

8. Vaccarezza and Niccoli (2019) make this same point about other-regarding virtues. They claim these virtues are good targets for moral education, because they are likely to elicit emulative envy rather than destructive envy, precisely because destructive envy would be self-defeating in such cases: "it would mean ipso facto missing any chance to equal the envied in relation to the envied trait" (2019, 341). I would add that the self-defeat is *most* glaring when there is a *match* between the envied virtue and the destructive vice (compassion and cruelty, honesty and deception). However, we can regard malicious moral envy as self-defeating more broadly, even when there is no such match, and even without a virtue theory framing. Even in a consequentialist picture, malicious moral envy can be seen as self-defeating: it obstructs both the subject and the target's ability to contribute to good outcomes.

9. Malicious leveling-down can be considered a degraded contribution to public moral discourse. "Moral grandstanding" is another such degraded contribution which is motivated by desire to be *recognized* rather than to be right (Tosi and Warmke 2016). Both behaviors reflect poorly on the subject. Unlike grandstanding, malicious moral envy would be driven by a sincere motivation to be morally better, rather than just to be *seen* as morally better. Thank you to Maria Silvia Vaccarezza for suggesting this connection.

10. I raise some worries for Wolf's argument and put forward real-life moral saints as potential counter-examples, in Carbonell (2009).

11. See Baron (1986), Flanagan (1986), and Louden (1988) for criticisms of Slote's argument here.

12. I thank Maria Silvia Vaccarezza and Ariele Niccoli for helping me see this important point.

13. Just as Trump's envy of Obama is tinged with racism, his criticism of Greta Thunberg is complicated by misogyny and ableism. See, for example, Nelson (2019) and North (2019). Is this a case of malicious moral envy? To be sure, Thunberg is not a peer to Trump. Still, sexism and ableism could amplify moral envy, in the sense that it may be even more enraging to Trump that someone "lower" than him on these other social hierarchies is regarded as morally superior.

14. I am grateful to participants in the Moral Psychology of Envy Workshop at the University of Puget Sound in May 2021, in particular Sara Protasi, Maria Silvia Vaccarezza, Ariele Niccoli, Neal Tognazzini, and Niels van de Ven for their helpful feedback on earlier drafts. Thanks also to James Carbonell, Jon Shaheen, Heidi Maibom, and Alex Plakias for helpful conversation.

REFERENCES

Abutaleb, Yasmeen, Josh Dawsey, and Laurie McGinley. 2020. "Fauci Is Sidelined by the White House as He Steps up Blunt Talk on Pandemic." *The Washington Post*, July 11, 2020. https://www.washingtonpost.com/politics/2020/07/11/fauci-trump-coronavirus/.

Baker, Sinead. 2021. "Trump Advisor Peter Navarro Went on a Wild Rant on Fox News, Calling Fauci the 'Father' of the Coronavirus." *Business Insider*, March 31, 2021. https://www.businessinsider.com/peter-navarro-trump-advisor-calls-fauci-father-of-coronavirus-fox-news-rant-2021-3.

Baron, Marcia. 1986. "On Admirable Immorality." *Ethics* 96 (3): 557–66.

Barr, Jeremy. 2021. "Lara Logan Draws Backlash for Comparing Fauci to Nazi Doctor Josef Mengele on Fox News." *The Washington Post*, November 21, 2021. https://www.washingtonpost.com/media/2021/11/30/media-lara-logan-fox-fauci-mengele-comparison/.

Ben-Ze'ev, Aaron. 2002. "Are Envy, Anger, and Resentment Moral Emotions?" *Philosophical Explorations* 5 (2): 148–54.

Blow, Charles M. 2020. "The Tanned Man Has a Green Monster." *The New York Times*, July 29, 2020. https://www.nytimes.com/2020/07/29/opinion/anthony-fauci-trump.html.

Bruni, Frank. 2021. "So Anthony Fauci Isn't Perfect. He's Closer than Most of Us." *The New York Times*, April 24, 2021. https://www.nytimes.com/2021/04/24/opinion/sunday/anthony-fauci.html.

C-SPAN. 2020. "President Trump Coronavirus News Conference." July 28, 2020. https://www.c-span.org/video/?474297-1/president-trump-coronavirus-news-conference. Minute 19:38.

Carbonell, Vanessa. 2009. "What Moral Saints Look Like." *Canadian Journal of Philosophy* 39 (3): 371–98.

———. 2012. "The Ratcheting-Up Effect." *Pacific Philosophical Quarterly* 93 (2): 228–54.

———. 2013. "*De Dicto* Desires and Morality as Fetish." *Philosophical Studies* 163 (2): 459–77.

Chamberlain, Samuel. 2021. "Rand Paul: 'Little Dictator' Fauci 'Acts Like an Ignoramus Every Day' Over Masks." *New York Post*, May 14, 2021. https://nypost.com/2021/05/14/fauci-acts-like-an-ignoramus-every-day-over-masks-rand-paul/.

Conway, George III. 2019. "Unfit for Office." *The Atlantic*, October 3, 2019. https://www.theatlantic.com/ideas/archive/2019/10/george-conway-trump-unfit-office/599128/.

Costa, Robert, Philip Rucker, Yasmeen Abutaleb, and Josh Dawsey. 2020. "Trump's May Days: A Month Of Distractions And Grievances as Nation Marks Bleak Coronavirus Milestone." *The Washington Post*, May 31, 2020. https://www.washingtonpost.com/politics/trumps-may-days-a-month-of-distractions-and-grievances-as-nation-marks-bleak-coronavirus-milestone/2020/05/31/123e7e6a-a120-11ea-81bb-c2f70f01034b_story.html.

D'Arms, Justin. 2017. "Envy." *The Stanford Encyclopedia of Philosophy* (Spring 2017 edition), edited by Edward N. Zalta. https://plato.stanford.edu/archives/spr2017/entries/envy/.

Engelen, Bart, Alan Thomas, Alfred Archer, and Niels van de Ven. 2018. "Exemplars and Nudges: Combining Two Strategies for Moral Education." *Journal of Moral Education* 47 (3): 346–65.

Dasgupta, Sravasti. 2021. "Donald Trump Jr. Sells T-Shirts Calling Dr. Fauci a 'Puppy Killer' After Outrage Over Alec Baldwin Merchandise." *The Independent*, October 28, 2021. https://www.independent.co.uk/news/world/americas/donald-trump-jr-fauci-tshirts-b1946755.html.

Exline, Julo, and Anne L. Zell. 2008. "Antidotes to Envy: A Conceptual Framework." In *Envy: Theory and Research*, edited by R. H. Smith, 315–31. New York: Oxford University Press. https://doi.org/10.1093/acprof:oso/9780195327953.003.0017.

Farley, Robert. 2020. "Trump's Nobel Nonsense." *Factcheck Posts*. (The Annenberg Public Policy Center.) September 23, 2020. https://www.factcheck.org/2020/09/trumps-nobel-nonsense/.

Flanagan, Owen. 1986. "Admirable Immorality and Admirable Imperfection." *The Journal of Philosophy* 83 (1): 41–60.

Kidder, Tracy. 2003. *Mountains Beyond Mountains*. Random House.

Kristjánsson, Kristján. 2006. "Emulation and the Use of Role Models in Moral Education." *Journal of Moral Education* 35 (1): 37–49.

———. 2017. "Emotions Targeting Moral Exemplarity: Making Sense of the Logical Geography of Admiration, Emulation and Elevation." *Theory and Research in Education* 15 (1): 20–37.

Louden, Robert. 1988. "Can We Be Too Moral?" *Ethics* 98 (2): 361–78.

MacFarquhar, Larissa. 2015. *Strangers Drowning: Voyages to the Brink of Moral Extremity*. London: Penguin Books Limited.

Millbank, Dana. 2021. "Why Is Anthony Fauci Trying to Kill My Puppy?" *The Washington Post*, October 25, 2021. https://www.washingtonpost.com/opinions/2021/10/25/fauci-puppy-experiments-conspiracy-republicans/.

Nelson, Camilla. 2019. "Misogyny, Male Rage and the Words Men Use to Describe Greta Thunberg." *The Conversation*, September 30, 2019. https://theconversation.com/misogyny-male-rage-and-the-words-men-use-to-describe-greta-thunberg-124347.

North, Anna. 2019. "Attacks on Greta Thunberg Expose the Stigma Autistic Girls Face." *Vox*, December 12, 2019. https://www.vox.com/identities/2019/9/24/20881837/greta-thunberg-person-of-the-year-trump.

Peiser, Jaclyn. 2020. "Twitter Bans Steve Bannon for Video Suggesting Violence Against Fauci, FBI Director Wray." *The Washington Post*, November 6, 2020. https://www.washingtonpost.com/nation/2020/11/06/twitter-bannon-beheaded-fauci-wray/.

Protasi, Sara. 2016. "Varieties of Envy." *Philosophical Psychology* 29 (4): 535–49.

———. 2021. *The Philosophy of Envy*. Cambridge, UK: Cambridge University Press.

Roberts, Robert C. 2003. *Emotions: An Essay in Aid of Moral Psychology*. Cambridge, UK: Cambridge University Press.

Sanger-Katz, Margot. 2020. "On Coronavirus, Americans Still Trust the Experts." *The New York Times*, June 27, 2020. https://www.nytimes.com/2020/06/27/upshot/coronavirus-americans-trust-experts.html.

Specter, Michael. 2020. "How Anthony Fauci Became America's Doctor." *The New Yorker*, April 20, 2020. https://www.newyorker.com/magazine/2020/04/20/how-anthony-fauci-became-americas-doctor.

Stein, Rob. 2020. "Fauci Reveals He Has Received Death Threats and His Daughters Have Been Harrassed." NPR. August 5, 2020. https://www.npr.org/sections/coronavirus-live-updates/2020/08/05/899415906/fauci-reveals-he-has-received-death-threats-and-his-daughters-have-been-harassed.

Tosi, Justin, and Brandom Warmke. 2016. "Moral Grandstanding." *Philosophy and Public Affairs* 44 (3): 197–217.

Vaccarezza, Maria Silvia. 2019. "Admiration, Moral Knowledge and Transformative Experiences." *HUMANA. MENTE Journal of Philosophical Studies* 12 (35): 150–66.

Vaccarezza, Maria Silvia, and Ariele Niccoli. 2019. "The Dark Side of the Exceptional: On Moral Exemplars, Character Education, and Negative Emotions." *Journal of Moral Education* 48 (3): 332–45.

Wagner, John. 2019. "Trump Says He Is Worthy of a Nobel Prize 'For a Lot of Things'—But Isn't Treated Fairly." *The Washington Post*, September 23, 2019. https://www.washingtonpost.com/politics/trump-says-he-is-worthy-of-a-nobel-prize-for-a-lot-of-things--but-isnt-treated-fairly/2019/09/23/e715baa2-de2c-11e9-b199-f638bf2c340f_story.html.

Williams, Bernard. 1981. *Moral Luck: Philosophical Papers 1973–1980*. Cambridge, UK: Cambridge University Press.

Wolf, Susan. 1982. "Moral Saints." *The Journal of Philosophy* 79 (8): 419–39.

Zagzebski, Linda. 2015. "Admiration and the Admirable." *Proceedings of the Aristotelian Society, Supplementary* 89: 205–21.
Zagzebski, Linda. 2017 *Exemplarist Moral Theory*. New York: Oxford University Press.

Chapter 8

"You're Just Jealous!"
On Envious Blame

Neal A. Tognazzini

Criticism often stings. Sometimes the pain derives from our knowledge that the criticism is unfair, that we didn't make the mistake we are being criticized for. But the sting is there, too, in cases where we know full well that we are criticizable. Those cases can be even more painful, in fact, since criticism compounds the sting of self-blame we're probably already feeling.

Not that criticism is always a bad thing: its sting can motivate self-improvement. Perhaps that's the most admirable way to respond to criticism, at least when the criticism is apt. But sometimes we try to *deflect* or *dismiss* the criticism instead, by calling into question the motivations or character of the person who voices it.

There are lighthearted examples of this, which involve unabashed *ad hominems*, like when my daughter tells me I smell bad after I've just finished exercising, and I respond with something like, "Oh yeah? Well, *you* stink too." (Some kids in my high school formed a band called "So's Your Face," an excellent all-purpose comeback. Great band, too.) But there are more serious examples, where the attempted deflection is sincere, like when we perceive that the criticizer is equally guilty of the thing they are complaining about, and we respond, "You're one to talk." The thought here isn't that the criticism they are offering is *false* but instead that their hypocrisy makes them ill-suited to be offering it.

It's puzzling exactly what it could mean for someone to be "ill-suited" to offer an apt criticism, and there is a burgeoning philosophical literature on this topic under the rubric of *the ethics of blame*.[1] There is widespread agreement that hypocrisy—or, rather, the fact that someone would be a hypocrite if they were to issue a rebuke of a particular wrong—undermines one's standing to blame, even if the would-be target is blameworthy.² The slogan that a wrongdoer seems entitled to invoke in these cases is something like, "Look who's talking!" or, "That's rich coming from you." At least sometimes, the accusation of hypocrisy seems to have bite.

In this chapter, I want to explore a different sort of deflection strategy, one that takes aim at *jealous* or *envious* criticism. This strategy also has a catchphrase, namely: "You're just jealous!" The person who makes this accusation may simply be grasping at straws in an attempt to avoid responsibility, but suppose that the person offering the criticism really *is* motivated by jealousy. Would that fact have any normative significance? Does an accusation of jealousy or envy, like the accusation of hypocrisy, ever have genuine force as a response to criticism? These are the questions I'm interested in exploring in what follows. My hope is that we'll learn something about the ethics of blame and about the dynamics of interpersonal relationships more generally.³

JEALOUSY OR ENVY?

Before trying to figure out what normative force, if any, is carried by the accusation, "You're just jealous!" let's start by asking whether it's really *jealousy* that's at issue, or whether this is one of those common cases where the word "jealous" is used to pick out envy instead. Here I rely on the work of Sara Protasi (2017, 2021), who defends a "lack vs. loss" model of the distinction between envy and jealousy.⁴ Roughly speaking, according to this model, despite their similarities as rivalrous and aversive emotions, the jealous person is most worried about *losing* something valuable that they perceive as already "belonging" to them, whereas the envious person is most bothered by the fact they *lack* something valuable that they perceive as "belonging" to someone else. (Note that the belonging at issue need not be a matter of literal ownership, so much as a loose sense in which the thing is seen as a part of your life or not.)

As Protasi and others point out, the "lack vs. loss" model of the distinction between envy and jealousy fits well with psychological and linguistic data, and has a good deal of explanatory power. I won't reproduce the arguments in favor of the model, but I do want to draw attention to one relevant data point, which is an asymmetry between how the two words get used. As Protasi (2017, 318) puts it, "'jealousy' encompasses a range of meanings that include those of 'envy,' but not vice versa." The "lack vs. loss" model can make sense of this linguistic asymmetry in the following way. Since it is less shameful to defend what you already own from threat than it is to pine after something that belongs to someone else, the concept of jealousy carries less moral and social baggage, which is why we tend to use the word "jealous" even for situations where what we are really feeling is envy.

So, the question for us is whether the accusation "You're just jealous!" is really about jealousy, or if instead it is about envy. If we adopt the lack vs. loss model, we can answer this question by figuring out whether the person in question is being accused of *guarding* something they already have or of *coveting* something that belongs to someone else.[5]

Here it will be useful to consider a few examples of the phenomenon in question. Not only will this help us to determine whether jealousy or envy is the central emotion at issue, but it will also help us to fix ideas for the discussion to follow.

Let me start with the title comic for cartoonist Tom Gauld's book *You're All Just Jealous of My Jetpack*. This is a single-panel comic with a person in a jetpack labeled "science fiction" and three people dressed in black labeled "proper literature." The three people—snooty professors, no doubt—are saying "tut tut," and the person in the jetpack responds, "You're all just jealous of my jetpack." My apologies to Tom Gauld for ruining the joke by explaining it, but the subtext here is that when literary critics look down on or otherwise criticize science fiction, those criticisms are inapt or somehow not worth listening to, since they are motivated by jealousy. Sci-fi is more "fun" than so-called proper literature—it has more jetpacks, for one thing—and deep down, literary critics wish they could have more fun too.

In this example, the accusation being lobbed at the snooty professors is not properly an accusation of *jealousy*, at least if we are operating with a lack vs. loss model of the difference between envy and jealousy. Proponents of so-called proper literature are being accused of having an aversive emotional response due to their perception that they *lack* the fun literary devices and plot points that show up in sci-fi stories. They wish they had something they don't; hence this cartoon depicts an accusation of envy.

For another example, consider an exchange from the popular TV sitcom *Friends*. Here's the background: after much romantic build-up in the first two seasons, Ross and Rachel finally get together in season 2, but then they break up again toward the end of season 3. Then in season 3, episode 22—"The One with the Screamer"—Rachel is dating a new man named "Tommy," and Ross is the only one of the friends who manages to see Tommy's dark side (he screams at people for no reason). Ross then tries to convince Rachel to stop seeing him but is aware he'll just get accused of jealousy. Here's the exchange (you'll have to provide the sarcasm to Rachel's and Chandler's responses yourself):

Ross: Look, I wasn't gonna say anything to you, but . . . all right, I don't think you should be seeing Tommy anymore.

Rachel: You don't?

Ross: No, the guy is mean. I mean, really mean. I think you should stay away from him.

Rachel: Hmm. Or maybe I should stay away from all men.

Ross: No. It's not just because I'm jealous. I mean, I'm not. I'm not jealous. Look, the guy screamed . . . he actually screamed at this couple sitting in our seats.

Chandler: Yeah, and at the end of the play, he got up, and he just started, like, banging his hands together.

In this example, no one explicitly accuses Ross of being motivated by jealousy, but they don't have to. He reads their facial expressions instead and offers a preemptive defense of himself. But is it jealousy or envy that he's being implicitly accused of?

I think it's possible to read this example either way, but the most plausible interpretation is that this is a case of jealousy proper, given the history between Ross and Rachel. Although they are broken up at the moment, Ross still hasn't fully "let go" of Rachel, and the worry is that his criticisms of her new boyfriend are motivated by his sense that he's finally *losing* her to a real-life rival, even though they are already officially broken up.

Let me outline one last example, because it will prove useful in the discussion below. This one is from the 2004 movie *Napoleon Dynamite*. In one scene, Napoleon has been asked to do a chore he doesn't feel like doing, and he gets frustrated with his brother Kip, who is just sitting around on the computer. When Napoleon expresses his frustration—"Stay home and eat all the freakin' chips, Kip!"—Kip responds: "Napoleon, don't be jealous that I've been chatting online with babes all day."

Like the sci-fi example from above, Kip's use of the term "jealous" here seems best interpreted as an accusation that Napoleon is *envious*. After all, what seems to be at issue here is a good thing that Kip has but Napoleon lacks, namely the opportunity to spend time on the computer talking to girls. Kip's response to Napoleon's rebuke is to highlight the "real" source of Napoleon's frustration, namely his envy.

What these examples make clear is that even though the accusation almost always features the word "jealousy," some cases are best interpreted as being about *envy* instead. But I'm interested in both types of situations. Suppose, then, that someone's criticism is motivated by envy or jealousy. So what? Why exactly would that be a problem, especially if the criticism is *apt*?

CRITICISM AS COMMUNICATION: THE TESTIMONIAL MODEL

One approach begins with the observation that criticism can be a form of communication. Regardless of whether the criticism is intended to sting, it is often intended to convey information, and so it can be thought of as a form of testimony. One way that envious criticism might go awry, then, is if the envy undermines the credibility of the testifier. Consider again the example from *Friends*. In that example, Ross is genuinely worried about Rachel's well-being, given the anger management problems of her new boyfriend, and when he says that Tommy is mean, he's simply trying to convey the information that Tommy is mean.

Right after he tells Rachel that Tommy is mean, though, Ross realizes that he has a credibility problem. As Rachel's very recent ex-boyfriend, any criticism that he lobs at her new boyfriend may very well be seen as an attempt to keep her from moving on, so that he can eventually win her back. Or, alternatively, his criticisms of the new boyfriend might be interpreted as a way for him to protect his own self-esteem, which is threatened by the ease with which Rachel seems ready to start dating other people. Ross's friends immediately adopt an interpretation along these lines, and as a result they think he is lying, or at least exaggerating, about Tommy's mean streak.

The jetpack cartoon can be fit into this framework as well, if we interpret the snooty professors' "tut tut" remark as an attempt to convey some information. Perhaps, for example, the professors are trying to convince the reading public that sci-fi literature is not worth purchasing or engaging with, that it is frivolous. When the jetpack person responds with the accusation of jealousy, then, the claim is that you, the reading public, shouldn't lend any weight to the professors' evaluation of the worth of sci-fi. Perhaps they genuinely think poorly of sci-fi, but that isn't because they have privileged access to truths about what makes for a good work of literature; instead, they are simply trying to knock sci-fi authors down a peg, so that so-called proper literature doesn't become an endangered species. As with the *Friends* example, the key point here is that we shouldn't take a jealous person's word at face value.

There is a large literature on the epistemology of testimony (e.g., Lackey 2008 and Goldberg 2010), but I think we can avoid the details here and instead focus on a more zoomed-out account of when someone's credibility as a testifier might legitimately be questioned. In general, what you want to know is whether the person is *telling the truth*. But there are two components to this: first, you want to be reasonably confident that the person is saying something that *they take to be true*—that is, that the person is being sincere, is testifying in good faith. In other words, you need to be reasonably confident that you aren't being lied to. But that's not quite enough by itself, because even sincere testifiers might lead you astray if they have no idea what they are talking about, or if their sincere judgment is compromised in some way. So, you also want to be reasonably confident that the person's take on the truth has been formed by their being in touch with the actual truth—that is, that the person is *competent*, that their sincere belief is somehow grounded in their experience with things of the sort they are talking about.

One nice way to summarize this is with the notion of explanation. When you are wondering whether to believe what someone has said, you should ask, first, whether the best explanation for why they said it is that they believe it (call this *the sincerity test*), and second, whether the best explanation for why they believe it is that their expertise or experience has put them in a good position to form true beliefs (this is *the competence test*).[6]

In this way of thinking about things, accusing a critic of jealousy or envy might be an attempt to impugn either the critic's sincerity or their competence. And in fact, it's not hard to think of both sorts of case. On the interpretation I suggested above, the *Friends* example falls on the sincerity side of things, whereas the jetpack example falls on the competence side of things. Ross's criticisms are not taken seriously because his friends think he's *lying*, whereas the criticisms of the snooty professors shouldn't be taken seriously because they are letting their professional self-interest cloud their judgments about quality.[7] Neither the negative evaluation of Tommy nor the negative evaluation of sci-fi ought to be taken seriously, since the criticisms fail one of the two tests for successful testimony.

But you can also imagine flip-flopping the examples, so that the *Friends* example falls on the competence side and the jetpack example falls on the sincerity side. Perhaps Ross isn't *lying* about Tommy's having a mean streak—that is, perhaps Ross genuinely believes that Tommy is mean—but his jealousy may nevertheless be pushing him to give an uncharitable interpretation to Tommy's behavior. He so badly wants Tommy to be an unsuitable partner for Rachel that he's convinced himself of Tommy's unsuitability. And in the jetpack example, you could imagine that the snooty professors don't *really* look down upon sci-fi literature, in their heart of hearts, but they feel they must present a negative judgment to the world around them in order to fit in, or something like that, so their "tutting" is just so much play-acting. Again, on either interpretation, the criticism's ability to transmit information has been compromised.

Here, then, is a straightforward way that the accusation of jealousy might have some genuine force. Call it "the testimonial model." In this model, criticism seeks uptake of the information it contains, and *felicitous* criticism offers its hearer a reason to believe the information it seeks to convey. But criticism manages to convey this reason only if it's coming from the mouth of someone we reasonably take to be both *sincere* and *competent*, and envy or jealousy might interfere with either or both. This is not to say that an insincere or incompetent speaker can't be speaking the truth, of course. It's only to say that even if the criticism is apt, *that this speaker is the one voicing it* is not a good reason to believe that it is.

CRITICISM AS REBUKE: THE EXPANDED TESTIMONIAL MODEL

So far, we've been working with a pretty thin notion of "criticism." We've said that Ross criticizes Tommy by *saying that he is mean*, and the snooty professors have criticized sci-fi literature by *implying that it is frivolous*. When criticism is taken to be a way of saying something negative about somebody, it's straightforward to apply the framework of the epistemology of testimony to the accusation that someone is criticizing out of jealousy or envy. If criticism is a type of assertion, then calling into question the motivations of the criticizer is just another way of questioning whether the assertion is one we have good reason to believe or accept.

But often criticism is more than a mere assertion. Consider now the example from *Napoleon Dynamite*, where Napoleon expresses anger at Kip for just sitting at home on the computer and eating all the chips, and where Kip responds by accusing Napoleon of being jealous that Kip has been "chatting online with babes all day." In this example, Napoleon's criticism isn't really meant to convey any information or make any sort of assertion that Kip might then come to believe on the basis of Napoleon's say-so. Instead, Napoleon's angry outburst seems more like a rebuke, something that's aimed at making Kip feel guilty for an apparent transgression. But the accusation of jealousy seems to work here too, so how should we understand it, if not as related to the conditions of reliable testimony?

Even here, though, I think we can press the testimonial model—or at least an expanded version of it—into service. When I'm wondering whether to believe something on the basis of your say-so, what I'm trying to figure out is whether *your saying it gives me a reason to believe it*. If you're only saying it because you're jealous and not because you believe it, then your saying it doesn't give me a reason to believe it. Likewise, if you only believe it because your jealousy is clouding your judgment, then even though you may be in earnest, your saying it still doesn't give me a reason to believe it. In the previous section we saw how this model applies to criticism understood as an attempt to convey reasons for belief. But we might also understand criticism as an attempt to convey reasons for *action*.

When criticism takes the form of a rebuke, I may be trying to get you to believe something—like, for example, that you've hurt my feelings, or that you had no good excuse for doing so. But often I'm also trying to get you to *do* something as well—like, for example, apologize or in some way acknowledge the way your behavior has damaged our relationship. Just as assertions can be used to give other people reasons to *believe* something, rebukes can be used to give other people reasons to *do* something. And what that means is that there may be a fruitful analogy between the epistemology of testimony and the ethics of blame.

To see what I have in mind, let's take a brief detour through the ethics of *hypocritical blame*, which, as I mentioned above, is widely taken to undermine one's standing to blame. What's not so widely agreed upon, however, is exactly *what it is* for a hypocrite to lose their standing to blame, beyond the vague thought that hypocritical blame is somehow inappropriate. But here's a thought I quite like: blame, at least overt blame, aims to convey reasons to the person being blamed: for example, reasons to apologize and make things right. And when someone loses their standing to blame, what they lose is their ability to convey those reasons. It may still be—in fact, it usually *will* be—that the person being blamed has *other* reasons to apologize and make things right, but the fact that they are being blamed (by a hypocrite) will not be among them.[8]

If that thought is on the right track, then there is a structural similarity between the aim of assertion and the aim of blame: whereas the first attempts to transmit a reason for belief, the second attempts to transmit a reason for action. And if an assertion is unable to fulfill its aim when it fails the sincerity or competence test, then we might expect that in cases where blame is unable to fulfill *its* aim, this is because it, too, has failed some version of the sincerity or competence tests.

When we examine the varieties of hypocritical blame, I think this is in fact what we find. Consider the following five hypocritical blamers:

1. *The clear-eyed hypocrite* is a hypocrite in the original sense of the term: they are merely play-acting, putting on a mask, wearing the trappings of blame in order to achieve a desired effect.
2. *The weak-willed hypocrite* is genuinely committed to the values they espouse but fails to act in accordance with those values due to weakness of will.
3. *The exception-seeking hypocrite* is also genuinely committed to the values they espouse but fails to act in accordance with those values because they mistakenly think those standards do not apply to them.
4. *The couldn't-care-less hypocrite* genuinely cares about the values that form the basis of their criticism, but they just aren't bothered by the fact

that they are enforcing those values in an unfair way, by blaming others who transgress while not blaming themselves when *they* transgress.
5. *The recently-converted hypocrite* is someone whose house is completely in order—there is complete alignment between how they act, the values they profess, and the way they dole out blame—but whose integrity is only very recently won due to a change of heart. Even if their change of heart is sincere (and so they aren't strictly speaking a hypocrite), there seems to be some sort of residue of their former commitments that make their current blame problematic in a way akin to hypocrisy.[9]

Suppose that each of these varieties of hypocrisy undermines the standing to blame. Is there a way to fit these varieties into our general testimonial model, such that each type of hypocrisy amounts to either a failure of sincerity or a failure of competence? I think so.

The clear-eyed hypocrite is perhaps the clearest case, since they are being insincere in a straightforward sense: they are not even committed to the values that they are purporting to enforce through their blame. But the couldn't-care-less hypocrite also seems to count as insincere in some sense, since they recognize that they are blaming in an unfair way but are doing it anyway. Perhaps we could cover both cases by saying that the clear-eyed and couldn't-care-less hypocrites are blaming *in bad faith*.

This distinguishes them from the weak-willed and exception-seeking hypocrites, who are both blaming in earnest. But whereas these two types of hypocrites seem to pass the sincerity test, they seem to fail the competence test. They are both, for different reasons, failing to uphold principles that they are genuinely committed to, one due to a volitional hiccup and the other due to misapplication of the relevant standards. Even the recently-converted hypocrite seems, in some sense, to run afoul of the competence test, since it seems like their past track record should encourage a bit of humility about how hard it is to get things right in this domain.

If the analogy I'm pushing works, it gives us a new model for trying to figure out why the hypocritical blamer lacks the standing to blame. *The case of testimony*: someone's say-so counts as a reason to believe what they say only if you can be reasonably confident that they aren't lying and, moreover, are well acquainted enough with the facts to be getting them right in this case. Insincerity and incompetence both render testimony incapable of transmitting a reason to believe the content of the testimony. *The case of blame*: the fact that someone is blaming you counts as a reason to acknowledge wrongdoing, apologize, and so on, only if you can be reasonably confident that they are blaming in good faith and, moreover, that they are well acquainted enough with the normative facts to be getting them right in this case. Bad faith and normative errors both render blame incapable of transmitting a reason to do the things that blame aims to inspire you to do.

Return now to the accusation of jealousy that comes up in the *Napoleon Dynamite* example. As I said above, Napoleon is not trying to get Kip to believe the content of his criticism; in fact, it's not clear that his criticism has any content at all. Instead, it's simply meant as a rebuke. On the expanded testimonial model, then, we should be able to explain what Kip is up to when he accuses Napoleon of jealousy in terms of either sincerity or competence. In this case, it seems like Kip is calling into question the reason-giving force of Napoleon's rebuke by invoking the competence test.

Perhaps Napoleon is right that Kip has been on the computer eating chips all day, but Napoleon's rebuke represents those facts as though they are bad things, worthy of criticism. Kip's response is intended to enlighten Napoleon, to let him know that his jealousy (envy, really) is compromising his ability to make an accurate evaluative judgment. Another way to put this is to say that when Kip accuses Napoleon of being jealous, he's pointing out that Napoleon's emotional reaction is *unfitting*: it represents the world inaccurately. And what's led him to have an unfitting emotion, on Kip's telling of it, is Napoleon's jealousy.[10]

So, this sort of rebuke—assuming Kip is right about Napoleon's motivations—seems to fail the competence test. But there will also be rebukes that fail sincerity test. A simple example might just be a reinterpretation of the jet-pack cartoon, where the snooty professors' "tut tut" is understood as a rebuke rather than an attempt to convey information. If the professors don't really think that sci-fi literature is frivolous, but they are tutting merely in an envious attempt to hurt the sales of widely adored sci-fi authors, then their tutting need not generate any reason for the sci-fi authors to change their ways.

There's another type of example, though, that would also illustrate the idea of a bad faith or insincere rebuke. This would be one where the blamer is genuinely committed to the values that their rebuke presupposes, and where the rebuke itself is fitting (the person being blamed has in fact behaved badly), but where the blamer's commitment to the values is *not* what explains why they have issued the rebuke.

Think, for example, of a case where a president of the United States has committed an impeachable offense, and where the members of the opposition party vociferously pursue impeachment and conviction, but where their pursuit of that goal is motivated primarily by the fact that they are envious of the power held by their colleagues across the aisle.[11] (We might describe the case in a way that highlights either envy or jealousy: envy if the opposition party lacks a majority in the Senate, and jealousy if the opposition party is trying to protect their majority in the Senate.) We can suppose for the sake of argument that the blistering rebukes of the president given in speeches on the

Senate floor are fitting, but the accusation of jealousy or envy might nevertheless make sense if the opposition party is wielding those rebukes, and the impeachment proceedings more generally, with the primary aim of regaining (or retaining) power, instead of with the aim of upholding the Constitution.[12]

So, it looks like the testimonial model can be expanded to accommodate not only jealous assertions, but jealous rebukes as well. In some cases, the accusation of jealousy is meant to be a way of pointing out that the person is criticizing in bad faith, either because they don't endorse the criticism or because their endorsement of the criticism isn't explaining why they are giving voice to it. In other cases, the accusation is meant to point out that the critic's view of the moral landscape is distorted by their jealousy. But in none of the cases is a genuine reason successfully conveyed to the person being criticized—not a reason to believe the content of the criticism, and not a reason for the person being criticized to shape up or apologize.[13]

Again, I haven't explained *how* the reason-giving force of hypocritical or jealous blame would get silenced in this way, and I'm not sure I have anything enlightening to say on that score. I'm only suggesting that the testimonial model can help us to make sense of what exactly is going on when someone says, "You're one to talk!" or, "You're just jealous!" These retorts, I'm suggesting, are ways of saying that whatever reasons you're offering, I'm not buying.

AN ALTERNATIVE MODEL: ABUSE OF NORMATIVE POWER

If we think of blame as a move in a moral conversation, then the testimonial model of hypocritical or envious blame seems promising.[14] But there's another model that is also worth exploring, so let me sketch its contours here. In brief, the idea is that to blame someone is to exercise a normative power, much like making a promise or issuing a command. In this model, the problem with hypocritical or envious blame would be that those ways of blaming amount to an *abuse of power*, and the accusation of hypocrisy or jealousy is way of calling out such abuse.

A normative power, according to David Owens, is "a power to change what people are obliged to do by communicating the intention of so doing" (2012, 128). For those who opt for a normative power account of phenomena such as promising, there are tricky questions about what it is in virtue of which we have such a power, but again, here I just want to sketch the contours of the idea so that we can apply it to the case of envious blame. The general idea is that promising—like the giving of consent or the issuing of commands—is a power we have to change the normative situation "at will," and the reason we acquire for performing as we have promised is "content-independent," in the sense that the reason-giving force of our promise does not derive from whether it would be a good idea to do the thing we have promised to do, but instead merely from the fact that we *have* so promised.

Like the offering of a promise, an expression of blame might be interpreted as an attempt to change the normative situation between blamer and blamee. Adopting the normative power framework then gives us another way to understand how blaming interactions can go awry due to hypocrisy or jealousy, because where there is power, there is *abuse* of power.

Consider first the broader notion of abuse of power. There are several courses of action that might legitimately count as abuses of power: (1) using your position of power to do immoral things; (2) using your position of power to do things that you weren't empowered to do; and (3) using your position of power to do something that is at odds with the legitimate source of your power. As an example of the first kind of abuse, think of the professor who exploits their graduate students; as an example of the second kind of abuse, think of the president who mobilizes the Department of Justice in an attempt to punish corporations for political reasons rather than for legitimate worries about monopolies (Krugman 2019); as an example of the third kind of abuse, think of the president who attempts to undermine the very democratic processes that put him in power in the first place.

Perhaps these three types of abuse are not exhaustive, and perhaps in the final analysis they aren't all distinct. But I want to focus on the second sort of abuse. In this sort of case, we might say that the powerful person is "weaponizing" certain tools that they would otherwise be perfectly within their rights to use. This person is deploying their power for purposes other than those it is intended to serve. And it is *this* sort of abuse of power that I suspect can teach us something about envious and hypocritical blame. Start with the case of hypocrisy.

Not all hypocritical blamers are cut from the same cloth, but one prominent variety—as discussed above—is the hypocrite who is merely play-acting, merely going through the blaming motions for some sort of personal benefit. If we take blame to be the exercise of a normative power, we might explain what goes wrong with this sort of hypocrisy as follows: instead of deploying blame for the purposes of moral conversation, the clear-eyed hypocrite is weaponizing the practice of blame for the sake of scoring points with onlookers or perhaps for the sake of wounding someone they take to be an enemy. This sort of hypocritical blame is an abuse of an otherwise legitimate power that we have to hold one another accountable for wrongdoing.

Perhaps, then, we can view *envious blame* as yet another way to abuse one's normative power. Again, assuming that one of the legitimate aims of blame is to transmit to the blamee a reason to apologize and make things right, accusing someone of being "just jealous" might be interpreted as the accusation that the person is acting in the role of a blamer not for the purpose of enforcing moral norms but instead to score points against a rival. In fact, envy is by definition a *rivalrous* emotion, and an envier sees their rival as superior in a certain respect. This can motivate the envier to knock their rival down a peg, to spoil their superior status. Blame, especially if it is voiced publicly, is a natural way that this action-tendency might manifest. When that happens, the blame is being weaponized, used as a status-leveler, rather than as a move in a genuine moral conversation.[15]

CONCLUSION

Often when someone is accused of being "just jealous," the accusation is false, and the accuser is simply trying to avoid coming to grips with the legitimate criticism being made. But in other cases, the accusation seems apt, and what I've tried to explore here are two models for explaining what exactly would be problematic about criticism that is motivated by envy or jealousy.

According to the testimonial model, the fact that a criticism is motivated by envy might impugn the critic's sincerity, or else it might cast doubt on the soundness of the evaluative judgment that the criticism presupposes. According to the abuse of normative power model, envy can co-opt the legitimate mechanisms that we use to hold each other accountable and weaponize them for personal gain. But on either model, to accuse a critic of jealousy or envy is to paint the critic as ill-suited to moral conversation. They may continue to talk *at* us, but their motivations undermine their ability to talk *with* us.[16]

NOTES

1. See, for example, Cohen (2006); Wallace (2010); Radzik (2011); Fritz and Miller (2018); and Todd (2019).

2. For important dissenting voices, see Bell (2013) and Dover (2019).

3. This question—in particular, about how being envied influences the dynamics of interpersonal relationships—is also helpfully explored by Jens Lange and Jan Crusius in their contribution to this volume, "How Envy and Being Envied Shape Social Hierarchies" (chapter 2).

4. Other philosophers also defend versions of this model. See, for example, Purshouse (2004) and Konyndyk DeYoung (2009).

5. Protasi does not *identify* coveting with being envious, and in fact she contends that "covetousness" is a "species of desire" rather than an emotion. However, she

does express the lack vs. loss model by using the motto: "envy covets what jealousy guards" (2021, 13).

6. This zoomed-out discussion of the epistemology of testimony is inspired by the account given in chapter 6 of Wright (2013).

7. Iago is right about this, at least: "oft my jealousy / Shapes faults that are not."

8. For development of this sort of account, see Herstein (2017) and Tognazzini (n.d.).

9. I borrow the first three varieties from Macalester Bell's taxonomy in Bell (2013). The fourth and fifth varieties are my own proposed additions to Bell's list.

10. There's a puzzle here about how it makes sense for Napoleon to feel envy, which involves a perception of Kip's superiority, while at the same time issuing a criticism, which implies a negative evaluative judgment. One way to resolve the puzzle is to say that Kip is wrong about Napoleon feeling envy, and another is to say that Napoleon's criticism is just so much play-acting. But a third resolution might simply appeal to a sort of ambivalence that Napoleon is feeling in the moment: perhaps he admires something he also perceives as laziness. For an excellent discussion of a similar sort of puzzle, see Vanessa Carbonell's contribution to this volume, "Malicious Moral Envy" (chapter 7).

11. This case is inspired by some remarks in Dover (2019). Perhaps, as Dover speculates, it accurately describes some Senate Republicans during the impeachment trial of Bill Clinton.

12. As Vanessa Carbonell has pointed out to me, politics is an arena both of rivalrous emotions and of coldly rational calculations, and the very same course of action might be recommended by each of those mental pathways. In practice, therefore, it will be difficult to determine whether a political agenda is being pursued in good faith.

13. It's worth noting that an accurate criticism may still manage to open the eyes of the person being criticized, even if it fails to convey this special sort of reason. (Thanks to Sara Protasi for pushing me to clarify this point.) So, it's not as though envious criticism will never be instrumentally valuable. For more on this line of thought, see La Caze (2001) and Frye (2016).

14. Various authors have defended the view that blaming interactions are like conversations. See, for example, Macnamara (2015), McKenna (2013), and Watson (1987).

15. It's worth noting that the *accusation* of envy or jealousy might be weaponized in a similar way, since envy or jealousy is taken to be a defect of character.

16. Thanks very much to Sara Protasi both for her editorial work and for extensive comments on a previous draft of this chapter. I'm also grateful to Christina Chuang, Hud Hudson, Andrew Law, Christian Lee, Niels van de Ven, Ryan Wasserman, Dennis Whitcomb, Isaac Wilhelm, and especially Vanessa Carbonell. Finally, thanks to Anna Tognazzini for suggesting the topic of this paper, and for helpful conversations about it.

REFERENCES

Bell, Macalester. 2013. "The Standing to Blame: A Critique." In *Blame: Its Nature and Norms*, edited by D. Justin Coates and Neal A. Tognazzini, 263–82. New York: Oxford University Press.

Cohen, G. A. 2006. "Casting the First Stone: Who Can, and Who Can't, Condemn the Terrorists?" *Royal Institute of Philosophy Supplement* 58: 113–36.

Dover, Daniela. 2019. "The Walk and the Talk." *The Philosophical Review* 128: 387–422.

Fritz, Kyle, and Daniel Miller. 2018. "Hypocrisy and the Standing to Blame." *Pacific Philosophical Quarterly* 99: 118–39.

Frye, Harrison. 2016. "The Relation of Envy to Distributive Justice." *Social Theory and Practice* 42: 501–24.

Goldberg, Sanford. 2010. *Relying on Others: An Essay in Epistemology*. Oxford: Oxford University Press.

Herstein, Ori. 2017. "Understanding Standing: Permission to Deflect Reasons." *Philosophical Studies* 174: 3109–32.

Konyndyk DeYoung, Rebecca. 2009. *Glittering Vices: A New Look at the Seven Deadly Sins and Their Remedies*. Grand Rapids: Brazos Press.

Krugman, Paul. 2019. "How Democracy Dies, American-Style." *New York Times*, September 9, 2019. https://www.nytimes.com/2019/09/09/opinion/trump-democracy.html.

La Caze, Marguerite. 2001. "Envy and Resentment." *Philosophical Explorations* 4: 31–45.

Lackey, Jennifer 2008. *Learning from Words: Testimony as a Source of Knowledge*. Oxford: Oxford University Press.

Macnamara, Coleen. 2015. "Reactive Attitudes as Communicative Entities." *Philosophy and Phenomenological Research* 90: 546–69.

McKenna, Michael. 2013. "Directed Blame and Conversation." In *Blame: Its Nature and Norms*, edited by D. Justin Coates and Neal A. Tognazzini, 119–40. New York: Oxford University Press.

Owens, David. 2012. *Shaping the Normative Landscape*. Oxford: Oxford University Press.

Protasi, Sara. 2017. "'I'm Not Envious, I'm Just Jealous!': On the Difference Between Envy and Jealousy." *Journal of the American Philosophical Association* 3: 316–33.

———. 2021. *The Philosophy of Envy*. Cambridge: Cambridge University Press.

Purshouse, Luke. 2004. "Jealousy in Relation to Envy." *Erkenntnis* 60: 179–205.

Radzik, Linda. 2011. "On Minding Your Own Business: Differentiating Accountability Relations within the Moral Community." *Social Theory and Practice* 37: 574–98.

Todd, Patrick. 2017. "A Unified Account of the Moral Standing to Blame." *Nous* 53: 347–74.

Tognazzini, Neal. n.d. "On Losing One's Moral Voice." Unpublished manuscript.

Wallace, R. Jay 2010. "Hypocrisy, Moral Address, and the Equal Standing of Persons." *Philosophy & Public Affairs* 38: 307–41.

Watson, Gary. 1987. "Responsibility and the Limits of Evil." In *Responsibility, Character, and the Emotions: New Essays in Moral Psychology*, edited by Ferdinand Schoeman, 256–86. Cambridge: Cambridge University Press.

Wright, Larry. 2013. *Critical Thinking: An Introduction to Analytical Reading and Reasoning*, second edition. New York: Oxford University Press.

Chapter 9

The Fact of Envy

Trends in the History of Modern Economics

Miriam Bankovsky

> Far from exhibiting generosity, kindness and concern for others, man is characterized by attitudes of envy and malice towards his fellows. And such a view would, it seems to me, have the added virtue of being more in keeping with the spirit of this dismal science, and with the nature of homo economicus as traditionally conceived.
>
> —Brennan (1973, 173)

> Envy can be a force for good, not just for evil, once a consequentialist view is taken.
>
> —Zizzo (2008, 205)

With only a small handful of varied exceptions (La Caze 2001; Bankovsky 2019; Protasi 2021), philosophers have long held envy to be irrational and immoral,[1] a view that regularly accompanies a popular political position (affirmed by both sides of politics) that envy is not a justification for redistributing material goods. But envy has enjoyed a more ambivalent interpretation in the history of modern economics, both with respect to its definitions, its ethical significance, and its material implications for the question of who should get what.

This chapter has two main objectives. The first is to provide a survey of the conceptual frameworks that underpin the various interpretations of envy that economists have offered since the 1940s, in a manner that identifies and compares the key assumptions and core commitments of each approach (but without the mathematical detail). The second objective is to reflect on the significance of these varied interpretations of envy in modern economics for the concern of this edited book, which investigates the moral psychology of envy. If moral psychology is defined as the study of human thought and behavior in contexts where those thoughts and behaviors are ascribed a particular moral value (Doris et al. 2020), then our second objective is to identify whether and how modern economists have conceptualized the moral value of envy.

What emerges, in first place, is a typology of at least four different concepts, which have been mobilized in the history of modern economics to explore or explain what envy is and its implications for patterns of production, consumption, and distribution. Envy has been defined, first, as a mere preference for the things that someone else happens to have; second, as a negative consumption externality; third, as a disposition whose effects can be manipulated to achieve certain objectives (in business organization, institutional design, or sales-marketing); and fourth (and quite oddly), as a commodity in families, where the production of envy in children can be increased or decreased through the distributions of a benevolent third party who seeks to maximize a family's utility function.

As for how economists have positioned the moral value of envy, two positions emerge. First, in contrast to the dominant tradition in both philosophy and politics (which mainly depict envy as immoral and imprudent), modern economists have mostly positioned envy as a matter of fact, avoiding a discussion of whether the disposition itself is good or bad. Modern economists have instead been interested in the effects that envy has on what gets produced, on who consumes the product, and on how resources are distributed. Second, even if economists do not assume positions about the moral nature of envy as an individual disposition, the studies still position envy as indirectly good or bad with respect to its effects on other objects (which, variously, include social welfare, productive activity, business organization, marketing success, and family utility).

In sum, in contrast to the dominant tendency—in both the history of political philosophy and in the language of politics—to dismiss envy as an immoral individual disposition that individuals themselves must overcome, modern economists provide a variegated picture, with intersecting and divergent implications for the question of who gets what. In what follows, we will turn to each concept of envy in chronological order, outlining its definition and material significance, so as to then identify the implications for a moral psychology of envy. An effort will also be made to place the emergence of the first concept of envy in historical context, suggesting an interaction between the concept-formulation of economists, on one hand, and the broader social and political problems of the period, on the other.

THE WELFARIST TRADITION: A MERE PREFERENCE FOR THE BUNDLE OF ANOTHER AGENT, IN VIEW OF JUSTICE AS "THE ABSENCE OF ENVY"

The first concept of envy belongs to social choice theory (which comprises part of what's known as welfare economics). This social choice version of envy has had a chequered past, formulated for the first time in three texts by Tinbergen (1930, 1946, 1953), explored by other scholars across the 1960s and into the early 1970s, comparatively forgotten for around a decade from the mid-1970s, and rehabilitated from the 1990s onwards in what remains a rather marginal part of welfare economics.[2] In this social choice version, envy is defined in technical terms as a mere preference that one agent has for another agent's bundle of goods (Hammond 1987). According to Jan Tinbergen (a Dutch economist who won the very first Nobel Prize in Economics in 1969), agent A is said to envy agent B if A prefers B's bundle of goods to the bundle that A has. For example, A might be envious of B if A prefers B's bundle of goods (which might include a Queen Anne mansion, a new Cadillac, and expensive food with colonial delicacies and a toffee apple) to their own (which might include a draughty tenement room, resoled boots, and cabbage, potatoes, and bread).

The larger purpose of this technical definition of envy was to introduce a theory of distributive justice as the "absence of envy," so as to avoid a major problem with the "disastrously restrictive" New Welfare economics of the 1930s and 1940s (Arnsperger and Van Parijs 1994, 4). The New Welfare economists had sought to restrict economics to identifying efficiency improvements, with the aim being to secure a greater number of satisfied preferences in an economy with the same resources. But the "absence of envy" economists felt that the New Welfare approach erred by ignoring the important question of how these preference satisfactions should be distributed among people.

To explain, in the 1930s, New Welfare economists like Lionel Robbins (1932) had chosen to follow logical positivist trends in the Vienna Circle (nicely articulated by A. J. Ayer in 1936) by presenting standards for interpersonal utility comparisons as merely subjective and merely emotive. This, in effect, denied any objective basis for making ethical judgments about how goods (and associated preference-satisfactions) should be distributed. For example, if one takes the toffee apple from agent B (who already enjoys expensive food with colonial delicacies) and gives this to agent A (who only has cabbage, potatoes, and bread), the New Welfare economists would say that there is no objective way to measure whether the toffee apple provides greater utility to agent A or to agent B (since experiences of utility are merely subjective). As Lionel Robbins famously put it, interpersonal comparisons of utility "cannot be justified by appeal to any kind of positive science" (1932, 125, see also 124 and 1938, 164). But the effect was that New Welfare economists could no longer justify prioritizing increases in agent A's bundle over increases in agent B's. The sole object of welfare economics became that of increasing the sheer number of preferences that were satisfied, in a manner that would not involve any loss to others, since the latter would then require controversial ethical judgments about whose experience of satisfaction was more significant (Hicks 1939; Kaldor 1939, 149; for a critical discussion, see Bankovsky and King 2017). For the "absence of envy" economists like Tinbergen, Arnsperger, Van Parijs, and many others, the New Welfare account was problematic because it expressly denied the possibility of working to secure a just distribution of goods among people themselves. Since a goal of satisfying more preferences said nothing about how preference-satisfaction should be distributed, it was entirely possible that efficiency-improvements could be compatible with the most advantaged agents (e.g., agent B) enjoying greater levels of preference-satisfaction with no improvements to the least well-off agents (e.g., Agent A).

The "absence of envy" literature sought to salvage a distributive role for economists, while continuing to avoid any re-introduction of "merely subjective" interpersonal comparisons of utility (Arnsperger and Van Parijs 1994). The task was to demonstrate the possibility of a distribution of goods in which every individual would be satisfied with their own bundle of goods. This re-introduced concerns for the distributions of the least well-off, who might reasonably or excusably find themselves envying the greater number of satisfied preferences enjoyed by the most advantaged. As Arnsperger puts it, envy-freeness became the idea of an equity criterion expressing *an ideal of equality in societies where preferences and endowments are heterogenous* (Arnsperger 1994, 158). This welfarist view was characterized, in general, by two postulates, which separated equitability from efficiency and combined them in a theory of fairness. The first said that that if there are no envious agents at allocation x, then allocation x is equitable. The second said that if allocation x is both equitable and Pareto efficient (in the sense that no further increases to preference satisfaction are possible for one party without associated decreases for another party), then allocation x is fair.[3]

Two implications follow from this social choice and welfarist definition of envy for a moral psychology. On one hand, the concept of envy as "preference for the bundle of another agent" does not position the disposition of envy as moral or immoral. In contrast to their counterparts in political philosophy and psychology, the "absence of envy" economists sought to avoid judging the moral nature of the emotional or psychological state of the envious party. These social choice economists have not asked, for example, whether an individual's envy manifests itself in immoral destruction of another's goods, or whether envy might rather promote positive forms of emulation. Nor have these economists asked whether envy was an unreasonable sentiment to experience or, conversely, whether envy might be excusable. Moreover, the social choice conceptions do not consider whether the envied individual's bundle is even worth envying. Envy remains a merely technical preference for another's bundle, without any moral overlay. On the other hand, there appears to be an implicit moral idea (one that lacks the necessary justification) that the existence of envy can indicate unfairness, and that people might reasonably want to live in a society that distributes resources in ways that reduce the likelihood of envy. In sum, these welfare economists implicitly depict envy-free distributions as a kind of moral social good, even if envy as an individual disposition is presented as morally neutral.

Before turning to the next concept of envy in modern economics, it is interesting to consider the possibility of a relation between trends in the elaboration of this first literature on envy with the larger global social and political context of economic development in post-World War II societies. Why was it that, from the late 1940s and across the 1960s, there was great interest in, and tolerance for, the idea that societies should be structured in ways that allowed individuals to be satisfied with their particular bundles (so that they did not experience envy)? And why was it that political tolerance for this idea collapsed from the late 1970s and into the 1980s? And finally, why is it that the "absence of envy" literature came to be rehabilitated in the 1990s in some more marginal areas of mainstream economics? The late 1940s to the 1970s were characterized by the "crucial reforms" of capitalism (Kalecki and Kowalik 1971) which sought, in the main, to institute post-Keynesian capitalist systems in which agents with different preferences and endowments could nonetheless achieve material fulfilment, with a role for government in boosting effective demand. It is against this broader tolerance for achieving societies in which all agents could achieve material fulfilment that the initial approach of Tinbergen and Dusenberry in the late 1940s became further developed in the 1960s and early 1970s by economists like Foley, Kolm, Varian, Thomson, and Moulin.

However, as Arnsperger notes (albeit without context or further discussion), interest in the social choice concept of envy died down from the late 1970s into the 1980s (1994, 155). This is the period in which the postwar reforms fell into decline, with the rise of neoliberal economic theory and governance from around 1974 onward. The objective of institutionalizing equality in the form of material fulfilment for all became steadily replaced by neoliberal and free-market institutions that instead embodied ideas of equality in the form of equal and reciprocal freedom from constraint. Indeed, it is at this point that the "absence of envy" literature became the primary target of the now popular political and theoretical rejection of egalitarianism for being purportedly grounded in envy, a view associated with conservative rejections of liberal egalitarianism as grounded in a "politics of envy" (de la Mora 1987).[4]

This comparative forgetting (and explicit rejection) of arguments in favor of envy as a ground for redistribution was relatively short-lived, with a revival of interest in the idea of the "absence of envy" from the 1990s onward. The 1990s revival of envy by Robert Frank, Claude Gamel, Claude d'Aspremont, Philippe Mongin, Hervé Moulin, Marc Fleurbaey, Christian Arnsperger, Philippe Van Parijs, and others effectively paved the way to several decades of ongoing (but politically marginal) work on how societies might achieve envy-free distributions (e.g., Cole and Tao 2021, etc.). Further historical and interview-based research is necessary to explore whether any interconnection existed between the revival of the 1990s, on one hand, and the experience of yet another global recession, on the other, an economic downturn that again disproportionately affected the least well-off. It is enough to note, however, that if the notion of envy-free distributions requires institutions to support the achievement of material fulfilment for all, then this would pose a significant challenge to the neoliberal defence of distributions that are the outcome of reciprocal freedom from constraint.

FROM WELFARIST TO BEHAVIORAL ECONOMICS: A NEGATIVE CONSUMPTION EXTERNALITY

From the late 1970s onward, another concept of envy emerged in economics, namely, the idea of envy as a negative consumption externality. This involved studying how envy distorted the level and type of consumption in an economy. The idea is visible in the work of scholars like Geoffrey Brennan (1973), A. Chaudhuri (1986), and Chal Sussangkarn and Steven M. Goldman (1983). This work says that envy is welfare-decreasing for the envious and can be represented in a utility function as a disutility. Although the individual disposition of envy is still viewed in morally neutral terms, the effort to increase the welfare of the envious through envy-mitigation is depicted as a broader social good, permitting a justification of redistribution that does not rely on the philanthropic benevolence of the envied.

To grasp these points, we need to begin by rehearsing our understanding of the concept of a consumption externality. In economics, an externality is the *indirect* effect of a transaction on the utility of a third party (i.e., someone who did not themselves participate in the producer-consumer transaction). Externalities are positive if they increase the utility of the third party and negative if they decrease that utility. In textbooks, classic examples of negative production externalities include air pollution as an effect of production, which harms the utility of third parties who are not involved in producing or consuming the product. The textbook solution is to design ways to ensure that the transaction between producer and consumer reflects the full-cost of producing or consuming the product, with a negative externality associated with a price-hike (e.g., through a tax), and a positive externality associated with a lowering of price (e.g., through a subsidy). Environmental economists, for example, have proposed that when products causing environmental damage are priced to reflect the full cost of the effect of that damage *on other humans*, then the demand for consuming damaging products will decrease. To position envy as a negative *consumption* externality is to say that envy is a decrease in utility experienced by a third party when someone else buys or consumes a good or service. Unlike pollution, envy is not usually depicted as an externality arising from production. Rather, envy is positioned as a consumption externality, because it is the increased consumption of the consuming party that gives rise to envy in the third party.

As a negative consumption externality, envy came to be represented in the social choice and welfare literature as a disutility for the envious subject. This is not a disutility that remains constant in the face of a difference between the envious and the envied. Rather, it is figured as a disutility that increases as a function of increases in utility of the envied. This is what Brennan (1973) does, depicting envy as "the increasing marginal disutility of others' income." It leads him to conclude that, "under the most reasonable assumptions" (174), envy "may establish a case for redistribution within the Pareto framework," a redistribution that "will be from rich to poor" (1973, 181).

Although this may appear similar, in its results, to the "absence from envy" literature, there are two differences. First, the theoretical representation of envy is different. Instead of simply asking whether people, at a given distribution x, are envious in that they would rather change bundles with someone else (Tinbergen 1946; Foley 1967; Kolm 1972; Varian 1974; and see Arnsperger 1994, 157–58 for further discussion), the negative externality approach includes envy in the utility function of the envious. As mentioned, it is depicted as an increasing marginal disutility experienced whenever another significant person's bundle of goods has increased.

The second difference is that the aim is not to ensure justice as "the absence of envy" but, rather, to identify distributions that maximize utility among plural agents. This means that some subjects may well remain envious, as long as the distribution represents the most utility for a set of agents, given the utility functions of those involved.

Finally, the contribution that Brennan understands himself to be making is not to the "absence of envy" literature, but rather to an alternative body of literature that sought to ground a defence of transfers from rich to poor on the altruistic utility functions of the rich. But Brennan thought that this sort of justification was unrealistic. Instead, he sought to justify transfers from rich to poor without requiring an unreasonable assumption that the rich be philanthropically motivated. His alternative is to assume that "individuals motivated by malice and envy may be prepared to contribute to redistributive programmes, not because they value increased consumption by the poor [the altruistic assumption] but because they value reduced consumption by the rich" (Brennan 1973, 182). He concludes that "All in all, it does appear as if malice and envy may not be wholly unmitigated evils—which is perhaps reassuring, since they do seem to exist in some abundance" (182).

Interestingly, this depiction of envy as a negative consumption externality does not lead to a view that the negative impact of envy should be costed and added to the price of the product that is consumed, as has elsewhere been proposed to manage the third-party harms of environmental damage. An "envy-tax" is not explicitly discussed, perhaps because it would be both politically untenable and methodologically unwieldy.

As for the implications for moral psychology, the individual disposition of envy as a negative consumption externality is again treated as a fact of human existence, without explicit moral overlay. However, if one goal is to increase welfare in a particular social distribution, there remains an implied judgment that envy is undesirable because it is welfare-reducing. The envier will need more goods to enjoy the same level of utility that they used to enjoy.

BEHAVIOURAL AND EXPERIMENTAL ECONOMICS: A DISPOSITION THAT CAN BE MANIPULATED TO ACHIEVE CERTAIN OBJECTIVES

From the 1980s onward, the discipline of economics became increasingly behavioral and experimental, as economists began to voice concerns about the ability of utility theory to predict the economic behavior of real-life agents (or, in our case, the behavior of real persons who are envious or envied). Welfarists like Brennan had sought to show how the overall utility in a group might be increased by mitigating the envy of those persons whose utility function was characterized by disutility proportional to the increasing utility of another person in the group. But behavioral economists worried that welfarist approaches were neglecting to study how envious persons behaved in the real world, faced with particular incentives. Indeed, one economist (e.g., Banerjee 1990) argued, counterintuitively, that envy might even be welfare-enhancing in the real world (and not a disutility at all), because envy might lead real persons to make choices that ultimately made them happier (for example, choosing leisure over labor).

The behavioral turn was oriented toward two objectives. The first was to understand how the envious and the envied behave, either in real life settings or in laboratory experiments. The second was to explore whether manipulating incentives could nudge the envious or the envied to behave in ways that support particular social objectives, including, for example, improvements to the organization of a firm, innovation compatible with reduced envy, and increased sales through marketing methods that encourage emulation.

Regarding the first objective (namely, to understand how envy functions in real-life settings), behavioral economists have studied the effects of envy on economic agents, both in laboratory games that simulate game theoretical scenarios (e.g., Kirchsteiger 1994; Zizzo 2008) and via the in situ observations of anthropologists and sociologists studying envy in real life (e.g., Frank 1985; Banerjee 1990; Mui 1995). In his consideration of the cognitive and behavioral economics of envy, Zizzo uses laboratory experiments to defend the view that simple models (like Brennan's) that depict envy as a disutility do not do justice to the real-world experiences of the envious and the envied. For Zizzo, it is important to study envy's empirical character through four interrelated lenses. First, there should be a specification of the reference group in relation to which the envious agent is competing for status. Second, attention must be paid to how envy operates between groups (and not just between individuals), a phenomenon that complicates the interactions between group identity and reference group (e.g., Bacharach 2006). Third, any representation of envy as a disutility should explain what it is about envy in particular that makes it utility-reducing and how this disutility is different to other utility-reducing dispositions (like the disutility of anger or jealousy or inequality aversion, etc.) (193–94). Fourth, envy also has a "thick" cognitive component—by which Zizzo means that envy is not interchangeable with the other disutilities mentioned, but rather has its own specific meaning. Unlike anger, jealousy, and inequality-aversion, envy involves an evaluation by the envious subject of their own deservingness for the income or consumption that the other party enjoys (see also Morgan-Knapp 2013), an element that makes envy different to the character of other disutilities (Zizzo 2008, 205–6). For Zizzo, experiments in laboratory and other settings can shine a light on how these factors work in the real world. Accepting that the data on the behaviors of envious and envied parties is still in its infancy and faces certain problems (including, for example, that it is not always clear that envy is at work in the behavior under observation), Zizzo nonetheless suggests that it is only through an exploration of the empirical effects of the cognitive dimensions of envy that we can really come to an understanding of topics like bargaining, firm structure, interindustry wage differentials, consumption, taxation, economic growth, and so on.

Other behavioral studies focus on how the envious and the envied behave as a function of differences in allocations which produce negative externalities of different strengths. Some studies account for distortions in the behavior of the envious, with others studying distortions in the behavior of the envied. Regarding the envious, Ahbijit Banerjee (1990) suggests that when the difference between the allocations of the envious and the envied is small, the negative consumption externality of envy leads the envious to distort their own consumption by engaging in "catch-up consumption." But when the difference between the allocations of the envious and envied is very large, the negative consumption externality produces a different sort of consumption distortion, namely, the envious person will likely give up on increasing their own income (and consumption) altogether, choosing leisure over labor. In this case, the envious person will accept their envy and find non-comparative modes of satisfaction through leisure. On one hand, this means that envy can unexpectedly be welfare-enhancing, if the envious try to improve their welfare through non-comparative means (i.e. Banerjee's suggestion is that choosing leisure over labor can be welfare-enhancing if the leisure produces more utility than the disutility of envy). On the other hand, this leads to the underemployment of human capital in an economy and to a decrease in overall consumption. Regarding the envied, Jon Elster (1991) argues that when the negative externality of envy manifests itself in destructive behavior on the part of the envious, then the envied are likely abstain from increasing their income and consumption, to avoid provoking the envy of others. Mui's analysis of envy in social and economic life (1995) cites supporting research in anthropology and sociology. Recounting several stories from the Communist Party newspaper (*Renmin Ribao*), Mui explains how specialized households in socialist countries had improved their outlooks only to find themselves subject to envious hostility and even attack from fellow villagers, leading them to "dare not work too hard to get rich again" (in Mui 1995, 313).

As for the second objective (namely, to explore how to manipulate incentives to nudge the envious and envied to behave in ways that support particular social objectives), a varied body of work now exists on how envy can be manipulated to improve the organization of a firm (Frank 1985; Banerjee 1990), or to develop an institutional framework to encourage innovation compatible with reduced envy (Mui 1995; Frank 1985), or to improve sales through marketing methods that encourage emulation through envy (Belk 2008; Mitsopoulos 2009).

With respect to firm organization, Robert Frank has drawn on the concept of envy to explain the empirical finding that wage structures within firms are more egalitarian than marginal productivity theory expects them to be.

Traditional economic theory says that a worker will be paid the value of their "marginal product" by a firm, where "marginal product" is understood in terms of the value by which the firm's production during each time period would decline if the worker were no longer employed in that firm. But, as Frank explains in *Choosing the Right Pond* (1985), wages rarely reflect "marginal productivity theory" in the everyday world of real work. He provides an anecdotal example of a university department being unwilling to increase the salary of one of its most original and productive scholars (perhaps a reference to himself?), on account of the university being unable to afford to handle the fifteen other salary increases that the productive scholar's raise would likely prompt (39). Frank then turns to a study of the pay schedules at a variety of firms to support an observation that, in practice, these "seem altogether more egalitarian than would be possible under marginal productivity theory" (42). Frank first considers and rejects various explanations that have been offered for this phenomenon, including that employers exploit worker inertia—the unwillingness of workers to move to other locations for better pay—by paying them substantially less than the economic value of what they contribute; or that employers conspire among themselves to hold down wages. These critical arguments, says Frank, are inconsistent with empirical studies—now *very* dated and perhaps less applicable to today's increasingly neoliberal economies—that found low-wage industries to be low-return industries, and wage rates to be positively influenced by profits (Stigler 1946; Seidman 1976). Instead, Frank argues that the internal wage structures of firms are far more egalitarian than one would think, not because of firm-worker exploitation but rather because the least productive workers are being paid *more* than the value of their marginal product, with the most productive workers receiving *less*. The alternative theory Frank proposes is that workers want to receive a higher internal status than their co-workers (which Frank defines as a desire to be envied, 1985, 47). This leads the most productive workers to accept *less* than the value of their marginal product on condition that they receive compensation in the form of a high internal ranking. And it leads the least productive workers to be paid *more* than the value of their marginal product in order to compensate them for not receiving the high internal ranking that they envy). In other words, if certain workers are to be kept at a low rank and endure envy, they must be paid a wage premium (and vice versa). The outcome of the working of envy, Frank argues, is wage compression within the firm, which marginal productivity theory is unable to explain.

A related preoccupation is that of Banerjee, who asks how envy might be manipulated within firms to achieve particular goals. Banerjee argues that firms can themselves influence the level of envy among their workers, by featuring or downplaying the importance of differences in rank; by creating an excessive amount of titled posts; by offering non-pecuniary awards for good performance; by changing the size of peer groups among workers; and by introducing someone who is more competitive into a peer group. On one hand, in cases where a difference in status within a group is perceived to be within the grasp of the envious, firms can stoke envy to promote greater productivity (while enjoying the additional benefits of not needing to increase wages). On the other hand, Banerjee warns that envy should not be increased to the point of undermining effort, because this would likely generate suboptimalities, with low-ranked workers opting to put less effort into their work (1990).[5] The take-home point is that behavioral economists have moved beyond utility theory to develop empirical theories of envy-influenced behavior under certain conditions, in this case with a view to increasing the efficiency and productivity of firms.

With respect to encouraging innovation compatible with reduced envy, Mui (1995) has studied the conditions under which an envious person will have a strong incentive to engage in the sabotage of an envied person's riches, as well as the conditions under which an envied person might voluntarily limit innovation in order to avoid provoking another's envy. Seeking to limit these undesirable effects, Mui studies how envious sabotage might be (partly) reduced in cases where the innovator voluntarily shares some of the benefits of the innovation, while also showing that the envious will not always support increases in the legal authority's propensity to punish envious sabotage (making that form of control ineffective).

With similar concerns for overall institutional design, but with a different focus on the phenomenon of conspicuous consumption (which Veblen [(1899) 2008] described as a public display of goods or services designed to show off one's social status), Robert Frank (1985) has argued that the drive for status is innate, underwritten by a desire to stoke the envy of others. He suggests that once we recognize this for what it really is (envy-stoking, rather than the satisfaction of preferences that reflect non-comparative needs that Frank views as more important), then we would want to limit this behavior. He thinks we should understand many of the laws in liberal democratic societies as an effort to reflect this recognition, and he encourages us to continue to consider how institutions might be designed to promote wiser forms of consumption. The take-home point of these studies is that behavioral economists have not just been interested in supporting business objectives through the manipulation of envy internal to the business. Rather, behavioral economists have also been interested in proposing institutional designs likely to keep the negative effects of destructive forms of envy at bay in society more broadly, in ways that generally promote an atmosphere of innovation.

Finally, with respect to how envy can be mobilized to increased sales through marketing methods that encourage emulation, a number of behavioural economists have studied how the manipulation of "benign" envy can increase consumption, a literature that is briefly considered by Belk, whose approach is more sociological than economic (Belk 2008; see also Mitsopoulos 2009).

As for the implications for a moral psychology of envy, clearly envy is again depicted as a disposition that is not good or bad in and of itself, but rather a phenomenon that should be studied for its effects on the sorts of larger objectives that businesses or societies are seeking to achieve. First, envy can be beneficial in promoting consumption, efficient business organization, and certain types of economic growth. Second, and conversely, envy can be detrimental in incentivizing undesirable forms of merely conspicuous consumption, in undermining innovation, and in leading to economic suboptimalities, if envious people decide not to put in effort when the desired higher status looks to be unattainable. Reflecting on these benefits and dangers of envy, Niels van de Ven has thus argued, in the present volume ("The Envious Consumer," chapter 12), that the manipulation of envy is thus a morally ambivalent phenomenon. Indeed, one of the more interesting insights of the economics literature is that envy can lead us to want things that we don't need, and overlook things that we *do* need, a position that requires teasing out using deliberative and philosophical considerations.

NEW HOUSEHOLD ECONOMICS: A COMMODITY IN FAMILIES, CONTROLLED BY A BENEVOLENT THIRD PARTY

One of the initially more puzzling deployments of envy in modern economics is found in the New Household Economics of Gary Becker, who won the Nobel Prize in Economics in 1992 for extending the concept of economic rationality to decisions relating to the formation and organization of families, to behaviors involved in racial discrimination, and to criminal activity (topics that had previously been beyond the domain of economists). Referring to Bentham's list of fifteen fundamental sources of "pleasure and pain," Becker defines envy as a basic "commodity" or Z-good, which he says is a fundamental source of "pleasure and pain" that contributes to a family's utility. By Z-good, Becker means a particular household-produced commodity that individuals don't simply purchase but also produce. In other words, individuals allocate both their income (through purchases) and their time to producing or controlling commodities that contribute to a family's utility. Z-goods are "numerous and include the quality of meals, the quality and quantity of children, prestige, recreation, companionship, love and health status" (1976, 307), and, for our purposes, Z-goods even include "altruism, envy and the pleasures of the senses" ([1981] 1991, 23–24).

But what exactly does this mean? I take Becker to mean that envy can actually be produced (or controlled) by households, so that families in effect choose to produce (or perhaps the words control and cultivate would be more appropriate) the amount, quality, and distribution of envy in families. Families do this because a certain amount, quality and distribution of envy can increase the family's utility. In other words, a certain amount, quality and distribution of envy can be utility-maximizing for the family. A household can produce high or low levels of envy, depending on the decisions of household members to invest time and income into controlling it in ways that serve the family's utility.

Although Becker details a number of ways that envy can be produced, controlled, and distributed in families, one example is particularly helpful in understanding his approach. This is the case in which there exists at least one altruistic parent that is willing and able to transfer resources to their children, where altruistic is defined not in philosophical terms but rather as a behavior that involves transfers to another person that increases their income, such that total income increases, even if the income of the altruist decreases somewhat. An altruist is thus someone whose utility is increased when they raise the family income (rather than their own personal income). The altruist (a) would refrain from actions that raise a's income if they lower the beneficiary's (b's) income, and a would take actions that lower a's income if they raise b's income by even more. In a multi-person household where an altruist has several beneficiaries (children, parents, siblings, spouses), Becker argues that an altruist would induce each beneficiary to internalize the effects of the beneficiary's actions on the altruist's own income and consumption (because even a selfish beneficiary knows that they are dependent on the altruist's transfers). To provide an example, if a child, Tom, is envious of his sister, he would still avoid taking actions that harm his envied sister and which appear to help him, if it looked like those actions would reduce the family's income (because the altruist would lower the consumption of family members if family income falls, and this would not be good for Tom as beneficiary). Tom knows that if he undertakes an action that reduces his sister's income by more than it increases his own income, then it will likely induce the altruistic parent to increase their contribution to Tom's sister and reduce their contribution to Tom, making Tom worse off than before. The altruistic parent thus helps to control the problem of envy, in ways that maximize the family's total income.

As for the implications of this idea of envy as a familial commodity for a moral psychology of envy, clearly the existence of envy in a family is depicted as a familial choice (or at least a choice on the part of the altruist). Envy is again something that is not necessarily good or bad in and of itself. It is rather a disposition whose function on the family's income and utility can be understood, with levels of intra-familial envy controlled by choices that the family altruist makes about who gets what.

CONCLUSION

Due to the rejection of envy as a ground for redistribution not just by conservative free-market thinkers (de la Mora 1987) but also in political philosophy (e.g., Rawls 1971), and in the language of everyday politics, I had expected to discover that envy was also rejected by mainstream modern economists (even in the face of the presumption that greed—and perhaps envy—can be good for economic growth). But my survey of envy in the history of modern economics suggests that economists have been more willing than philosophers to accept the "fact of envy" and analyze its effects on human interaction and economic behavior. That said, even if economists do not explicitly assume positions about the moral nature of envy as an individual disposition, the studies still position envy as indirectly good or bad with respect to its effects on other objectives.[6]

NOTES

1. For a critical summary of the extensive philosophical literature on the irrationality of envy, please see Protasi (2021).

2. Please see Heilmann and Wintein (2021) for an explanation of the key ideas in Tinbergen 1930, 1946, and 1953, as well as how they compare with the theories of the 1960s and early 1970s. Heilmann, Wintein, Hinz, and Dekker have recently drawn attention to the existence of Tinbergen 1930, by providing an English translation of the Dutch original. Prior to the English translation of Tinbergen's 1930 article, most scholars attributed the first welfare formulation of the 'no-envy' criterion to Tinbergen 1946 and 1953. See Tinbergen [1930] 2021.

3. It should be noted, however, that the welfarist version of fairness as "the absence of envy" is different from John Rawls's pre-distributive notion of justice as fairness (Rawls 1971). The welfarist view not only continued to avoid standards for interpersonal comparison but also limited its analysis to utility (defined as mere preference-satisfaction). In contrast, Rawls introduced interpersonally comparable standards (albeit not of utility) that parties behind a veil of ignorance would find it reasonable to accept and the theory thus sought agreement on principles for the institutions of the basic social structure (exceeding the welfarist concern to merely ensure satisfaction with particular bundles of goods).

4. Alfred Archer, Alan Thomas, and Bart Engelen present a criticism of this conservative position in their contribution to this volume, titled: "The Politics of Envy: Outlaw Emotions in Capitalist Societies" (chapter 10).

5. For a similarly motivated study (i.e., studying the likely effect of envy on effort), but one that focuses not on the effort of workers within a business and rather on the decision of workers in an economy to choose leisure over income, see Barnett et al. (2010).

6. The person I would most like to thank is Dr. Sara Protasi. They are possibly the most organized editor that I have had the pleasure to be involved with. The approach allowed scope for invited contributors to follow our own interests, while also providing careful and considered assistance to frame our work, in support of the broad goals of the volume. The reviewing and sharing process meant that we also learned from each other's work as we progressed. I also acknowledge the many contributors to two virtual workshops that Protasi organized, who also provided me with valuable feedback. A big thank you to two economists and historians of economic thought, Professor John E. King and Professor Michael Howard, for providing me with reassurance. I am particularly grateful to John King for talking through aspects of my interpretation on a number of occasions. The usual caveats apply: all errors remain my own.

REFERENCES

Arnsperger, Christian. 1994. "Envy-Freeness and Distributive Justice." *Journal of Economic Surveys* 8 (2): 155–86.

Arnsperger, Christian, and Philippe Van Parijs. 1994. "La justice économique comme absence d'envie." *Recherches Economiques de Louvain* 60 (1): 3–7.

Ayer, A. J. 1936. *Language, Truth and Logic*. London: Penguin.

Banerjee, Ahbijit. 1990. "Envy." In *Economic Theory and Policy: Essays in Honour of Dipak Banerjee*, edited by Bhaskar Dutta, Shubhashis Gangopadhyay, Dilip Mookherjee, and Debraj Ray, 91–111. Bombay: Oxford University Press.

Bankovsky, Miriam, and John E. King. 2017. "Reviving the Living Dead: Economic Policy with Ethical Values." *Journal of Australian Political Economy* 80: 178–200.

Bankovsky, Miriam. 2018. "Excusing Economic Envy: On Injustice and Impotence." *Journal of Applied Philosophy* 35 (2): 257–79.

Barnett, Richard C., Joydeep Bhattacharya, and Helle Bunzel. 2010. "Choosing to Keep Up with the Joneses and Income Inequality." *Economic Theory* 45: 469–96.

Becker, Gary. 1976. *The Economic Approach to Human Behaviour*. Chicago: University of Chicago Press.

Becker, Gary. (1981) 1991. *A Treatise on the Family*. Cambridge MA: Harvard University Press.

Belk, Russell W. 2008. "Marketing and Envy." In *Envy: Theory and Research*, edited by R. H. Smith, 211–26. Oxford: Oxford University Press.

Brennan, Geoffrey. 1973. "Pareto Desirable Redistribution: The Case of Malice and Envy." *Journal of Public Economics* 2: 173–83.

Chaudhuri, A. 1986. "Some Implications of an Intensity Measure of Envy." *Social Choice and Welfare* 4: 255–70.

Cole, Richard, and Yixin Tao. 2021. "On the Existence of Pareto Efficient and Envy-Free Allocations." *Journal of Economic Theory* 193: 1–20.

de la Mora, Gonzalo Fernandez. 1987. *Egalitarian Envy: The Political Foundations of Social Justice.* New York: Paragon House Publishers.

Doris, John, Stephen Stich, Jonathan Phillips, and Lachlan Walmsley. 2020. "Moral Psychology: Empirical Approaches." In *The Stanford Encyclopedia of Philosophy* (Spring 2020 edition), edited by Edward N. Zalta. https://plato.stanford.edu/archives/spr2020/entries/moral-psych-emp/.

Elster, Jon. 1991. "Envy in Social Life." In *Strategy and Choice*, edited by Richard Zeckhauser, 49–82. Cambridge, MA: MIT Press.

Fernandez de la Mora, Gonzalo. 1987. *Egalitarian Envy: The Political Foundations of Social Justice.* New York: Paragon House Publishers.

Foley, Duncan. 1967. "Resource Allocation and the Public Sector." *Yale Economic Essays* 7: 45–98.

Frank, Robert H. 1985. *Choosing the Right Pond: Human Behaviour and the Quest for Status.* New York: Oxford University Press.

———. 1988. *Passions within Reasons: The Strategic Role of the Emotions.* New York: W. W. Norton & Company.

Goel, Anand M., and Anjan V. Thakor. 2005. "Green with Envy: Implications for Corporate Investment Distortions." *The Journal of Business* 78 (6) (November): 2255–88

Hammond Peter J. (1987) 2016. "Envy." In *The New Palgrave Dictionary of Economics*, edited by J. Eatwell, M. Milgate, and P. Newman. London: Palgrave Macmillan.

Heilmann, Conrad and Stefan Wintein. 2021. "No Envy: Jan Tinbergen on Fairness." *Erasmus Journal for Philosophy and Econmoics* 14 (1): 222–245.

Hicks, John R. 1939. "The Foundations of Welfare Economics." *Economic Journal* 49 (196) (December): 696–712.

Kaldor, Nicholas. 1939. "Welfare Propositions of Economics and Interpersonal Comparisons of Utility." *Economic Journal* 49 (195) (September): 549–52.

Kalecki, Michał and Tadeusz Kowalik. 1971. "Observations on the 'Crucial Reform.'" *Politica ed Economica* 2–3: 190–96.

Kirchsteiger, Georg. 1994. "The Role of Envy in Ultimatum Games." *Journal of Economic Behavior and Organization* 25: 373–89.

Kolm, S. C. 1972. *Justice et Equité.* Paris: Editions du CNRS.

La Caze, Marguerite. 2001. "Envy and Resentment." *Philosophical Explorations* 4 (1): 31–45.

Mitsopoulos, Michael. 2009. "Envy, Institutions and Growth." *Bulletin of Economic Research.* 61 (3): 201–22.

Morgan-Knapp, Christopher. 2014. "Economic Envy." *Journal of Applied Philosophy* 31 (2): 113–126.

Mui, Vai-Lam. 1995. "The Economics of Envy." *Journal of Economic Behavior and Organization* 26: 311–36.

Protasi, Sara. 2021. *The Philosophy of Envy.* Cambridge MA: Cambridge University Press.

Rawls, John. 1971. *A Theory of Justice.* Cambridge, MA: The Belknap Press.

Robins, Lionel. 1932. *An Essay on the Nature and Significance of Economic Science*. London: Macmillan & Co.

Stigler, George. 1946. "The Economics of Minimum Wage Legislation." *The American Economic Review* 36 (3): 358–365.

Sussangkan, Chal and Steven Goldman. 1983. "Dealing with Envy." *Journal of Public Economics* 22: 103–112.

Tinbergen, Jan. (1930) 2021. "Mathematical Psychology." Translated by Conrad Heilmann, Stefan Wintein, Ruth Hinz, and Erwin Dekker. *Erasmus Journal for Philosophy and Economics* 14 (1): 210–221.

Tinbergen, Jan. 1946. *Redelijke Inkomensverdeling*. Haarlem: N.V. De Gulden Pers.

Tinbergen, Jan. 1953. *Redelijke Inkomensverdeling*. 2nd edition. Haarlem: N.V. De Gulden Pers.

Varian, H. 1974. "Equity, Envy and Efficiency." *Journal of Economic Theory* 9: 63–91.

Veblen, Thorstein. (1899) 2008. *The Theory of the Leisure Class*. Oxford: Oxford University Press.

Zizzo, Daniel. 2008. "The Cognitive and Behavioural Economics of Envy." In *Envy: Theory and Research*. Edited by Richard Smith, 190–210. Oxford: Oxford University Press.

Chapter 10

The Politics of Envy

Outlaw Emotions in Capitalist Societies

Alfred Archer, Alan Thomas, and Bart Engelen

A common critique made by conservatives against those who support economic egalitarianism is that they are engaging in "the politics of envy." For example, Margaret Thatcher (1974), the former prime minister of the United Kingdom and leader of the Conservative Party, dismissed egalitarianism as "the politics of envy, the incitement of people to regard all success as if it were something discreditable." Similarly, Winston Churchill (1950, 347), another conservative former UK prime minister, called socialism "the gospel of envy." This critique is not only to be found in political rhetoric. The economist and philosopher, F. A. Hayek (1978, 93) claimed that demands for the redistribution of wealth "rest on the discontent that the success of some people often produces in those that are less successful, or to put it bluntly, on envy." In a recent book, Anne Hendershott (2020, chapter 6) describes egalitarian proposals to redistribute wealth and reorganize the economy as "the ultimate act of envious revenge." The basic idea behind these critiques is that those with fewer resources are claimed to simply be envious of those who have more and that envy, due to its destructive nature, is deemed to be an illegitimate basis of political critique (Morgan-Knapp 2014).

Our aim in this chapter is to investigate how egalitarians can respond to this critique. Some have sought to defend egalitarianism by defending the role of envy in politics (Bankovsky 2018; Frye 2016). Our aims are similar, though we take a different approach toward this goal. We argue that envy for the rich actually plays a crucial role in supporting unequal capitalist societies. We start by examining the criticism that political envy is irrational in more detail. We then draw on William Reddy's (2001) concept of *emotional regimes*, the set of norms governing emotional life that will underpin any stable political regime. We argue that envy for the wealthy plays a crucial role in the emotional regime of capitalist societies, as it encourages people to engage in conspicuous consumption and to compete with others for honor and esteem. Those who support capitalist societies with high levels of economic inequality, we argue, are therefore in no position to criticize egalitarians for promoting a politics of envy. We finish by drawing on Alison Jaggar's (1989) work to argue that economic envy should be seen as an "outlaw emotion" that can play an important role in helping people to recognize injustice.

POLITICAL ENVY AND IRRATIONALITY

Egalitarians are criticized for promoting the politics of envy, being motivated by envy for the rich themselves, and inciting such feelings in others. By itself, though, this doesn't provide any reason to reject egalitarianism. For this to count as a proper criticism of egalitarianism, and not simply an attempt to dismiss egalitarian concerns without properly considering them, some reason needs to be given for thinking that envy is an illegitimate source of political motivation.

The first step in this argument is to describe the nature of envy. Emotions typically involve distinctive evaluations, phenomenologies, eliciting conditions and action tendencies. Envy involves a judgement of positive value. When someone feels envy for another person, they view that person as having something or being someone of value. Importantly, it's also a comparative judgment, as it involves the judgement that the other person has something valuable that the envier lacks. As Aaron Ben-Ze'ev (2000, 282) explains, "The person we envy has personal attributes (such as beauty, patience, or intelligence), possessions (such as a car), or positions (being the boss) that we lack but desire." Envy is also an unpleasant emotion. As Sara Protasi (2016, 536) articulates the consensus position, envy is "an aversive reaction" to this perceived inferiority.[1] The unpleasantness of envy is emphasized in Aristotle's (*Rhetoric* II 10) definition of envy as "pain at the good fortune of others," and also Kant's (*Metaphysics of Morals* 6:459) claim that envy is "a propensity to view the well-being of others with distress."

Envy also seems to involve social comparison. As Jon Elster (1999, 70) puts the point, envy involves the thought that "it could have been me." Similarly, Aristotle (*Rhetoric* 1388a) claims that "we envy those who are near us in time, place, age, or reputation," and Aaron Ben-Ze'ev (1992, 556) claims that "in envy, our attention is focused on those perceived to be immediately above us." Studies conducted by Niels van de Ven and Marcel Zeelenberg (2015) found that envy was indeed more likely to be elicited when participants judged themselves to be closer to the position of the envied person. Finally, in order to eliminate the gap between themselves and the person they envy, envious people can try to bring themselves up to the same level as the latter. This form of envy is called "benign envy" (Van de Ven, Zeelenberg, and Pieters 2009). Alternatively, they may bring the envied person down to their level. This is called "malicious envy" (see also Protasi 2016). Clearly, conservative critics of egalitarianism take it to be motivated by malicious rather than benign envy.

The reason that critics of egalitarianism provide for dismissing envy for the rich as a legitimate source of political motivation is that such envy is an irrational emotion. Christopher Morgan-Knapp (2014) provides a detailed argument for this position. The starting point of his argument is the following characterization of envy:

> Envy's characteristic presentation is of the subject lacking some good that her rival possesses, of this difference between them being bad for the subject, of this difference reflecting poorly on the subject's worth, and of the difference being underserved. (2014, 118)

Morgan-Knapp then argues that no distribution of material possessions can possibly satisfy all of these features. There is no issue with satisfying the first two features. Some people may possess more of some good than others and this can be bad for the person who has less. As Morgan-Knapp (2014, 120) points out, this will be the case for positional goods and positionally distributed goods.

When goods are (physically or socially) scarce, the fact that others have more money than you can indeed come at your expense, so the difference in wealth can indeed be bad for you. However, Morgan-Knapp argues that someone's possession of a good cannot both be deserved and reflect badly upon those who lack it. If someone's possession of a good is undeserved then it does not reflect poorly on the worth of the envier. On the other hand, if the difference does reflect poorly on the subject's worth then this is because the difference is deserved in some way. This means that economic envy will always be misrepresenting the situation and so is never a fitting response to differences in material possessions. If we accept this argument then it seems reasonable to think that the envy people feel toward the rich should not influence political theorizing. Those who believe that egalitarianism is motivated by envy, then, have little reason to take this view seriously.

There are several ways egalitarians might respond to this argument. One is to argue that envy can be a morally justifiable emotion when it's a response to injustice (La Caze 2001). Miriam Bankovsky (2018), for example, argues that envy can be a perfectly rational response if the envier accurately judges that the envied person does not deserve their success but that success still reflects badly on the self-esteem of the envier. In societies where wealth is a major source of self-esteem and poverty a source of shame, it is not irrational to feel envy toward those whose privileged start in life makes it much easier for them to acquire wealth. This means that an envier could meet all of Morgan-Knapp's criteria for envy without misrepresenting the situation. Another way to respond is to argue that egalitarians are motivated by resentment rather than envy. For example, Robert Young (1987) has argued that the emotions underpinning egalitarian concerns are better characterized as resentment rather than envy.[2] This means that these concerns are not vulnerable to the criticisms made of the envious.

Our aim in the remainder of this chapter is to provide a different way for egalitarians to respond to this criticism. We grant, for the sake of the argument, that some egalitarians may be partially motivated by envy. However, we argue that those who endorse capitalist societies with high levels of economic inequality are in no position to criticize egalitarians for promoting a politics of envy. Our first step will be to explain the role that envy plays in the social structures that underpin capitalist society.

EMOTIONAL REGIMES

Envy, we argue, plays a key role in the emotional regime of capitalist societies. The term "emotional regime" was coined by William Reddy (2001). Reddy argued that emotions have a universally-applicable core biological foundation but are nevertheless culturally flexible. Key to his account is the concept of *emotives* (Reddy 2001, 105), which are expressions, usually verbal, of emotions, for example: "I am happy," "I am sad," and "I admire you." According to Reddy, however, these speech acts do not only describe the world (i.e., express a specific experience); they also change it (105). The way in which people label and express their emotions then plays an important role in determining their affective experiences. Importantly, the culture in which people live will have a major influence in shaping their emotional experiences and expressions.

This reveals the political significance emotions can have as they can and should be managed to ensure a stable political order. Reddy introduces the idea of an "emotional regime" to describe this normative process of shaping people's emotional experiences. He defines an emotional regime as: "The set of normative emotions and the official rituals, practices, and emotives that express and inculcate them; a necessary underpinning of any stable political regime" (Reddy 2001, 129). While these regimes may vary, some form of effective emotional regime are an essential component of any stable political regime.[3] A society, then, is not only governed by institutions and rules but also by an emotional regime—that is, by norms and expectations about the kind of emotions society can instill in its citizens and deem appropriate and inappropriate.

ENVY, ADMIRATION, AND THE EMOTIONAL REGIME OF CAPITALISM

Now that we know what an emotional regime is, we can ask what's involved in the emotional regimes that underpin capitalist societies. We follow the precedent of John Rawls (2001) in his definition of a capitalist society as one in which a minority of citizens control the major means of production in a way that allows them to monopolize the terms on which other people labor for a wage. As Luc Boltanski and Eve Chiapello (2005) point out, the emotional appeal of capitalism needs to be powerful enough to ensure the stability of capitalism in light of the inherently unattractive features of the system:

> In many respects, capitalism is an absurd system: in it, wage earners have lost ownership of the fruits of their labour and the possibility of pursuing a working life free of subordination. As for capitalists, they find themselves yoked to an interminable, insatiable process, which is utterly abstract and dissociated from the satisfaction of consumption needs, even of a luxury kind. For two such protagonists, integration into the capitalist process is singularly lacking in justifications. (7)

Material incentives and the threat of unemployment and poverty may be able to explain some form of engagement in the labor force. However, these incentives by themselves will not be able to generate the kind of active engagement and voluntary sacrifices that are increasingly required from all wage earners (8). Moreover, appeals to economic self-interest by themselves will unlikely be enough to generate sufficient active engagement from members, which is why emotional engagement is needed to stabilize the capitalist order.

While the emotional regimes of capitalist societies vary, it's possible to investigate some general features that tend to characterize the emotional life of such societies.[4] Eva Illouz (2007), for example, has analyzed the way in which capitalism is increasingly justified in emotional terms while at the same time colonizing and marketizing emotional life. Similarly, Martijn Konings (2015) has investigated how the ideals of self-sufficiency and personal responsibility combined with a scorn toward dependency are at the core of the emotional logic of capitalist societies. Our aim is not to contradict either of these compelling analyses, or to offer a complete analysis of the emotional regime of capitalism.[5] Instead, we focus on one part: the mandated feeling rules towards the wealthy. Drawing on Adam Smith and Thorsten Veblen's accounts of the important role that emulation for the rich plays in capitalist societies, we argue that envy, alongside admiration, for the rich plays an active role in supporting and stabilizing capitalist societies.

In his *The Theory of the Moral Sentiments* (hereafter *TMS*, 1759), Smith outlines a view of morality based on sympathy. According to Smith, we have a natural tendency to sympathize with other people's emotions. This sympathy is based on imagining what we would feel if we were in another person's situation and approving the other agent's feelings as appropriate for the situation. Sympathy also plays an important role in thinking about how we should feel in a particular situation, as we have a desire to be approved of by others. The approval by others provides us with an incentive to act or feel in specific ways. However, Smith claims that we do not only desire to be approved of by other people, but also to be *worthy* of that approval (*TMS* III).

Smith claims that we find it easier to sympathize with those experiencing joy than with those experiencing sorrow, because it's pleasant to share in another's happiness, whereas sharing in another's pain is unpleasant (*TMS* I.iii.1.5). This tendency leads the rich to flaunt their wealth, as it will lead others to pay attention to them and admire them:

> The rich man glories in his riches, because he feels that they naturally draw upon him the attention of the world, and that mankind are disposed to go along with him in all those agreeable emotions with which the advantages of his situation so readily inspire in him. (*TMS* I.iii.2.1)

Meanwhile, the poor hide their poverty because it will not receive the sympathetic attention of other people. This results in a distorted moral outlook.

First, admiration for the rich leads those with fewer resources to feel deference toward those with more (*TMS* I.iii.2.3) and to develop a desire to emulate the rich (*TMS* I.iii.3.7). This deference allows the tastes of the rich to determine what is fashionable and the behavior of the rich to determine the behavior people seek to emulate, even when this behavior is immoral or foolish. To make matters worse, the rich need not worry about acting virtuously in order to secure the admiration of others, as their wealth will secure it for them. The ability of the rich to secure admiration without virtue encourages others to try to become wealthy as well: if successful, they too should no longer worry about acting decently in order to receive the admiration of others (*TMS* I.iii.3.8). This encourages us to emulate immoral people. It's also harmful for our well-being, as it encourages people to spend their lives laboring hard to achieve material possessions that do little to increase their happiness. However, it's also an important driver of the economy: "It is this deception which rouses and keeps in continual motion the industry of mankind" (*TMS* IV.1.10).[6]

Importantly for our purposes, the inequalities in wealth that characterize capitalist societies trigger widespread admiration for the rich, which in turn encourages people to defer to them, emulate them, and strive to attain a similar status. As capitalist societies run on the promise of increasing material wealth for all parties involved, the hope of becoming richer is a crucial motivator for people to engage in the labor market. Admiration for the rich thus plays a key role in ensuring its stability.

Like Smith, Thorstein Veblen (1899) thought that the rich become objects of emulation. However, Veblen provides a wider account of the emotional reactions that people may be seeking to provoke through their wealth: not just admiration but also envy. According to Veblen, a key motivation driving people to acquire wealth is that "wealth confers honor" (1899, 35). In capitalist societies, social comparisons will be based on private property, as these become the signs that one has power, authority, and superior status over others. Eventually wealth transforms into becoming worthy of esteem for its own sake and not just as a sign of power. This leads, according to Veblen (1899, 39) to "pecuniary emulation": the "desire to excel in pecuniary standing and so gain the esteem and envy of one's fellowman." In other words, people attempt to equal or surpass the wealth of others in order to be deemed worthy of honor, admiration, or envy. Of course, it's not enough for the rich to simply possess more wealth than others do, they must also display it. They do so by engaging in conspicuous consumption, the buying of goods and services with the aim of displaying one's wealth.[7] Conspicuous consumption shows others that they are fitting targets of esteem and envy. To signal their superiority, the rich display their wealth through expensive status symbols such as high-priced suits, cars, and houses, competing between themselves for their own turn in the limelight in the economy of attention and celebrity.

According to both Smith and Veblen, the envy and admiration people feel toward the rich is an unfortunate result of the way in which people seek esteem in capitalist societies. To stress that they are not merely incidental features but rather key components of the emotional regimes of capitalist societies, it's important to note how these emotional responses are actively encouraged by media representations of wealth. As Diana Kendall explains in her book *Framing Class: Media Representations of Wealth and Poverty in America*, the American media typically encourages a desire to emulate the rich by encouraging people to identify with them:

In a mass-mediated culture such as ours, the media do not simply mirror society; rather, they help to shape it and to create cultural perceptions. The blurring between what is real and what is not encourages people to emulate the upper classes and shun the working class and the poor. Television shows, magazines, and newspapers sell the idea that the only way to get ahead is to identify with the rich and powerful and to live vicariously through them. From sitcoms to reality shows, the media encourage ordinary people to believe that they may rise to fame and fortune; they too can be the next winner of the lottery of *American Idol*. (2011, 211)

Kendall explains various ways in which the framing of class in the media encourages a desire to emulate the rich. One is *consensus framing*, which encourages people to see the wealthy as like everyone else by downplaying or obscuring differences in wealth between different social classes (Kendall 2011, 29–34). Another is *emulation framing*, which focuses on the achievable nature of the wealthy's achievements by emphasizing humble origins and encouraging others to aspire to the same (39–42). Finally, there is *price tag framing*, which focuses on the cost of the items bought by the wealthy (42–49) and encourages a view "according to which a person's worth is measured by what he or she owns" (212). All these presentations of wealth encourage, in different ways, people to view the pursuit of wealth as valuable and worthwhile.

We can see how these media frames encourage envy by returning to our account of the nature of envy. Price tag framing encourages viewers to value the luxury items possessed by the wealthy.[8] Emulation framing encourages people to close the gap between themselves and the wealthy by acquiring the same goods and achieving the same successes. Consensus framing encourages people to believe that the rich are counterfactually close to them and that they too could achieve this wealth. This is important because the thought that "it could have been me" is one of the key eliciting conditions for envy (van de Ven and Zeelenberg 2015). In their framing of wealth, the media help create, shape, maintain, and reinforce the desire to emulate the rich. As Gregory Mantsios (2003, 518) points out, this aligns with the ideological outlook of those who run the media and entertainment industry: "The presentation of the rich as worthy of emulation is simply a reflection of the (upper) class outlook of those with prominent roles in the media."

As we can see, the envy and admiration that is felt toward the rich is not simply the result of a natural tendency, as Smith claims. While such a natural tendency probably exists, these emotional reactions are likely to be particularly strong and geared toward a particular group, namely the rich, in capitalist societies. Admiration and envy for the rich then form a key part of the emotional regime of such societies. The ideology of consumerism encourages people to value material possessions, which in turn encourages people to desire to emulate the wealthy and to defer to them. This helps to maintain the power of the wealthy and helps to ensure the stability of the capitalist system.[9]

IMPLICATIONS FOR POLITICAL ENVY

Having explained the role of envy for the rich in the emotional regime of capitalist societies, we can now respond to those who endorse capitalism and dismiss egalitarianism as a politics of envy. Our main claim here is that these authors are *themselves* endorsing a politics of envy, as they are supporting a political and economic system in which the promotion of envy for the rich is integral to its stability and continued existence. As such, they are in no position to criticize egalitarians for endorsing a politics of envy, as envy also has a key role to play in the very system they are promoting.

In response, it might be objected that there is an important difference between the envy for the rich that egalitarians are accused of and the kind of envy for the rich promoted under capitalism. As we have already pointed out, philosophers and psychologists distinguish between benign envy, which aims at improving the position of the envier, and malicious envy, which aims at bringing the envied person down to the same level as the envier. The envy for the rich that features in the emotional regime of capitalism arguably involves a desire to become more like the person being envied. It's not a desire to bring the envied person down to the same position as the envier. Those wishing to defend capitalism, then, may point out that the benign form of envy for the rich that features in capitalism's emotional regime is not the same as the destructive form of malicious envy that they claim is motivating egalitarians.

This distinction matters because benign envy is argued to be a morally permissible and perhaps even virtuous emotion (Protasi 2016, 2021, chapter 3), while malicious envy is generally viewed as a morally bad emotion. Sara Protasi (2021, 80), for example, argues that those who experience certain forms of benign envy provide a model for how to engage in fair competition with others and will be motivated to improve both themselves and society as a whole. Malicious envy, on the other hand, is "radically vicious" as it is bad both for the envier and for others (Protasi 2021, 93). The envy endorsed by defenders of capitalism, then, would be less morally objectionable (and may even be morally desirable in itself) than the envy they claim motivates egalitarians.

One reply here is that, however plausible it may be, this distinction still involves conceding that those who endorse free-market capitalism are also engaging in the politics of envy. This seems to take away much of the force from the criticism of egalitarians. "You are engaging in the politics of envy" on closer inspection is revealed to include the caveat "and so are we but in a different way." This undermines some of the rhetorical strength of the conservative's dismissal of egalitarianism.

The more important point, though, is that this reveals the true nature of the criticism, namely that egalitarians feel the wrong kind of envy toward the rich. Instead of feeling malicious envy, they should be feeling benign envy toward the rich. Putting the criticism in these terms reveals that it's functioning to enforce the emotional regime of capitalism. This emotional regime mandates that the rich should be admired, envied benignly, and emulated. The concerns of egalitarian critics are dismissed precisely because they don't comply with these feeling rules.

The significance of this point becomes clear when we consider the different eliciting conditions of benign and malicious envy. Several psychological studies have found that malicious envy is more likely to occur than benign envy when the envier judges that the envied person's success is undeserved (Lange and Crusius 2015; Lange et al. 2016; Van de Ven et al. 2012; Van de Ven 2016).[10] This suggests a connection between the thesis that benign envy is key to capitalism and the controversial thesis that market entitlements are deserved. A person may be entitled to a substantial economic reward for allowing a company to take a short cut over a piece of land that was, hitherto, being put to no productive use. As Amartya Sen points out, it's difficult to see how merely permitting the use of one's property is a form of productive contribution meriting economic reward (Sen 1985, 15–17) The thesis that benign envy is a key motivation in capitalist society, then, cannot be detached from the thesis that such societies are meritocratic. The rich, so the capitalist emotional regime tells us, should be admired and emulated because they deserve to be rich. This is controversial because, as the example shows, merits and market entitlements can easily come apart. The same applies to the rich who acquire their wealth through rent-seeking: as this wealth is undeserved, malicious instead of benign envy might be more appropriate here.[11] This is an echo of Smith's claim that the idea of markets as rewarding the bourgeois virtues is a fiction. To this, Amartya Sen adds that "it might . . . be seen as a 'convenient fiction,' but that fiction is a whole lot more convenient for some than for others" (1985, 16). This puts the envy critique in an even clearer light. Egalitarians are likely to view the wealth of the rich as undeserved and may, as a result, feel malicious envy. Dismissing these concerns as the politics of envy is simply a convenient way to avoid engaging with the claim that this wealth may not be deserved.[12] The conservative dismissal of malicious envy is a way of changing the subject from whether or not the rich deserve the wealth to the emotional states of those claiming they do not.[13]

Alison Jaggar's concept of "outlaw emotions" can help us understand the nature of this move. Outlaw emotions are those that contravene a society's emotional rules (Jaggar 1989, 166). For example, in a society that demands gratitude from welfare recipients, some people may instead feel resentment when they receive their welfare payment. In the same way, feelings of malicious envy toward the rich can be viewed as an outlaw emotion that is prohibited by the emotional regime underpinning capitalist societies in which admiration and benign envy toward the rich are mandated. Outlaw emotions are more likely to be experienced by those in subordinate positions who do not benefit from the existing social structures. While they are often confusing and disorienting, Jaggar (1989, 167) argues that these emotions can also be epistemically valuable, as they enable and motivate new ways of seeing the world. The clash between the resentment felt by the welfare recipient and the gratitude they are supposed to feel can be the first step toward taking a critical stance to the dominant societal values and to a welfare system that stigmatizes recipients. Similarly, the clash between feeling malicious envy toward the rich and the socially prescribed feelings of admiration and benign envy can prompt an investigation into the causes of economic inequality and capitalist exploitation.[14] This doesn't mean that we should always encourage such feelings or accept them uncritically. Rather, we should attend to outlaw emotions carefully and seriously, instead of dismissing, suppressing, or condemning them from the start (Jaggar 1989, 169). We should not, then, be too quick to dismiss feelings of malicious envy toward the rich.

Attending to the outlaw emotion of malicious envy may lead us to question the extent to which the rich really are deserving of our admiration and benign envy. Sure, the rags to riches entrepreneur who achieves wealth through the exercise of qualities of character, from ingenuity to hard work and determination, in the overcoming of obstacles may well be worthy of admiration or benign envy. But in other cases, admiring the rich as wealth creators, risk takers, and suppliers of enterprise to the productive process is simply mistaken, as it misrepresents the way in which contemporary political institutions favor not the heroic figure of the entrepreneur but rather the "insider" figure of the rent seeker. Of course, much more can and should be said about the many mechanisms that cause wealth concentration at the top and growing economic inequalities without those being deserved, here. The short version, however, is that we live under "rentier capitalism" (Christophers 2019), which is marked by a hugely "unfair distribution of the benefits and costs of economic production" (Scanlon 2018, 152). The rent seeking that many of the rich are engaged in turns economic competition from win-win, to win-lose, as the rent seeker gains at the expense of her fellow citizens via her insider status in economic institutions.

While many wealthy people in capitalist societies have strong work ethics, which undoubtedly informs their self-proclaimed ethos of meritocracy, that does not come close to justifying the gaps. Many people, rich and poor alike, work very long hours: the differentiating factor is the structure of our economic institutions that sees, for example, American CEOs paid more than their median worker by a factor of one thousand (Leder 2021). The idea that the wealthy are worthy targets of admiration and benign envy and that the rest should therefore try to emulate them assumes a highly idealized—and indeed mostly fictional—view of how wealth accumulation works. While benign envy for the rich may be unobjectionable in those cases where it is fitting, we are skeptical that this applies for most of the rich in our own highly unequal capitalist societies.

When the personal qualities of the rich are not admirable qualities, then malicious envy might well be an appropriate response. If the superior status of the rich has been derived from exploiting an unfair institutional set up, such that they enjoy goods that others would have received under an alternative, just institutional set-up, then an attitude of malicious envy is appropriate. If restitution or redress is unavailable, we see no objection to seeing the unfair gains of the rent seeker confiscated even if they cannot be redistributed. The malicious envy we feel toward the rent seekers enables us to view leveling down as a justifiable option in this case.

Does this mean that egalitarians ought to always express their malicious envy and perhaps even promote it in others? Not necessarily. As Amia Srinivasan (2018) has argued, victims of oppression often find themselves in situations where they must choose between a fitting emotional response to injustice and the emotional response that best advances their cause.[15] For example, victims of racism may feel justified anger (or outrage) in response to their oppression, but expressing this anger in public discussions could make others feel less sympathetic to their situation. Here, victims of racism face an *affective injustice* of having to manage the psychological conflict between a legitimate emotional response and the emotional response that would best advance their cause. Malicious envy may well be a fitting but counterproductive response to the rent-seeking rich that is unlikely to advance the egalitarian cause. If this is correct, egalitarians are also faced with the affective injustice of having to manage the conflict generated by their apt but counterproductive malicious envy.

That said, one can also argue the egalitarian cause would indeed be advanced by promoting malicious envy. According to contemporary neo-Machiavellians, our politics needs to be less civil, more agonistic, and more open to the channeling of emotions such as envy, rancor, outrage, and anger against socioeconomic elites (Green 2016; McCormick 2011). A conception of political civility that dismisses such outlaw emotions can be interpreted as obstructing the needed development of fairer political and economic institutions. Outlaw emotions such as malicious envy can trigger skepticism as to whether the wealthy really deserve their status as role models, innovators, and cultural legislators. It is in this context that the policing of emotions that occurs when legitimizing benign envy and dismissing malicious envy is not a neutral activity. Dismissing, discrediting, or banishing envy, animosity, and rancor from politics serves to reinforce an unfair institutional structure that systematically advantages those who can extract rents (insiders) at the cost of those are unable to do so (outsiders).

CONCLUSION

We have investigated how egalitarians should respond to the criticism that they are engaged in a destructive and irrational politics of envy. We argued that inducing envy for the rich plays a key role in the emotional regime underpinning and stabilizing capitalist societies. This means that those who endorse capitalism are endorsing a political and economic system in which the promotion of envy for the rich is integral to the stability of the system. They are, then, are in no position to criticize egalitarians for endorsing a politics of envy. Critics of egalitarianism can respond by pointing to an important difference between the kinds of envy involved here. While capitalist societies promote benign envy for the rich, egalitarians are arguably motivated by malicious envy.

However, we argued that this response helps to reveal the true nature of this criticism of egalitarians. This criticism serves to enforce the emotional regime underpinning capitalist society by dismissing the concerns of those who violate its feeling rules. Moreover, we argued that malicious envy for the rich is aptly understood as an outlaw emotion in capitalist societies. Given the potential for outlaw emotions to motivate new investigations and enable new ways of perceiving the world, we should attend carefully to such feelings rather than dismissing them. Like anger and outrage, malicious envy can trigger critical investigations of how capitalist institutions unfairly favor rent seekers and of the extent to which the rich really are really deserving of our admiration after all.[16]

NOTES

1. This condition is also endorsed by Bankovsky (2018), Morgan-Knapp (2014), and Rawls (1971, 535).

2. For further discussion see Protasi (2021, 127).

3. See Hochschild's (1983) work on feeling rules, Ahmed's (2004) work on the way emotions function as cultural practices, and Jaggar's (1989) work on emotional hegemony, which we discuss in the fourth section.

4. The emotional regime of a particular society will also change over time. See Boltanksi and Chiapello's (2005) account of how the spirit of capitalism has adapted in response to anti-capitalist critiques.

5. We provide a more complete analysis in Thomas, Archer, and Engelen (forthcoming). Here we discuss shame for the arguably deserved poor, status anxiety among those competing for scarce status goods and envy, and admiration for the rich.

6. The claim that the pursuit of wealth is a private vice that brings collective benefits was outlined by Bernard Mandeville ([1732] 1989), first published in 1714, more than forty years before Smith's *Theory of the Moral Sentiments*.

7. For a detailed discussion of the problems caused by conspicuous consumption, see Frank (2000).

8. For more on these issues, see the contributions in this volume from Miriam Bankovsky ("The Fact of Envy: Trends in the History of Modern Economics," chapter 9) and Niels van de Ven ("The Envious Consumer," chapter 12).

9. Though, this may not promote the well-being of the rich. We explore this issue in Thomas, Archer, and Engelen (forthcoming).

10. Some studies also found that benign envy is more likely to be elicited when the envier judges the envied person's success to be deserved (van de Ven et al 2012; van de Ven 2016), though other studies didn't find this (Lange and Crusius 2015; Lange et al. 2016). For further discussion, see Protasi (2021, 36–37).

11. Technically economic rent is income derivable merely from owning an asset and controlling the permissions that this grounds (such as giving a person a right of way over one's own land). As Bill Edmundson explains: "To say that a doctor has a basic right to own a stethoscope is to obscure what is important, namely, the excellence that a competent doctor manifests in skillfully making use of [it]. . . . The right to profit from the sale or lease of medical instruments is another matter. In this sense of ownership, 'ownership is not a productive activity' as Cambridge economist Joan Robinson (1966) put it. Rawls coined the term 'pure ownership' to capture the idea" (Edmundson 2017, 26–27). The interpolated references are to Robinson (1966, 18) and Rawls (2007, 350). (Robinson actually says that "*owning* capital is not a productive activity.")

12. An alternative way to understand how emotional norms are violated here is that egalitarians feel the moral emotion of resentment, which is wrongly categorized as malicious envy. For a related discussion, see Protasi (2021, chapter 5). Alternatively, we might think that the emotion mischaracterized as envy is disgust. Thanks to Sara Protasi and Imke von Maur for suggesting these possibilities.

13. Compare this with Marilyn Frye's (1983, 84) claim that men often respond to women's anger by treating it as revealing something about the nature of women's psychology rather than something about the world. Similarly, Audre Lorde's (1984, 118) discussion of the demand that victims of racism get rid of their anger before discussing racism in feminist settings. According to Shiloh Whitney (2018, 497), when such dismissals are widespread across society, they constitute a form of affective injustice that she calls *affective marginalization*. When being thus deprived of uptake, people cannot emotionally influence others. Note, though, that according to

our interpretation of the phenomenon, the conservative dismissal of egalitarianism acknowledges egalitarian envy, but denies its fittingness or moral appropriateness.

14. Compare with Bankovsky's (2018) claim that envy can be a rational response when the envied person doesn't deserve their success but that success still reflects badly on the self-esteem of the envier, and Harrison Frye's (2016, 522–23) claim that envy for the rich can play a useful role in triggering reflection on one's social situation, which may raise awareness of injustice.

15. For further discussion of this point, see Archer and Mills (2019).

16. Thanks to participants in the Moral Psychology of Envy Workshop and the seventh European-American Online Workshop in Philosophy of Emotion for helpful discussion of these ideas. Special thanks to Sara Protasi for incredibly helpful feedback and suggestions. This publication was made possible through the support of a grant from The John Templeton Foundation. The opinions expressed in this publication are those of the authors and do not necessarily reflect the views of The John Templeton Foundation.

REFERENCES

Ahmed, Sara. 2004. *The Cultural Politics of Emotion*. Edinburgh: Edinburgh University Press.

Archer, Alfred, and Georgina Mills. 2019. "Anger, Affective Injustice, and Emotion Regulation." *Philosophical Topics* 47 (2): 75–94.

Bankovsky, Miriam. 2018. "Excusing Economic Envy: On Injustice and Impotence." *Journal of Applied Philosophy* 35 (2): 257–79.

Ben-Ze'ev, Aaron. 2000. *The Subtlety of Emotions*. Cambridge MA: MIT Press.

Boltanski, Luc, and Eve Chiapello. 2005. *The New Spirit of Capitalism*. Translated by Gregory Elliott. London: Verso.

Christophers, Brett. 2019. *Rentier Capitalism: Who Owns the Economy and Who Pays for It?* London: Verso.

Churchill, Winston. 1950. *Europe Unite Speeches 1947 & 1948*. London: Cassell.

Edmundson, William A. 2017. *John Rawls: Reticent Socialist*. Cambridge: Cambridge University Press.

Frank, Robert. H. 2000. *Luxury fever: Money and Happiness in an Era of Excess*. Princeton NJ: Princeton University Press.

Frye, Marylin. 1983. *The Politics of Reality: Essays in Feminist Theory*. Berkeley CA: Crossing Press.

Frye, Harrison. P. 2016. "The Relation of Envy to Distributive Justice." *Social Theory and Practice* 42 (3): 501–24.

Green, Jeffrey E. 2016. *The Shadow of Unfairness: A Plebeian Theory of Liberal Democracy*. Oxford: Oxford University Press.

Hayek, Friedrich H. 1978. *The Constitution of Liberty*. Chicago: University of Chicago Press.

Hendershott, Anne. 2020. *The Politics of Envy*. Manchester, NH: Crisis Publications.

Hochschild, Arlie R. 1983. *The Managed Heart*. Berkeley CA: University of California Press.
Illouz, Eva. 2007. *Cold Intimacies: The Making of Emotional Capitalism*. Polity.
Jaggar, Alison M. 1989. "Love and Knowledge: Emotion in Feminist Epistemology." *Inquiry* 32 (2): 151–76.
Kandall, Diana E. 2011. *Framing Class: Media Representations of Wealth and Poverty in America*. London: Rowman & Littlefield.
Konings, Martijn. 2015. *The Emotional Logic of Capitalism: What Progressives Have Missed*. Palo Alto, CA: Stanford University Press.
La Caze, Marguerite. 2001. "Envy and Resentment." *Philosophical Explorations* 4 (1): 31–45.
Lange, Jens, and Jan Crusius. 2015. "Dispositional Envy Revisited: Unravelling the Motivational Dynamics of Benign and Malicious Envy." *Personality and Social Psychology Bulletin* 41 (2): 284–94.
Lange, Jens, Jan Crusius and Birk Hagemeyer. 2016. "The Evil Queen's Dilemma: Linking Narcissistic Admiration and Rivalry to Benign and Malicious Envy." *European Journal of Personality* 30 (2): 168–88
Leder, Michelle. 2021. "Is a CEO Worth 1000 Times the Average Worker?" *Bloomberg.com*, June 1, 2021. https://www.bloomberg.com/opinion/articles/2021-06-01/is-a-ceo-worth-1-000-times-the-median-worker.
Lorde, Audre. (1984) 2019. *Sister Outsider* London: Penguin.
Mandeville, Bernard. (1732) 1988. *The Fable of The Bees, or, Private Vices, Publick Benefits*, edited by F. B. Kaye, 2 vols., Indianapolis: Liberty Fund.
Mantsios, Gregory. 2003. "Media Magic: Making Class Invisible." In *Privilege: A Reader*, edited by Michael S. Kimmel and Abby L. Ferber, 99–109. Boulder CO: Westview.
McCormick, John. 2011. *Machiavellian Democracy*. Cambridge: Cambridge University Press
Morgan☐Knapp, Cristopher. 2014. "Economic envy." *Journal of Applied Philosophy* 31 (2): 113–26.
Protasi, Sara. 2016. "Varieties of Envy." *Philosophical Psychology* 29 (4): 535–49.
———. 2019. "Happy Self-Surrender and Unhappy Self-Assertion." In *The Moral Psychology of Admiration*, edited by Alfred Archer and Andre Grahle, 45–60. London: Rowman & Littlefield.
———. 2021. *The Philosophy of Envy*. New York: Cambridge University Press.
Rawls, John. 1971. *A Theory of Justice*. Cambridge MA: The Belknap Press of Harvard University Press.
———. 2001. *Justice as Fairness: A Restatement*. Edited by John Kelly. Cambridge MA: Harvard University Press.
———. 2008. *Lectures on the History of Political Philosophy*. Edited by Barbara Herman. Cambridge MA: Harvard University Press.
Reddy, William M. 2001. *The Navigation of Feeling: A Framework for the History of Emotions*. Cambridge: Cambridge University Press.
Robinson, Jon. 1966. *An Essay on Marxian Economics*. Basingstoke: Macmillan.

Scanlon, Timothy M. 2018. *Why Does Inequality Matter?* Oxford: Oxford University Press.
Sen, Amartya. 1985. "The Moral Standing of the Market." *Social Philosophy and Policy* 2 (2): 1–19.
Srinivasan, Amia. 2018. "The Aptness of Anger." *Journal of Political Philosophy* 26 (2): 123–44.
Smith, Adam. (1759) 2007. *The Theory of Moral Sentiments*. Cosimo.
Thatcher, Margaret. 1974. "Britain Can Win." *The News of the World*, September 22, 1974. https://www.margaretthatcher.org/document/102398.
Thomas, Alan, Alfred Archer, and Bart Engelen. Forthcoming. *Extravagance and Misery: The Emotional Regime of Market Societies*.
van de Ven, Niels. 2016. "Envy and its Consequences: Why It Is Useful to Distinguish Between Benign and Malicious Envy." *Social and Personality Psychology Compas* 10 (6): 337–49
———. 2017. "Envy and Admiration: Emotion and Motivation Following Upward Social Comparison." *Emotion and Cognition* 31 (1): 193–200.
van de Ven, Niels, and Marcel Zeelenberg. 2015. "On the Counterfactual Nature of Envy: "It Could Have Been Me." *Cognition and Emotion* 29 (6): 954–71.
van de Ven, N., Marcel Zeelenberg, and Rik Pieters. 2009. "Leveling Up and Down: The Experiences of Benign and Malicious Envy." *Emotion* 9 (3): 419–29.
———. 2012. "Appraisal Patterns of Envy and Related Emotions." *Motivation and Emotion* 36 (2): 195–204.
Whitney, Shiloh. 2018. "Affective Intentionality and Affective Injustice: Merleau-Ponty and Fanon on the Body Schema as a Theory of Affect." *Southern Journal of Philosophy* 56 (4): 488–515.
Young, Robert. 1987. "Egalitarianism and Envy." *Philosophical Studies* 52 (2): 261–76

Chapter 11

To Envy an Algorithm

Alison Duncan Kerr

In March 2016, a computer program, AlphaGo, beat professional Go player, Lee Sedol. This was the first tournament where a computer beat a 9-dan professional, which is the highest rating possible. Could Sedol have felt a fitting bout of envy at AlphaGo? Various constraints must be met for a bout of envy to be fitting. In particular, one's envy is commonly thought to be fitting roughly when one's rival has some good, one lacks that good, and the difference is genuinely bad for the envier. This chapter aims to consider the potential emotional relations between a computer and a person. I argue that people can fittingly envy algorithms.

One of the biggest concerns for artificial intelligence (AI) is the interaction between humans and artificially intelligent agents. There is no evolutionary precedent that dictates how these interactions ought to take place or how best to understand these interactions. We are still learning as a species how to *socially* interact with AI. Within this context, it is natural to emphasize the elements of human experience, like emotions, that are usually only directed at other humans. Emotions are commonly thought of as a uniquely human phenomenon—though there is strong evidence that other animals experience emotions as well (Paul and Mendl 2018). In particular, social emotions (e.g., envy, jealousy, guilt, embarrassment) are especially difficult to understand in the context of interactions with AI agents.

This chapter focuses on one aspect of this challenge: the propriety of feeling envy toward an algorithm, a computer programme, a machine, or a robot. By "propriety" I mean whether it can be *fitting* to feel envy toward an AI agent. In what follows, I will focus on the AI agent AlphaGo, as a case study where it might appear reasonable for one to feel envious of AI.

A CASE STUDY: ALPHAGO

Artificial intelligence is rapidly and steadily advancing, but not all terminology has been yet consistently adopted amongst AI scholars often due to various specializations within AI (Eaton et al. 2015). Leading AI scholar, Alison Adams, offers an overview, explaining that AI:

> refers to a class of computer systems designed to model some aspect of human intelligence, whether it be learning (machine learning), moving around and interacting in the world (robotics and vision), reasoning towards a solution to a problem (search strategies), using natural language, modelling intelligence according to neural models (neural networks or connectionism) or having expert knowledge of some subject (expert of knowledge-based systems). (1998, 1)

It seems then, that AI now has an impact on nearly every aspect of our lives through, for example, digital assistants (e.g., Siri and Alexa), search engines (e.g., Baidu, DuckDuckGo, Gigablast, and Google), games (e.g., Go and chess), autonomous vehicles (e.g., self-driving cars and drones), military applications (e.g., autonomous weapon, drones, and threat identification), mass surveillance (e.g., facial recognition), robots (factory, sex, and pet robots), and health care (e.g., diagnosis, identifying treatments, surgery, and dosages). A large percentage of the world population owns a smart phone that can carry out many of these activities. We use AI to improve our knowledge, move about the world, manufacture our goods, assist with overall health, keep us safe, and for mere enjoyment. Despite often being unnoticed, AI is ubiquitous and deeply embedded in human reality.

All processing by computers, machine learning, and AI employs algorithms. An algorithm is simply a finite step-by-step procedure that can be followed mechanically without any ingenuity (Dean 2016). Games are considered an ideal venue for assessing the strength, responsiveness, and performance of AI algorithms. The AI required for chess became particularly well known with Deep Blue. IBM's AI expert, Murray Campbell explains, "[Chess is] known as a game that requires strategy, foresight, logic—all sorts of qualities that make up human intelligence. So, it makes sense to use chess as a measuring stick for the development of artificial intelligence" (Greenemeier 2017). In 1997, Deep Blue was the first AI to defeat a reigning world champion—beating Garry Kasparov was a momentous event for AI.

Nonetheless, there is some controversy about what counts as AI within the gaming world, with a focus being on not merely being composed of predetermined inputs but rather being composed of machine learning intelligence—the ability to continue to develop. Go has long been considered a difficult challenge in the field of AI and is considerably more difficult to solve than chess.

In 1965, British mathematician I. J. Good considered what it would be like to have a computer play Go. He wrote, "Go on a computer?—In order to programme a computer to play a reasonable game of Go—rather than merely a legal game—it is necessary to formalise the principles of good strategy, or to design a learning programme. The principles are more qualitative and mysterious than in chess, and depend more on judgment. So I think it will be even more difficult to programme a computer to play a reasonable game of Go than of chess" (Good 1965). The game Go was deemed as requiring a rigorous, highly advanced machine learning AI. Like chess, Go is a strategy, two-person board game. It is perhaps the world's oldest continuously played game—it "is thought to have originated in China some 4,000 years ago" (*Britannica* 2021). Go is

> of East Asian origin, it is popular in China, Korean, and especially Japan, the country with which is most closely identified.... Traditionally, go is played with 181 black and 180 white go-ishi (flat, round pieces called stones) on a square wooden board (goban) checkered by 19 vertical lines and 19 horizontal lines to form 361 intersections.... Each player in turn ... tr[ies] to conquer territory by completely enclosing vacant points with boundaries made of their own stones. A player's final score is his number of walled-in points less the number of his stones lost by capture. Go demands great skill, strategy, and subtlety and is capable of infinite variety, yet the rules and pieces are so simple that children can play. (*Britannica* 2021)

Go has an official ranking with about one thousand professional Go players in China, Japan, Korea, and Taiwan. Professional players range between 1-dan and 9-dan, the very best being 9-dan. Given the necessity of creativity and skill, and the extensive different possible moves and outcomes, the reality of a meaningful virtual opponent seemed far off—Go was the holy grail of AI.

DeepMind Technologies is a British company that focuses on AI and created the computer programme AlphaGo. In March 2016, when AlphaGo beat world champion Lee Sedol, there was world-wide publicity of the tournament and a movie covering the momentous occasion (AlphaGo 2017). Sedol entered the tournament thinking he would win. He said, "I have heard that Google DeepMind's AI is surprisingly strong and getting stronger, but I am confident that I can win at least this time" (Rundle 2016).

The tournament consisted of five matches. When Sedol lost the first match, he explained how surprised he was but that the loss would not affect his play for the following match. When Sedol lost the second match he said, "Yesterday, I was surprised, but today, I am quite speechless." When Sedol lost the third match, he said, "I want to apologize for being so powerless. I've never felt this much pressure, this much weight." When he won the fourth match, he said, "I couldn't be any happier! The victory is so valuable that I wouldn't exchange it for anything in the world." Sedol lost the final match, with an overall score of four to one. Later, in 2019, after widespread adoption of AI into Go games (e.g., AlphaGo and now its predecessors) and the evident proficiency of AI, Sedol declared that since AI is an entity that can no longer be defeated, he will retire from professional Go play.

THE TRADITIONAL ASSESSMENTS OF ENVY

Presumably, both Kasparov and Sedol felt a range of emotions after their losses. They likely felt emotions like anger, disbelief, embarrassment, grief, heartbreak, and sadness. Perhaps they each felt envy for the AI. Nonetheless, what precise emotions were felt by Kasparov or Sedol is not the topic here. Instead, it is relevant to consider the varieties of emotions that are commonly felt in intense competition with a worthy rival and how best to understand them—for example, envy is understood as a "competitive emotion" by the Stoics (Konstan 2006). One commonly envies those who would be suitable as a competitor. On this, Aristotle explains,

> We compete with those who follow the same ends as ourselves: we compete with our rivals in sport or in love, and generally with those who are after the same things; and it is therefore these whom we are bound to envy beyond all others. Hence the saying: Potter against potter. We also envy those whose possession of or success in a thing is a reproach for us: these are our neighbors and equals. ([350 BCE] 1941, 1388a).

When is envy appropriate? Emotion theorists commonly assess emotions along three dimensions. While the terminology sometimes differs, the *traditional assessments* are: fit, warrant, and benefit. Consider each in turn.

An emotion is *fitting* in a certain situation if and only if the emotion corresponds to the relevant features of the agent's situation.[1] A fitting emotion is roughly analogous to a true belief in the sense that the emotion has gotten the situation correct.[2] For example, when one feels fear, one's fear is fitting when one is, indeed, in danger. Similarly, anger is fitting when one has been wronged.

An emotion is *warranted* in a certain situation if and only if the person feeling the emotion has sufficient evidence for the fittingness of the emotion in the situation.[3] When a wave slams one's kayak into a rock and one then sees water pouring into the kayak through the new hole, one has good evidence of impending danger. One's fear in this situation is warranted.

There are multiple possible combinations of fit and warrant. In the case of the broken kayak, one's fear would be both warranted and fitting. In contrast, imagine one's friends aim to tease by staging a fake, but highly compelling, kayak leak following a fake kayak collision. Though one is not in genuine danger (i.e., fear is unfitting), still one's fear in face of such strongly persuasive evidence is warranted.

Third, an emotion is beneficial if and only if the emotion contributes to the agent's well-being.[4] Imagine one feels fear when seeing a leak in their kayak causing them to grab their things and leap out before it sinks. Perhaps if the kayaker had not felt fear, they would not have acted so fast to save their items before fleeing In this scenario, one's fear (both fitting and warranted) of the leaking kayak is beneficial.

When would envy be appropriate? Aristotle writes, "Envy is also a disturbing pain excited by the prosperity of others" ([350 BCE] 1941, 1386). Envy is roughly pain felt toward a competitor's more favorable good fortune/achievement. Envy involves some sense of competition between the envier and the envied pertaining to age, disposition, place, reputation, or wealth.[5] Hume famously wrote, "A poet is not apt to envy a philosopher, or a poet of a different kind, of a different nation, or of a different age" ([1739] 2007, 271). Thus, one does not appropriately envy another with whom one is not in competition. The envier and the envied are near equal in some relevant regard. A person feels fitting envy roughly when their rival has something good that envier lacks, and the envier negatively evaluates this difference in possession. If the envier and the envied are not rivals, then envy is not fitting. For example, it would be unfitting for French professional footballer, Kylian Mbappé, to feel envy toward Maria Ressa for winning the Nobel Peace Prize in 2021—there is no sense in which Mbappé and Ressa are competitors/rivals. Ressa's achievement of the Nobel Peace Prize is not bad for Mbappé such that it would be reasonable for him to envy her.

Envy can fail to be fitting in other ways. If the rival does not possess the good or if the "good" is not genuinely good, then the envier's envy is not fitting. For example, imagine that Pat and Alex each applied for a promotion. One day, Pat mishears a conversation that Alex got promoted, and feels envious of Alex. Pat's envy of Alex is not fitting because Alex did not get promoted. If the overheard conversation concerned a different applicant named "Alex," then perhaps Pat's envy would be warranted, despite being unfitting.

Because envy is a painful emotion, one might be tempted to conclude that it is never beneficial to feel envy. Contrary to this view, many emotion theorists have shown there are various ways that negative or painful emotions (e.g., envy) are beneficial.[6] For example, envy tends to involve a motivation to improve so as to surpass the rival's advantage—thus, envy can be beneficial when it motivates a person to improve herself.[7] There is also evidence that envy sometimes helps improve one's memory and attention (Hill, DePriore, and Vaugh 2011; van de Ven, Zeelenberg, and Pieters 2011). A silver medalist may feel envious of the gold medalist, and then be motivated to improve and achieve gold in the following Olympics. The silver medalist's envy is beneficial in this situation.

In addition to the traditional assessments, envy is frequently assessed according to a moral dimension. Immanuel Kant argues that envy "aims, at least in terms of one's wishes, at destroying others' good fortune" ([1797] 2000, 459). Envy is understood as invidious when the envier has the desire that the envied no longer have the relevant thing they possess. Then, it might be understood as always immoral to feel envy. Nonetheless, one's feeling envy need not necessarily involve appraising the difference between the envier and the envied as an injustice. The envier may deem the difference to be bad for the envier, but not unjust. Furthermore, the envier need not dislike the envied; competitors are often friends. Perhaps it is always morally problematic to feel envy, but even if that is so, it might remain true that some bouts of envy are fitting, warranted, and beneficial.

Envy is sometimes confused with longing, admiration, or jealousy. At times, one might use "envy" when they merely long for another's possession. Emotion researchers acknowledge that while natural language is not always precise about emotion attributions, there is an important distinction between envy and jealousy. Justin D'Arms explains that both jealousy and envy are three-place relations,

> Jealousy involves three parties, the subject, the rival, and the beloved; the jealous person's real locus of concern is the beloved, a person (or being) whose affection he is losing or fears losing. The locus of concern in jealousy is not the rival. Whereas envy is a two-party relation, with a third relatum that is a good (albeit a good that could be a particular person's affections); and the envious person's locus of concern is the rival. (D'Arms 2017)

So, while both envy and jealousy have a three-place relation, jealousy is a three-party relation that involves three people (or beings). For jealousy, there is a person feeling jealousy that the beloved is giving attention to a rival. The jealous person would likely still feel jealous if the beloved is giving attention to a different rival. Thus, D'Arms argues that the rival is fungible but the beloved is not fungible for the jealous person. D'Arms differentiates envy from jealousy through the claim that envy is only a two-party relation, though envy does have a three-place relation, with the good as the third element.

In new work on envy, Sara Protasi (2021) holds that jealousy and envy have three-party relations and differentiates the two emotions in a way that diverges from that of D'Arms. She writes, "envy and jealousy are rivalrous painful emotions involving a three-party relation, which are directed at a competitor and are concerned with a good, and which often arise together" (Protasi 2021, 11). For Protasi, the fundamental distinction between envy and jealousy is that envy concerns the *lack* of a valuable good and jealousy concerns the *loss* of a valuable good. Another important difference is that a modest amount of jealousy is often socially viewed as reasonable or understandable, whereas envy is often socially viewed as admitting an inferiority (Parrot and Smith 1993).

An exhaustive understanding of the division between jealousy and envy would take us too far astray for the topic at hand. For my purposes, envy is a three-place relation: (1) the agent/person/subject/envier, (2) the subject/rival/competitor/envied, and (3) the good. The envy felt for the lack of a good that the competitor possesses is painful for the agent. The envier and the envied are rivals. To understand envy in terms of the traditional assessments, these assumptions are presupposed. Accordingly, a bout of envy is fitting when the envy corresponds to the relevant features of the agent's situation—an agent's envy of a subject is fitting just in case (i) the subject has a good that the agent lacks, (ii) the lack of the relevant good is bad for the agent in some regard, and (iii) the agent and the subject are genuine rivals relevant to the good.

ALGORITHMS AND EMOTIONS

There is a flourishing research programme endeavoring to design AI that possesses the ability to interact with human emotions. Theorists are developing AI agents that can identify, experience, express, and respond to various emotions.[8] It is still very controversial whether emotional bonds can be made between humans and AI:

> The fact that emotion is so intimately bound up with conscious feeling is considered by some to be a block on the possibility that robots could ever be considered properly emotional. This concern rests on a more general scepticism about the idea that consciousness could emerge from "mere" information processing, the stock in trade of artificial intelligence. . . . No amount of "mere" information can account for the experiences of seeing a charging bull, of consciously judging it to be a danger or, most pertinently, of being afraid of it. So, if these considerations are along the right lines, robots need emotions yet could never have them. (Smith and Farina 2018)

Perhaps AI agents' experience of emotions could never correspond to the way in which humans experience emotions. Nonetheless, AI agents/robots are becoming more successful at identifying emotions in humans. When AI agents can effectively recognize human emotions, the AI agents can better interact with humans. Scientists are developing algorithms to determine which emotions a given human is expressing and how to use this information to predict what a human will do next (or purchase next). This information, concerning occurrent emotions and predictions of future actions, already impacts what advertisements can be found across the internet and on social media. These focused advertisements relate to purchases, of course, but also advertisements connected to the politics of major voting issues and elections. Research on AI and emotions is being done in a dizzyingly wide range of fields from computer science, mathematics, neuroscience, kinematics, cognitive science, economics, and psychology.

It is up for debate whether a requirement of the AI agent is that it is able to identify, experience, and express various emotions itself. For my purposes, here, I am concerned with whether it makes sense to feel an emotion (e.g., envy) toward an AI agent. Is there something required of AI for it to makes sense for a human to feel an emotion toward it?

Clearly, humans feel emotions toward other entities that are not humans. For example, when my dog Carbon climbs onto my lap during a Zoom meeting, I see my colleagues' joy. When Carbon performs complicated tricks, while the neighbors are watching (some of whom are not nice and have poorly behaved dogs), I feel a deep pride for Carbon. I recognize the neighbor's envy as Carbon sits quietly while their dogs behave wildly—it almost appears that Carbon exhibits a sense of pride in this scenario as well. When Carbon diligently switches between playing aggressively with my partner and playing tenderly with my young daughter, I feel love for Carbon. My daughter feels jealous that Carbon follows me adoringly; she longs for Carbon to follow her adoringly instead. Conversely, some dogs will display jealousy if someone gets too close to their beloved. When playing catch with Carbon and my children, my young daughter might feel envious that Carbon can catch the ball better than she can. People frequently claim the ability to perceive a dog's love, in addition to guilt, jealousy, joy, and grief. There is plenty of research suggesting that animals do, indeed, feel emotions (e.g., de Vere and Kuczaj 2016; Correia-Caeiro, Guo, and Mills 2020). Humans are not the only entities that feel emotions, and humans feel emotions toward nonhuman entities.

While it seems relatively uncontroversial to imagine that humans feel a range of emotions toward animals (e.g., dogs) and that animals (e.g., dogs) also feel a range of emotions, humans clearly feel emotions toward non-animals as well. For example, one might feel sad about one's plant dying or angry at one's bike for breaking. One is likely to feel rage toward a computer that perpetually freezes, especially if it freezes and dies just before the submission of a big project. So, one can feel an emotion toward a nonhuman entity like a computer. A separate question is whether one can feel a *fitting* emotion toward nonhumans. While my anger at a cat for spitefully using my shoe as a toilet after an undignified bath could arguably count as fitting—the cat did indeed wrong me, my anger at my bike for breaking is not fitting—there is no way of understanding a bike as having wronged me. Martha Nussbaum describes this sort of scenario,

> Notoriously, however, people sometimes get angry when they are frustrated by inanimate objects, which presumably cannot act wrongfully. . . . In 1988, the *Journal of the American Medical Association* published an article on "vending machine rage": fifteen injuries, three of them fatal, as a result of angry men kicking or rocking machines that had taken their money without dispensing the drink. . . . We tend to think that we have a right to expect "respect" and cooperation from the inanimate objects that serve our ends, and in the moment we react as if they were bad people, since they clearly are not doing "their job" for us. We quickly realize this doesn't make sense—most of the time. (2016, 18–19)[9]

In some sense, we find this sort of anger as understandable—we can all sympathize with a friend who feels angry at a malfunctioning machine at an inopportune moment. While this anger seems understandable, given some measurement, it is clearly not fitting. The vending machine has not wronged the man no matter how much money it takes without dispensing a drink. The vending machine does not have an intention to steal from others, though perhaps an artificially intelligent agent could be designed in this manner.

While perhaps artificially intelligent agents are capable of emoting or getting closer to having this capability, this does not matter for our purposes. Humans can feel emotions toward AI. Nonetheless, feeling simple emotions like joy and anger might appear less controversial than more complex social emotions like envy. Recall world champion 9-dan professional Go player Lee Sedol. Sedol and the algorithm, AlphaGo, are apparently competitors or rivals.[10] This was a genuine tournament that gripped the global Go community.

While in all of the interviews it is not clear Sedol explicitly stated that he felt envy toward AlphaGo, he was patently pained by AlphaGo's success and said so unequivocally. In light of the events and Sedol's emotional responses, it is reasonable to imagine a scenario in which Sedol felt envious toward AlphaGo concerning the good of being the best (i.e., winning the tournament). If Sedol felt envious of AlphaGo, would his envy be fitting? Recall that envy is fitting just in case it satisfies the three constraints such that it would correspond to the relevant features of the agent's situation. For (i), the subject, AlphaGo, has a good (winner of the tournament) that Sedol lacks. For (ii), the lack of this good is bad for Sedol—he is no longer the "best" at Go. For (iii), Sedol and AlphaGo are genuine rivals relevant to the good (winner of the tournament). At the time of the tournament, Sedol and AlphaGo were genuine rivals. While both Sedol and media spectators thought Sedol would win the tournament, the AlphaGo team were confident that they would at least win at least a match or so. In the end, AlphaGo and Sedol were genuine competitors—Sedol won one of the five matches, so the difference in their playing abilities was not tremendous. Recall, though, this is not an empirical claim about whether Sedol actually felt envy (or resentment, profound sadness, grief, etc.). It is, though, meant to be a case for the conceivability that someone in Sedol's position could feel envious of AlphaGo and do so fittingly. Satisfying all three constraints on a fitting bout of envy, Sedol's circumstances exhibits a plausible scenario of a human feeling a fitting bout of envy toward an algorithm.

PROTASI ON ENVY

Sara Protasi (2021) recently published an extensive treatment on envy where she argues that there are four distinct kinds of envy: (i) inert, (ii) emulative, (iii) spiteful, and (iv) aggressive. In her view, the kind of envy is determined through various combinations of two variables: focus of concern and perceived obtainability of the good. The first variable is about what is the agent's concern—the good (independently of the envied) or the envied. For example, an agent might independently value the good but also be pained by the rival possessing it. The agent's focus of concern might be on the good in this case, and then be more intent to *obtaining the good* rather than depriving the rival of the good. In contrast, if the agent's focus of concern is on the envied, then the agent will be more intent on taking away the good from the envied. Protasi explains the second variable, perceived obtainability of the good, as: "if I perceive myself as capable of taking away the good and acquire it myself, then I will try to steal (either literally or figuratively) the good; but if I perceive myself as incapable of doing so, I will try to spoil the good" (Protasi 2021, 42). Perceived obtainability is influenced by one's confidence and skills and also by the nature of the good. Some goods are exclusive (e.g., the president of an organization, the gold medallist of a race). According to Protasi, the various combinations between these variables generates the four types of envy. She offers an extensive discussion and thorough argument for the plausibility of each in turn.

An agent who feels *emulative* envy focuses on the good and deems the good to be obtainable. When an agent feels emulative envy, she takes her rival to be an ideal worth emulating. If the agent responds to her painful envy with motivated efforts to improve herself and then she is successful in her efforts to emulate her rival, then her envy is beneficial.[11] An agent who feels *inert* envy focuses on the good and deems the good to be unobtainable. Inert envy is a passive and self-defeating emotion due to the agent having little concern toward the rival and considering the good as unachievable. An agent who feels *aggressive* envy focuses on the rival and deems the good to be obtainable. Aggressive envy is actively malicious—an agent feeling aggressive envy is motivated to steal the good from the rival. Finally, an agent who feels *spiteful* envy focuses on the rival and deems the good to be unobtainable. Spiteful envy has the likelihood of extreme maliciousness, seeing as the agent may focus on bringing the rival down while not holding oneself as capable of obtaining the good, so also is not motivated to improve oneself. It is important to note that Protasi acknowledges that there are certainly borderline cases between these four types of envy.

Protasi's illuminating scheme explains the differences in various envy experiences in one framework. It emphasizes when there is a propensity for the envier to focus on the good and when there is a propensity for the envier to focus on the rival. Her account is further motivated through highlighting the related action tendencies associated with each kind of envy.

HOW TO ENVY AN ALGORITHM

In light of Protasi's four kinds of envy, what type of envy would Sedol feel in this scenario? Recall that shortly after AlphaGo's win, Sedol publicly retired from the professional life as a Go player because AI is an entity that can no longer be defeated by humans. Well, after the end of the tournament, it would seem that Sedol holds that a good (defeating all other rivals) is not obtainable—this points to either inert envy or spiteful envy. Nonetheless, it is helpful to consider first Sedol and AlphaGo around the time of the tournament in light of each of Protasi's kinds of envy—let us take into account at the middle of the tournament when AlphaGo had already won three matches, Sedol had one one match, and there was a single match remaining.

Consider first aggressive envy, where an agent deems the good obtainable and takes herself to be capable of stealing the good from her rival. In Protasi's account, aggressive envy is actively malicious and may try to spoil the good for the envied. For a person in Sedol's position to feel a bout of aggressive envy, the person could be motivated to win through sabotage AphaGo (e.g., unplug the computer, get fed suggested Go moves). This seems like a highly implausible description of Sedol, who appears far more interested in a fair determination of which 9-dan professional player is the legitimate best. Next, consider spiteful envy, where an agent deems the good unobtainable, where an agent has extremely malicious action tendencies. For a person in Sedol's position to feel a bout of spiteful envy, the person could be motivated to win by any means (e.g., delete the entire AlphaGo algorithm, destroy all notes or information connected to the algorithm). For similar reasons given with respect to aggressive envy, this seems like an extraordinarily implausible description of Sedol. To be clear, though, neither aggressive envy nor spiteful envy seem entirely farfetched as a possible kind of envy. Moreover, neither aggressive envy nor spiteful envy seem entirely farfetched for some other person in a position like Sedol's to have, though it would certainly be a deeply undesirable emotion to experience for the envier or for anyone in the nearby vicinity.

Instead, consider inert envy where the agent deems the good unobtainable and has little concern for the rival. An agent with inert envy feels a hopeless despair toward the notion that it is impossible to obtain the good. This is an improbable description of Sedol's envy going into the final match. Sedol expressed clear hope after having won the fourth match. Furthermore, Sedol did not hold that the good was unobtainable, he showed great effort in the final match. Finally, consider emulative envy where an agent deems the good obtainable and the agent takes the rival worth of emulation. After Sedol had won a single match against AlphaGo but lost three others, perhaps Sedol thought he might be able to come close with a two to three outcome. At this point, there was still hope of some redemption. A person in Sedol's position is likely to feel the related emotions that Protasi characterizes of emulative envy—the envy is a painful feeling combined with shame at the inferiority of having lost three matches to AlphaGo thus far and with hope of improving in the final match to win at least one more. Of Protasi's four kinds of envy, only emulative envy is a reasonable characterization of Sedol's emotion in the midst of the tournament between him and AlphaGo.

Reflecting on Sedol at a later date is likely to bring different results. Sedol declared that his departure from professional Go life was due to the existence of undefeatable AI. Since he deemed that it was no longer in the realm of possibility that he could be the world's best, he did not want to participate. At this stage, a few years after the tournament when Sedol retires, imagine that he again feels envy of the most recent AI Go algorithm, AlphaGoZero. "After just three days of self-play training, AlphaGoZero emphatically defeated the previously published version of AlphaGo—which had itself defeated eighteen-time world champion Lee Sedol—by one hundred games to zero. After forty days of self-training, AlphaGoZero became even stronger, outperforming the version of AlphaGo known as 'Master,' which has defeated the world's best players and world number on Ke Jie" (Silver and Hassibis 2017). AI Go algorithms continue to develop at a dramatically rapid rate. If retired Sedol feels envious of AlphaGoZero, then what kind of envy does retired Sedol feel?

Again, consider first aggressive envy, where an agent deems the good obtainable and takes herself to be capable of stealing the good from her rival. Retired Sedol is not actively malicious and is not trying to spoil the good for AlphaGoZero. Moreover, retired Sedol has retired because he does not deem the good (being world champion) genuinely obtainable. Retired Sedol does not feel aggressive envy for AlphaGoZero. For spiteful envy, where an agent deems the good unobtainable and extremely malicious action tendencies, the latter seems implausible. While retired Sedol does deem the good unobtainable, he is acting with composed and reasonable tendencies through his retirement. Retired Sedol does not feel spiteful envy of AlphaGoZero. Consider again emulative envy where an agent deems the good obtainable and the agent takes the rival worth of emulation. Retired Sedol does not deem the good (being a world champion) obtainable. Perhaps AlphaGoZero is worthy of emulation, but retired-Sedol does not think that he can match the skill of AlphaGoZero. Retired-Sedol does not feel a bout of emulative envy. Lastly, consider inert envy where the agent deems the good unobtainable and has minimal concern for the rival. Retired Sedol does feel a hopeless despair toward the notion that it is impossible to obtain the good (being a world champion). Retired Sedol does show minimal concern for AlphaGoZero. He no longer wants to engage in a competition with an algorithm that retired Sedol deems a legitimate competitor—AI development has advanced to this point and continued advancement is inevitable. Of Protasi's four kinds of envy, only inert envy is a reasonable characterization of retired Sedol's envy of an algorithm like AlphaGoZero or its descendants.

At the end of the second section of this chapter, I argued that Sedol's envy of AlphaGo is fitting, seeing that it meets the three constraints on a fitting instance of envy. Sedol and AlphaGo were genuine rivals, at that time. When the tournament occurred, Sedol and AlphaGo had comparable, competitive, skill levels within the field of Go. Is retired Sedol's envy of AlphaGoZero also fitting? A few years following their tournament, as Go algorithms and AI continued to develop, the level of skill of retired Sedol versus AlphaGoZero is now dramatically dissimilar. AI steadily improves at a pace that cannot be matched by a human. Retired Sedol and AlphaGoZero are no longer true competitors or genuine rivals. It seems then, that retired Sedol's envy is unfitting—(i) AlphaGoZero does have a good (prestige of world champion skills) that retired Sedol lacks, (ii) the lack of this good is bad for retired Sedol, but (iii) retired Sedol and AlphaGoZero are not genuine rivals—their Go skills are no longer comparable.

CONCLUSION

While it is natural for one to hold that people cannot envy non-persons, I have argued against this position. I have argued that, in the right circumstances, one can feel a fitting (and warranted) bout of envy toward an algorithm. An especially interesting result of this investigation is that a person can feel fitting envy for an algorithm at one point in time, but at another point in time, it may be unfitting for that same person to feel envy for the algorithm. For my purposes, here, I have not considered whether it would make sense, or is indeed possible, for an AI agent like AlphaGo to feel envy. There is plenty of developing research investigating whether AI agents can feel emotions, merely appear to feel emotions, or cannot feel emotions at all. This is a topic for a further project. It is clear, for my arguments here, that having an emotion toward an object need not require the object capable of feeling an emotion itself. One can feel envy toward an algorithm, like AlphaGo; this bout of envy can be both fitting and warranted.

NOTES

1. The term "fitting" used in this manner comes from D'Arms and Jacobson (2000). This term has become standardly used (e.g., Kerr 2021; Protasi 2021) but some employ different terms, for example, Greenspan (1988) uses "applicable," de Sousa (1987) uses either "objectively correct," "appropriate," or "rational," and Gibbard (1990) and Jones (2003) use "apt."

2. This statement is offered as an intuitive and uncontroversial analogy, and does not commit me to a cognitivist view of emotions. My aim here is to remain neutral on the nature of emotions.

3. The term "warrant" used in this manner comes from D'Arms and Jacobson (2000), though they differ slightly in their definition—see Kerr (2021) for discussion. Other theorists also endorse this sort of definition but use different terminology, for example, Greenspan (1988) uses "appropriate" and Jones (2003) uses "reasonable."

4. In D'Arms and Kerr (2008), we use "prudential" and gloss it as concerned with the self-interested advisability of the emotion; this use of "prudential" is analogous to my use of "beneficial" here and throughout the chapter. My use of "prudential" and the like is quite different here and in Kerr (2021). For assessments similar to this use of "beneficial," Greenspan (1988) uses "adaptive," Gibbard (1990) uses both "advantageous" and "pragmatic," and Jones (2003) uses "strategically wise."

5. For discussion, see Aristotle ([350 BCE] 1941), Bacon ([1597] 2005), Konstan (2006), Nietzsche ([1878] 1996, [1887] 1998), and Plato ([380 BCE] 1961, [380 BCE] 2007).

6. For example, see the collection of papers in Parrott (2014).

7. See Exline and Zell (2008) for discussion on envy and motivation.

8. See Chakriswaran et al. (2019), Sánchez-Escribano (2018), and Bosse et al. (2014) for overview.

9. In this quote, Nussbaum references the studies from Tarvis (1982, 164n72) and Averill (1982, 166).

10. It is interesting to think about necessary conditions for rivalry. Are all rivals also competitors? Are all competitors also rivals? Must one or both rivals judge of one another as rivals? Are the conditions on rivalry for individuals (e.g., siblings) the same as the conditions for groups (e.g., sports teams)? Not all dictionary entries assume personhood for rivalry. The vast literature discussing rivalry seems to assume that all theorists are referring to the same concept. I am going to follow the standard assumptions here with the intention to consider these important concerns in future work.

11. In contrast with my earlier work (D'Arms and Kerr 2008), Protasi (2021) argues that emulative envy is not even implicitly malevolent and gives a convincing argument for the possibility of genuinely benign envy. A thorough engagement of this dispute would be good fun but will have to wait for future work. For more on the benign/malicious envy distinction, see in this volume Vanessa Carbonell's on "Malicious Moral Envy" (chapter 7) and Niels van de Ven on "The Envious Consumer" (chapter 12).

REFERENCES

Adams, Alison. 1998. *Artificial Knowing*. New York: Routledge.
AlphaGo. 2017. *AlphaGo Movie*. https://www.alphagomovie.com/.
Aristotle. (350 BCE) 1941. "Rhetoric." In *The Basic Works of Aristotle*, edited by R. McKeon and translated by W. D. Ross. New York: Random House.
Averill, James. 1982. *Anger and Aggression*. New York: Springer.
Bacon, Francis. (1597) 2005. *The Essays*. Sioux Falls, SD: NuVision Publications.
Bosse, Tibor, Joost Broekens, João Dias, and Janneke van der Zwaan. 2014. *Emotion Modeling: Towards Pragmatic Computational Models of Affective Processes*. London: Springer.
Britannica. 2021. "go." Encyclopedia Britannica. https://www.britannica.com/topic/go-game. Accessed October 28, 2021.
Carbonell, Vanessa. 2022. "Malicious Moral Envy." In *The Moral Psychology of Envy*, edited by Sara Protasi. London: Rowman & Littlefield International.
Chakriswaran, Priya, Durai Raj Vincent, Kathiravan Srinivasa, Vishal Sharma, Chuan-Yu Chang, and Daniel Gutiérrez Reina. 2019. "Emotion AI-Driven Sentiment Analysis: A Survey, Future Research Directions, and Open Issues." *Applied Sciences* 9 (24): 5462.
Correia-Caeiro, Catia, Kun Guo, and Daniel S. Mills. 2020. "Perception of Dynamic Facial Expressions of Emotion Between Dogs and Humans." *Animal Cognition* 23: 465–76.

D'Arms, Justin. 2017. "Envy." In The Stanford Encyclopedia of Philosophy (Spring 2017 edition), edited by Edward N. Zalta. https://plato.stanford.edu/archives/spr2017/entries/envy/.

D'Arms, Justin, and Daniel Jacobson. 2000. "The Moralistic Fallacy: On the "Appropriateness" of Emotions." *Philosophy and Phenomenological Research* 61: 65–90.

D'Arms, Justin, and Alison Duncan Kerr. 2008. "Envy in the Philosophical Tradition." In *Envy: Theory and Research*, edited by Richard H. Smith, 39–59. New York: Oxford University Press.

Dean, Walter. 2016. "Algorithms and the Mathematical Foundations of Computer Science." In *Gödels Disjunction: The Scope and Limits of Mathematical Knowledge*, edited by Leon Horsten and Philip Welch, 19–66. Oxford: Oxford University Press.

de Sousa, Ronald. 1987. *The Rationality of Emotion.* Cambridge, MA: MIT Press.

de Vere, Amber J. and Stan A. Kuczaj II. 2016. "Where Are We in the Study of Animal Emotions?" *WIREs Cognitive Science* 7 (5): 354–62.

Eaton, Eric, Tom Dietterich, Maria Gini, Barbara J. Grosz, Charles L. Isbell, Subbarao Kambhampati, Michael Littman, Francesca Rossi, Stuart Russell, Peter Stone, Toby Walsh, and Michael Wooldridge. 2015. "Who Speaks for AI," *AI Matters* 2 (2): 2–14.

Exline, Julie Juola, and Anne L. Zell. 2008. "Antidotes to Envy: A Conceptual Framework." In *Envy: Theory and Research*, edited by Richard H. Smith, 315–34. New York: Oxford University Press.

Gibbard, Allan. 1990. *Wise Choices, Apt Feelings: A Theory of Normative Judgments.* Cambridge, MA: Harvard University Press.

Greenspan, Patricia. 1988. *Emotions and Reason: An Inquiry into Emotional Justification.* London: Routledge & Kegan Paul.

Good, Irving J. 1965. "The Mystery of Go." *The New Scientist*, January: 172–74.

Greenemeier, Larry. 2017. "20 Years after Deep Blue: How AI Has Advanced Since Conquering Chess," *Scientific American*, June 2, 2017. https://www.scientificamerican.com/article/20-years-after-deep-blue-how-ai-has-advanced-since-conquering-chess/.

Hill, Sarah E., Danielle J. DePriore, and Phillip W. Vaugh. 2011 "The Cognitive Consequences of Envy: Attention, Memory, and Self-Regulatory Depletion." *Journal of Personality and Social Psychology* 101 (4): 653–66. doi: 10.1037/a0023904.

Hume, David. (1739) 2007. *A Treatise of Human Nature.* Sioux Falls, SD: NuVision Publications.

Jollimore, Troy. 2015. "'This Endless Space between the Words': The Limits of Love in Spike Jonze's *Her.*" *Midwest Studies in Philosophy* 39: 120–43.

Jones, Karen. 2003. "Emotional Rationality as Practical Rationality." In *Setting the Moral Compass: Essays by Women Philosophers*, edited by Cheshire Calhoun, 333–52. Oxford: Oxford University Press.

Kant, Immanuel. (1797) 2000. *The Metaphysics of Morals*, translated by Mary Gregor. Cambridge: Cambridge University Press.

Kerr, Alison Duncan. 2021. "On the Rationality of Emotion Regulation." *Philosophical Psychology* 34 (4): 453–73.

———. 2020. "Artificial Intelligence, Gender, and Oppression." *Encyclopedia of the UN Sustainable Development Goals*, edited by W. L. Filho. Springer.

Konstan, David. 2006. *The Emotions of the Ancient Greeks: Studies in Aristotle and Classical Literature.* Toronto: University of Toronto Press.

Levy, David. 2009. *Love and Sex with Robots: The Evolution of Human-Robot Relationships.* Gerald Duckworth & Co.

Nietzsche, Friedrich. (1887) 1998. *On the Genealogy of Morality,* translated by Carol Diethe. Cambridge: Cambridge University Press.

Nussbaum, Martha. 2016. *Anger and Forgiveness: Resentment, Generosity, and Justice.* New York: Oxford University Press.

Parrott, W. Gerrod. (Ed). 2014. *The Positive Side of Negative Emotions.* Guilford Press.

Parrott, W. Gerrod, and Richard H. Smith. 1993. "Distinguishing the Experiences of Envy and Jealousy." *Journal of Personality and Social Psychology* 64: 906–20.

Paul, Elizabeth S., and Michael T. Mendl. 2018. "Animal Emotion: Descriptive and Prescriptive Definitions and their Implications for a Comparative Perspective." *Applied Animal Behaviour Science* 205: 202–9. doi: 10.1016/j.applanim.2018.01.008.

Plato. 1961. "Lysis." In *The Collected Dialogues of Plato*, edited by Edith Hamilton and Huntington Cairns. Princeton, NJ: Princeton University Press.

———. (360 BCE) 2007. *Philebus*, translated by Benjamin Jowett. Charleston, SC: BiblioBazaar.

Protasi, Sara. 2021. *The Philosophy of Envy.* New York: Cambridge University Press.

Rundle, Michael. 2016. "DeepMind Will Fight Go World Champ Live on YouTube," *Wired Business*, May 2, 2016. https://www.wired.co.uk/article/deepmind-go-match-live-stream.

Sánchez-Escribano, M. Guadalupe. 2018. *Engineering Computational Emotion—a Reference Model for Emotion in Artificial Systems.* Cham, Switzerland: Springer.

Smith, J. and L. Farina. 2018. "A Puzzle about Emotional Robots: Could a Robot Truly Experience Human Emotions?" *iai News* 69. 17 October 2018. https:// iai.tv/articles/a-puzzle-about-emotional-robots-auid- 1157?_ga1/42.23632122.15798741 12.15399506€4- 1317334097.1539950664.

Silver, David, and Demis Hassibis. 2017. "AlphaGo Zero: Starting from Scratch." *DeepMind* (blog post), October 18, 2017. https://deepmind.com/blog/article/alphago-zero-starting-scratch.

Sullins, John P. 2012. "Robots, Love, and Sex: The Ethics of Building a Love Machine." *IEEE Transactions on Affective Computing* 3 (4): 398–409.

Tarvis, Carol. 1982. *Anger: The Misunderstood Emotion.* New York: Simon & Schuster.

van de Ven, Niels. 2022. "The Envious Customer." In *The Moral Psychology of Envy*, edited by Sara Protasi. London: Rowman & Littlefield International.

van de Ven, Niels, Marcel Zeelenberg, and Rik Pieters. 2011. "Why Envy Outperforms Admiration." *Personality and Social Psychology Bulletin* 37 (6): 784–95. doi: 10.1177/0146167211400421.

Chapter 12

The Envious Consumer

Niels van de Ven

"All you need is envy." This is how Young and Rubicam, a global marketing agency, opens their 2006 report on how brands can position themselves to sell more products. The advertising agency argues that envious desire can motivate consumers to buy, and provides advice on how brands can harness the power of envy to increase sales. A thought-provoking claim, as the typical view of envy throughout history has been far more negative (see Smith and Kim 2007 for an overview). Young and Rubicam knew that many people hold a negative view on envy, as they also added a section on whether their envy-building strategy is evil. So, why would a brand want to trigger envy, if envy has long been condemned as something evil?

In this chapter, I provide an answer to this question, by focusing on the emerging research in psychology and marketing on how envy drives consumers. I describe the functional view of envy that argues that it, like any emotion, serves an important function to people: envy helps protect our relative position (status) in a group (see Van de Ven 2015; Lange, Weidman, and Crusius 2018). The functional approach makes a distinction in a benign and malicious subtype of envy. The malicious type of envy is the one people traditionally think of: a destructive, begrudging feeling that the other should lose the advantage that triggered the envy. For consumers, it leads to negative perceptions and communication about the person and the brand owned by the envied person. Benign envy is still a negative and frustrating feeling to experience, but the goals and motivations are aimed at acquiring whatever the envied person has. In this sense, the envious desire motivates people to achieve more themselves.

After providing the overview on the empirical research on envy in consumption from the psychology and marketing literature, I reflect on whether people also consume to be envied themselves. Finally, I describe how the empirical findings based on the functional account of envy might further the thinking on the role envy plays in response to inequality in society. For example, the different antecedents for benign and malicious envy might help gain a better understanding of not only consumer envy but also help to shed light on how people deal with inequality.

BENIGN ENVY

The most straightforward way envy is important for consumption is that envy can fuel the desire for goods that others have. The anthropologist George Foster (1972) argued that getting what others have is one possible way to get rid of the frustrating feeling of envy. The frustrating feeling of envy arises because someone else is better off in a domain that is important to oneself. Rawls (1971) and Taylor (1988) called this "emulative envy." Research in psychology indeed found that envy can be seen as having two subtypes, that differ in how they deal with this frustration (Van de Ven, Zeelenberg, and Pieters 2009; Lange et al. 2018). First, malicious envy is the stereotypical destructive type of envy, that resolves the frustration by pulling down the other from their superior other. The envied person is then no longer superior, so the source of frustration is gone. The other subtype is benign envy, which motivates someone to improve their own position. By moving up to the same level as the superior other, the frustration is also resolved. It is this latter type of envy that motivates people to strive for the coveted advantage someone else has, which likely fuels consumption. Indeed, academic research found that when students saw a video of a fellow student who enthusiastically described his new iPhone, this triggered benign envy in the study respondents and made them willing to pay more for the product themselves (Van de Ven, Zeelenberg, and Pieters 2011).

It's to be noted that there is an alternative view on subtypes of envy, according to which there is only one envy that it can lead to both more constructive and destructive behavior depending on the circumstances (Cohen-Charash and Larson 2017 and Tai, Narayanan, and McAllister 2012). I think this view is compatible with the view that distinguishes subtypes of envy. It just depends on the level at which one zooms in (or out) of the experience. In the emotion literature behavioral tendencies are typically seen as an integral part of the emotional experience (e.g., Frijda 1988), which is why I prefer to distinguish envy as having subtypes (see Van de Ven 2015 and Crusius et al. 2020 for more on this discussion).

The tendency to improve one's position as a response to envy has been discussed in economics and sociology as well, for example under the name of keeping-up-with-the-Joneses (Matt 2003). People want to keep up with what their neighbors have, and they feel bad (likely envy) if they fall behind (Frank 2013). Although benign envy thus motivates to improve one's position (they try to achieve what others have), it should be stressed that this is not necessarily positive. As Frank argued, the continuous motivation to need more can lead to overconsumption and a chronic dissatisfaction with one's current state. This is also known as the "hedonic treadmill" (Brickman and Campbell 1971), the idea that after getting more goods the expectations and desires increase again. As soon as people have acquired something, they become habituated to that situation and set their eyes on a next target, creating a perpetual sense that one is lacking the things that one wants (or needs). The function of benign envy is to solve the frustration that arises because someone else is better off by improving one's own position. And although this sounds as self-improvement and thus something positive, the hedonic treadmill example suggests this need not be positive. There are more such possible negative consequences of benign envy. Consider the work by Sharma, Singh, and Sharma (2020) who found that players of online computer games that felt more benign envy were more likely to attempt to cheat in these games. Note that this was general cheating to improve one's chance of winning the game, not cheating to specifically hurt the envied other. Exactly the strong desire to improve their own position that was triggered by envy made the gamers try to cut corners in the game. Both Crusius and Mussweiler (2012) and Van de Ven, Zeelenberg, and Pieters (2011) found that envious people were suddenly willing to pay more for a good if they saw someone else having it and felt envy as a result, and whether such social effects actually are in the best interest of the person is questionable. A final example of negative consequences (from a legal perspective) of benign envy is that envious consumers were more willing to buy counterfeit goods, again as a method to reduce the difference between oneself and the envied person (Loureiro, Pinero de Plaza, and Taghian 2020).

All these possible negative consequences of benign envy in the domain of consumption are important in more academic discussions of envy. Some argued that the proponents of benign envy claim that benign envy is a very positive experience, but this is not what the proponents of the subtype approach actually claimed (see the discussion in Crusius et al. 2019). When psychologists talk about a positive motivation in benign envy, this is not intended as an evaluation of whether the outcome is good or bad, but rather in the sense that it motivates people to get more of something compared with what they currently have. Perhaps striving for other goals (instead of the one triggered by benign envy) could have made people happier, or the additional consumption might create a temporary boost in happiness for the individual but harms society as it might lead to overconsumption. For most empirical psychologists studying envy it is clear that benign envy feels negative (i.e., painful) and triggers a motivation to improve one's position. This latter motivation can lead to positive and negative outcomes (for broader discussions on how philosophers have seen envy as something positive and negative, see Taylor 1988; La Caze 2001; Thomason 2015; D'Arms 2017; Protasi 2021).

Belk (2009) wrote an excellent article, arguing that in the last century benign envy has largely replaced malicious envy. Due to marketing efforts, easier access to consumer goods that makes many more products available, and unprecedented economic growth, the idea took hold in society that it is possible to attain what others have (where in the past many products were simply out of reach for the masses and especially the poor). Belk argued that in the past one's position in life was largely fixed, and envy would thus mainly be outed in its malicious form as self-improvement was often not possible. But for modern consumers much more is attainable, which is why benign envy has largely replaced malicious envy. We'll come back to this later in the section on the relation between envy and inequality, but from all this work it is clear that benign envy plays a large role in consumption.

MALICIOUS ENVY

Where benign envy contains motivational tendencies to reduce the gap to the envied other by improving one's own position, malicious envy does so by trying to hurt the position of the envied person (Van de Ven, Zeelenberg, and Pieters 2009). Zizzo and Oswald (2001) found that envy can be so malicious, that people are willing to give up some of their money if doing so allows them to destroy even more money from the envied person. Malicious envy also made people gossip more about the envied person (Wert and Salovey 2004) and was found to lead to negative behavior toward the envied person in the workplace (Duffy, Shaw, and Schaubroeck 2008). In marketing, it is also clear that the negative effects of malicious envy are not only aimed toward the envied person: malicious envy is typically felt toward the superior person, but it was also found to increase dissatisfaction with the brand/product that the envied other owns, and make the envious person less likely to recommend the product to others (Anaya et al. 2016; Wobker, Kopton, and Kenning 2013). In other words, the negative attitudes thus extend to the *object* of envy in these consumer settings.

Besides the possible destructive consequences of envy, marketing research sometimes also found more constructive (motivating) responses from the malicious form of envy. For example, Kristofferson, Lamberton, and Dahl (2018) found that when people were maliciously envious of another consumer who owned a superior product, those with generally low self-esteem disliked the brand of the product more, while those that generally have high self-esteem actually liked the brand *more.* This is a surprising finding for two reasons. First, people with low self-esteem tend to experience more malicious envy in general (Smith et al. 1999), and if malicious envy typically leads to negative behavior toward the envied person it is unclear *why* self-esteem would moderate the effect of malicious envy on brand liking as Kristofferson et al. (2018) found. Second, people with a high self-esteem are more likely to think that the coveted object is attainable for themselves and perceived attainability makes benign envy more likely (Van de Ven, Zeelenberg, and Pieters 2012). Therefore, one would be more likely to expect that those with high self-esteem would like the brand more because of (benign) envy. How the findings of Kristofferson et al. (2018) thus fit in this broader range of findings remains somewhat of an open question.

Another interesting finding on consumer envy by Salerno, Laran, and Janiszewski (2018) is that with benign envy people focus on the *process* on how to improve their own situation. This makes sense given the different motivations that are triggered by the subtypes of envy, as benign envy motivates to improve and a focus on the process how something can be attained will likely help to do so. But for malicious envy they found that consumers focused on the eventual *outcome* (who gets what in the end), and that consumers who experienced malicious envy actually sought out direct rewards that would help them improve their position. In other words, benign envy led to a more intrinsic motivation for self-improvement, while malicious envy led to more direct search for gratification by rewarding oneself. At first sight this seems to conflict with the findings of Crusius and Lange (2014), who found that it is benign envy that tends to focus someone's attention to the object of envy (the outcome), while malicious envy tends to focus attention toward the other person. However, this search for gratification might well be a way to resolve the frustrating feeling as people typically try to get rid of negative feelings by seeking instant gratification (Malesza 2019).

An interesting question is whether malicious envy might sometimes fuel a desire to *overtake* and outperform the superior other. Malicious envy often results in a strong dislike of the envied person and a desire to degrade the other (Parrott and Smith 1993). Outperforming them, not just getting what the other has, might help satisfy that motivation as well as overtaking the other person also reduces the status and position of the envied other. The difference with benign envy then is that benign envy motivates to improve one's position (and when one outperforms the other it is a side effect that the position of the envied person is harmed), while for malicious envy the harm to the position of the other is the primary driver of motivation (and the resulting improvement to the envier's position is the side effect). In situations of competition the realization that others are doing well has been found to fuel a desire to outperform them (Chan and Briers 2018; Wolf et al. 2020). So, does this occur via the motivation to improve oneself (from benign envy) or from a motivation to put down the other (from malicious envy)? Lin (2018) studied responses to social media posts and found that it actually seemed to be malicious envy that led to a motivation to outperform the other.

WHEN DOES (EACH TYPE OF) ENVY ARISE?

The literature on how people make social comparisons suggests that envy is more intense for things that are (a) important to our self-view and (b) when we compare ourselves to people who are initially thought to be similar to us (Festinger 1954; Tesser 1988). Furthermore, envy is typically stronger toward people who are (initially) similar to us. The more people think, "that could have been me!" the stronger their envy is (Van de Ven and Zeelenberg 2015). Interestingly, in society this means that envy is often felt more toward others that are relatively close to us in for example social rank, rather than towards the super-rich.

The fact that we typically compare ourselves (and feel envy toward) those who are initially close to us does not mean that the super-rich, that are more visible to us now in times of television and social media, do not have an effect on us via social comparison and envy. As Frank (1999) argued, many goods get their value from their *relative* worth, rather than their absolute worth. The 400,000-euro car is better than the 100,000-euro car; but the difference between these two in the absolute value of the car (how it can get us from *A* to *B*) is very small, and most of its price premium buys a relative rank difference that shows off one's social status. The super-rich still sets a standard for others that "trickles down" to people's desires at lower levels of income.[1] Frank argued that many luxury goods are positional, and thus get most of their value from the social rank they provide. This is also why many people that are financially well-off still feel that they do not have enough, as they need to keep spending to keep up in status with the people around them. This phenomenon seems particularly apparent in the United States: the website Financial Samurai shows how a couple that makes $500,000 a year (compared to a US median household income of $68,000) can still feel that their budget is really tight as they try to keep up with the spending of their equally affluent neighbors (Financial Samurai 2021).

Positional goods, those that derive value from their relative rank more than their absolute benefit, need not be consumer products: some areas that people themselves indicated to be positional are grades in school, investing for future prosperity, intelligence, physical fitness, weight, and attractiveness (Hillesheim and Mechtel 2013). As an example, most people prefer getting a

B as a grade when everyone else has a C, than to receive an A when everyone else gets an A+. For such positional goods envy is found to be stronger (Boardman, Raciti, and Lawley 2018), likely because what the other has also has a negative effect on the person who is worse off. One of Frank's points in his book is that much more (luxury) goods in rich countries are positional than might appear at first sight, and based on the findings of Boardman and colleagues thus have much potential to trigger envy as well. All in all, the fact that much luxury consumption is positional (Frank 1999) and that positional goods trigger envy (Boardman, Raciti, and Lawley 2018), makes it not so surprising that in this era of excess envy over consumption is on the rise (see Belk 2009).

Aside from the psychological literature on when envy is likely to be more intense, it is also important to look at when the benign and malicious forms of envy are more likely to occur. For a more thorough overview, see Van de Ven and Zeelenberg (2020) but the most important is the deservingness of the advantage of the other: When the position of the superior other is deserved, benign envy is more likely, when it is undeserved malicious envy is more likely to result (Smith et al. 1994; Van de Ven, Zeelenberg, and Pieters 2012; Ferreira and Botelho 2021; but for a critique, see Protasi 2021). Other than this, for example, the relationship with the envied person matters: if people have a better bond with others benign envy is more likely when these others are better off (e.g., Lin and Utz 2015; Lee and Eastin 2020), and if we dislike them malicious envy is more likely (Ferreira and Botelho 2021). Perceived control (being able to obtain the outcome of the envied person as well) is more likely to lead to benign envy (Van de Ven, Zeelenberg, and Pieters 2012), and focusing on the object of envy leads to more benign envy while focusing on the person tends to lead to more malicious envy (Crusius and Lange 2014; Protasi 2021).

These are the most important antecedents that have been identified that distinguish benign from malicious envy. Note that the empirical support for this is initially derived from studies that asked respondents to recall instances of benign and malicious envy, after which these respondents rated several questions about the situation that had elicited these emotions. Such studies for example found that for malicious envy respondents had thought the situation to be undeserved. Based on appraisal theory (see Moors et al. 2013 for an overview), which argues that the initial perception of a situation (the appraisal) gives rise to a specific emotion, these findings were interpreted as if the appraisal (undeservedness) causes the emotion (malicious envy). Still the causality is not fully confirmed as a change in perceptions of deservingness could also technically be a *consequence* of the emotion, rather than an antecedent. Especially for perceived undeservedness, there is some debate on whether this might be a consequence of malicious envy (see Miceli and

Castelfranchi 2007; Protasi 2021), but note that there are studies (e.g., Van de Ven, Zeelenberg, and Pieters 2011) in which perceived deservedness was manipulated after which differences in benign and malicious envy (and subsequent behavioral intentions) were found and causality was thus more strongly confirmed.

All in all, thinking about the possible antecedents of the envy subtypes is important, because by understanding this better we can also make predictions in how people typically react to others that are better off than we are and thus to inequality in general. I come back to this later in the section on how research on envy might inform the thoughts on responses to inequality, but let me first focus on how people respond to being envied themselves.

DO PEOPLE WANT TO BE ENVIED?

Besides the direct motivations that envy triggers in people, there is another way that envy might affect consumers: a consumer might respond to *being* envied. Young and Rubicam, the branding agency that argued that all a brand needs is envy, assumed that consumers also buy products because they want to be envied by others. But is this the case? Foster (1972) argued that being envied triggers feelings on two dimensions: a competition axis (where you feel happy as your status increases) and a fear axis (when you worry about the other's negative behavior that might result from envy). Consistent with this is that Rodriguez Mosquera, Parrott, and Hurtado de Mendoza (2010) found that being envied is an ambivalent feeling: people might feel good for being better off but worried about the possible negative feelings it triggers in others.

The key to understanding the possible negative response to being envied is the model of Exline and Lobel (1999) on how people respond to being the target of an upward social comparison. When people feel that they are the target of an upward social comparison, they make an evaluation whether the other person (a) feels threatened by this comparison (and is thus potentially envious) and (b) whether they care about the other person's response. This latter can be a care for the well-being of the outperformed (and thus potentially envious) person, care for the relationship one has with the other, or a care for one's own well-being. For example, this model can help explain why many students prefer private praise over public recognition (Exline et al. 2004), as private (in contrast to public) praise helps to prevent negative consequences to others or in their relationship to the other students.

Based on this model by Exline and Lobel (1999), Van de Ven, Zeelenberg, and Pieters (2010) predicted that people would not mind being benignly envied but would feel worried when others were maliciously envious of them. After all, benign envy would not typically lead to negative behavior toward the envied person, while malicious envy does. They indeed found that when others were thought to be maliciously envious, the envied person would put in extra effort to help the envious person in an attempt to ward off the negative consequences of malicious envy. Consistent with this idea that being benignly envied is less bad than being maliciously envied, Feng et al. (2021) found that when a consumer is benignly envied their bond with the brand of the owned product increases, but when consumers think they are maliciously envied for owning a brand, they feel more anxious and get a worse connection with the brand.

The empirical support for Foster's (1972) fear axis, that people sometimes worry when they are being envied, is thus quite clear. But what about the competitiveness axis? Does being envied feel good? Situations in which we are envied can indeed have positive consequences as being envied was associated with having a higher self-confidence (Rodriguez Mosquera et al. 2010). Similarly, Lee et al. (2018) found that people who feel they are envied at work also experience positive feelings. However, is this *because* someone is envied? Or do people feel good because they are in a situation that makes them stand out positively? This seems like an important distinction: people want to have high status and want to be admired, and feel good when they have this. But these are also the situations that might trigger envy. It might thus well be that sometimes people feel good in situations in which they are envied, but that does not mean that people feel good *because* they are envied. Fileva (2019) argued that some people might want to provoke envy, but to the best of my knowledge there is no support for this claim, nor do I think there is a good reason to expect that this would be the case.

From a functional perspective, it makes sense to expect that people feel good when they do well and are assigned high status by others.[2] After all, having a high status confers benefits (e.g., consumers who buy luxury products are seen as having higher status and are treated better as a result, Nelissen and Meijers 2011). But why would people want to be envied? As discussed earlier, it creates a negative feeling in others, and either a motivation to pull the superior person down from their positions or a motivation in the envious to improve their situation. The first two are clearly negative outcomes, the third one is more neutral from the perspective of an envied person (although it has a clear functional benefit to the envious person). There is thus no clear reason to expect that people want to be envied (other than it being a side-effect of for example striving for status). Rawls (1971) argued that some people in superior positions are jealous (defined as a situation in which people are not willing to give up some of their advantage to others, see also Taylor, 1988), and do not want others to improve. Although I agree that something like this might happen at times, I again do not think that this supports an idea that people want to be envied. Simply the fact that they want to keep their superior position and status seems a sufficient explanation and it is not needed for people to want to be envied to explain that they strive for more.

So far, I have not seen empirical support for the argument that sometimes people want to be envied (as suggested in Fileva 2019). In Lin, Van de Ven, and Utz (2018) we had tested why people post about material and experiential purchases on social media, and how they respond to others doing so. We found that people expect others to be more envious of material purchases, but, contrary to this expectation, it turns out that people are actually more envious of experiential purchases. We had added a few exploratory questions on why people post about their purchases (see the appendix of that paper for the full list) that we ended up not reporting on, but one question explicitly asked respondents whether they post their purchases because they want to be envied. On a scale from -3 (disagree) to +3 (agree) with 0 as a neutral midpoint, we found that respondents from the United States, on average, disagreed with this statement as the mean score is significantly below the neutral midpoint ($M = -0.22$, $SD = 1.83$, $t(405) = 2.45$, $p = 0.012$, $d = 0.24$). The effect is small, but on average people thus disagreed with the idea that they like to be envied. Of course, this is a self-report measure, and people might not want to admit that they want to be envied, but to me it at the very least indicates that people do not strive to be envied, and perhaps even prefer to generally avoid it. It seems more likely that being envied is a side effect of our actual desire for status.

Lin, Van de Ven, and Utz (2018) thus found that on average people do not want to be envied, but this does not mean that there are no people that would like to be envied. The variation in responses to that question was quite large, and there are generally some clear differences in how people respond to receiving preferential treatment. For example, Butori and De Bruyn (2013) found that some customers dislike receiving preferential treatment from a service provider, while others actually love this. Perhaps people with strong narcissistic traits actually like to be envied (although again the question should be raised whether it is a side effect of their desire for status, or a pure desire to be envied). Furthermore, if we strongly dislike someone we would not care much about their well-being or our relationship with them, and we might actually like it that we cause negative feelings in them. To summarize this point, it is an empirical claim that people want to be envied and further work to test this is very welcome, and could focus for example on testing whether people actually want to be envied and whether possible moderators exist that are related to for example culture, personality traits, or sociological factors.

ENVY AND CONSUMER INEQUALITY

The previous overview of the empirical literature on envy and its relation to consumption clearly shows that envy is an important response to consumer inequality. In mild forms unequal outcomes often exist: the rich can buy more (and better) goods, a regular customer might receive a free upgrade to their hotel room that others do not get, and there might only be one table in the restaurant with the best view. In all these cases some inequality exists in the outcomes of consumers, and we've discussed that envy can play a role in situations such as these. But inequality in society is clearly a bigger issue with far-reaching (moral) implications, as was for example argued by Rawls (1971) and many others. Does envy play a role in responses to societal inequality? Should it?

Some philosophers have argued that all envy is irrational (e.g., Morgan-Knapp 2014; Nozick 1974). Nozick argued that the only reason the superior position of another person can be painful to us is if the other's position is deserved. After all, if it was not deserved, it should not negatively affect our self-view. Any envy, that he defined as malicious envy in the sense that it leads to a preference that the superior other loses their advantage, is thus by his definition misguided and irrational. From a functional, psychological perspective this does not make sense. Envy is an emotion, and all emotions evolved because they helped humans adapt to their (social) environment (Keltner and Gross 1999). If someone else undeservedly receives a promotion that I coveted, my self-esteem might be protected a bit by the fact that the other did not deserve their advantage, but it still rattles me that I did not have the promotion. That frustration, that pain, is still the fuel of (malicious) envy. As discussed before, malicious envy can still have useful functions by restoring the imbalance by pulling down the other, or by motivating the better off to share some of their superior position (see also Foster 1972). Furthermore, both Nozick (1974) and Morgan-Knapp (2014) ignored the possible benefits of benign envy, namely that exactly the frustration that someone else is better off can actually be a motivation to improve oneself.

Does this mean that envy *should* play a role in redistributive policies in society, as for example Bankovsky (2018) argues? I do not know. But I certainly do not think we should condemn any envious response to those in a superior position as being derived from irrational envy. People have sexual desires. Whether these are acted upon in a healthy way depends on individual characteristics, social norms, and a societal structure. The same holds for an emotion like envy: it exists and evolved because it is functional to help monitor and protect one's status in a group. Whether it is acted upon in a healthy way depends on a combination of individual characteristics, social norms, and societal structures. I think that such a functional perspective to analyze the emotion can help in gaining a better understanding of the role envy plays in the responses to inequality. Let me point to a few areas where I think combining the psychological and philosophical viewpoints might be worthwhile.

A key to understanding the responses to inequality is that envy, like other emotions, is not driven mainly by the objective situation, but rather by one's *perception* of the situation (Roseman 1991). People are not averse to inequality, as long as it perceived as fair and deserved (Starmans, Sheskin, and Bloom 2017). Obviously, the *perception* of undeservingness is often related to actual undeservingness, but these do not always map nicely onto each other. For example, people that have a high "belief in a just world," in the sense that they believe that people tend to get from life what they deserve based on their input, are also more likely to accept inequality (Garcia-Sanchez et al. 2021). Bénabou and Tirole (2006) argue that this is why people in the US accept inequality more than they do in Europe (and dislike redistributive tax policies), because in the US they more strongly believe that people deserve their socioeconomic position despite the fact that social mobility is actually higher in Europe. In other words, their work finds that doing well in the US is much more based more on the social rank you already had as a kid than it is in Europe, but people in the US actually think that the better off deserve their position in the social hierarchy more. This difference in perception might likely give rise to different likely envious responses toward the super-rich in Europe versus the US, as discussed earlier that perceptions of deservedness are actually one of the key factors that determine whether the resulting envy will be of the benign or malicious type.

Perhaps another point that might be interesting to political philosophers is that besides perceived deservedness, this chapter highlighted some other antecedents that are thought to determine whether envy would likely be of the benign or malicious type. First, the relationship with the envied other matters; if people have a better bond with others benign envy is more likely (e.g., Lin and Utz 2015; Lee and Eastin 2020), and if we dislike them malicious envy is more likely (Ferreira and Botelho 2021). Consistent with this is that, if the better off are more humble about their accomplishments, benign envy is more likely, while if they behave more arrogantly, malicious envy is more likely (Lange and Crusius 2015; Lin 2018). A society in which the general atmosphere is more friendly and optimistic, and in which the better off do not show off in an arrogant manner will thus be more likely to trigger benign envy over existing inequality. We also know that people feel less bad over being benignly envied than over being maliciously envied (Van de Ven, Zeelenberg, and Pieters 2010), so in a society in which the better off actually deserve their advantage (or at least are perceived to deserve their advantage) the better off also feel less bad over being envied as they expect others to be benignly envious (and not maliciously envious).

Another factor that can play a role is perceived control: when people think it is feasible that they can improve their own situation, benign envy is more likely (Van de Ven, Zeelenberg, and Pieters 2012). Note that Boardman Raciti, and Lawley (2018) did not find an effect of controllability, so it remains a question how important this is in responses to inequality. Interestingly, Smith (2004) argued that if someone feels envy for a longer period of time, the experience can also "transmute" into other emotions. Specifically, if obtaining the desired outcome is impossible to people, they might give up and either accept the situation or they might start to develop resentment toward the superior person or the society that creates the inequality. Our understanding of envy might help to predict how people behave following the inequality.

Finally, although I strongly think that envy is functional in how it helps a person achieve their social goals, fully giving in to its action tendencies is not always objectively best. Acting very negatively toward those with high status might backfire, as other people might actually look favorable on those with high status and might dislike you for trying to sabotage these better off. Following our passions and intuition often points us in the right direction, but adding some thoughts, consideration, and restraint at time helps as well. I therefore agree with Protasi (2021) and Morgan-Knapp (2014) that we would often do well to regulate our envious experience, as we are not always accurate in our perceptions or they might not be in our best interest given the circumstances. By listening to envy as a signal that we apparently find something really important, by careful questioning of our own assumptions on whether it is deserved or undeserved that the other has their advantage (and thus potentially transform out malicious envy into the benign form), and by realizing that we do not always need to compare ourselves to others, we might regulate our envy and resolve the frustration that gave rise to the envy as well.

CONCLUSION

Envy serves a clear function: it monitors our social status and signals when our status is threatened by others that do better than us. It is therefore an important emotion that reacts to situations of inequality. Envy can motivate people to improve their position, or be more malicious and be aimed at pulling down the superior other. This latter has no absolute benefit to an envious person, but it does have the indirect benefit that by pulling down the superior other the status gap is reduced again. Furthermore, the fear of being envied might actually make the better off share some of their advantage, especially in situations in which their advantage was undeserved. This has clear benefits to a group as well. I hope this functional perspective of envy, based on empirical work in psychology and consumer research that has revealed much of the antecedents of these subtypes of envy, can help to further the (political) philosophical thinking on the role envy plays (or should play) in the responses to societal inequality.

NOTES

1. Alfred Archer, Alan Thomas, and Bart Engelen talk about how the rich influence the tastes and aspirations of the lower classes in their contribution to this volume: "The Politics of Envy: Outlaw Emotions in Capitalist Societies" (chapter 10).

2. For an in-depth discussion of this aspect, see Jens Lange and Jan Crusius's contribution to this volume: "How Envy and Being Envied Shape Social Hierarchies" (chapter 2).

REFERENCES

Anaya, G. Joel, Li Miao, Anna S. Mattila, and Barbara Almanza. 2016. "Consumer Envy During Service Encounters." *Journal of Services Marketing* 30 (3): 359–72. doi: 10.1108/JSM-03-2015-0121.

Bankovsky, Miriam. 2018. "Excusing Economic Envy: On Injustice and Incompetence." *Journal of Applied Philosophy*, 35 (2): 257–79. doi:10.1111/japp.12194.

Belk, Russell W. 2011. "Benign Envy." *AMS Review* 1 (3): 117–34. doi: 10.1007/s13162-011-0018-x.

Benabou, Roland, and Jean Tirole. 2006. "Belief in a Just World and Redistributive Politics." *The Quarterly Journal of Economics* 121: 699–746.

Boardman, Darren, Maria M. Raciti, and Meredith Lawley. 2018. "Outperformed: How the Envy Reflex Influences Status Seeking Service Consumers' Engagement." *Journal of Service Theory and Practice* 28 (6): 752–73. doi: 10.1108/JSTP-08-2018-0179.

Brickman, Philip, and Donald T. Campbell. 1971. "Hedonic Relativism and Planning the Good Science." In *Adaptation Level Theory: A Symposium*, edited by Mortimer H. Appley, 287–302. New York: Academic Press.

Brown, Jonathan D. 1986. "Evaluations of Self and Others: Self-Enhancement Biases in Social Judgments." *Social Cognition* 4: 353–76. doi: 10.1521/soco.1986.4.4.353.

Butori, Raphaella, and Arnaud De Bruyn. 2013. "So You Want to Delight Your Customers: The Perils of Ignoring Heterogeneity in Customer Evaluations of Discretionary Preferential Treatments." *International Journal of Research in Marketing* 30 (4): 358–67. doi: 10.1016/j.ijresmar.2013.03.004.

Chan, Elaine, and Barbara Briers. 2019. "It's the End of the Competition: When Social Comparison Is Not Always Motivating for Goal Achievement." *Journal of Consumer Research* 46 (2): 351–70. doi: 10.1093/jcr/ucy075.

Cohen-Charash, Yochi, and Elliott C. Larson. 2017. "An Emotion Divided: Studying Envy is Better than Studying 'Benign' and 'Malicious' Envy." *Current Directions in Psychological Science* 26 (2): 174–83. doi:10.1177/0963721416683667

Crusius, Jan, and Jens Lange. 2014. "What Catches the Envious Eye? Attentional Biases Within Malicious and Benign Envy." *Journal of Experimental Social Psychology* 55: 1–11. doi: 10.1016/j.jesp.2014.05.007.

———. 2021. "Counterfactual Thoughts Distinguish Benign and Malicious Envy." *Emotion*. doi: 10.1037/emo0000923

Crusius, Jan, and Thomas Mussweiler. 2012. "When People Want What Others Have: The Impulsive Side of Envious Desire." *Emotion* 12 (1): 142–53. doi: 10.1037/a0023523.

Crusius, Jan, Manuel F. Gonzalez, Jens Lange, and Yochi Cohen-Charash. 2020. "Envy: An Adversarial Review and Comparison of Two Competing Views." *Emotion Review* 12 (1): 3–21. doi: 10.1177/1754073919873131.

D'Arms, Justin. 2017. "Envy," *The Stanford Encyclopedia of Philosophy* (Spring 2017 Edition), editor Edward N. Zalta, plato.stanford.edu/archives/spr2017/entries/envy/.

Duffy, Michelle K., Jason D. Shaw, and John M. Schaubroeck. 2008. "Envy in Organizational Life." In *Series in Affective Science. Envy: Theory and Research*, editor Richard H. Smith, 167–89. New York: Oxford University Press

Exline, Julie J., and Marcia Lobel. 1999. "The Perils of Outperformance: Sensitivity About Being the Target of a Threatening Upward Comparison." *Psychological Bulletin* 125 (3): 307–37. doi: 10.1037/0033-2909.125.3.307.

Feng, Wenting, Irina Y. Yu, Morgan X. Yang, and Mengjie Yi. 2021. "How Being Envied Shapes Tourists' Relationships with Luxury Brands: A Dual-Mediation Model." *Tourism Management* 86: 104344. doi: 10.1016/j.tourman.2021.104344.

Ferreira, Kirla, and Delane Botelho. 2021. "(Un)deservingness Distinctions Impact Envy Subtypes: Implications for Brand Attitude and Choice." *Journal of Business Research* 125: 89–102. doi: 10.1016/j.jbusres.2020.12.008.

Financial Samurai. 2021. "Scraping By on $500.000 a Year: Why It's So Hard to Escape the Rat Race." https://www.financialsamurai.com/scraping-by-on-500000-a-year-high-income-earners-struggling/.

Foster, George M. 1972. "The Anatomy of Envy: A Study in Symbolic Behavior." *Current Anthropology* 13 (2): 165–202.

Frank, Robert H. 1999. *Luxury Fever: Why Money Fails to Satisfy in an Era of Excess*. New York, NY: Free Press.

———. 2013. *Falling Behind: How Rising Inequality Harms the Middle Class*. University of California Press.

Frijda, Nico H. 1988. "The Laws of Emotion." *American Psychologist* 43 (5): 349–58. doi: 10.1037/0003-066X.43.5.349

García-Sánchez, Efraín, Isabel Correia, Cicero R. Pereira, Guillermo B. Willis, Rosa Rodríguez-Bailón, and Jorge Vala. 2021. "How Fair Is Economic

Inequality? Belief in a Just World and the Legitimation of Economic Disparities in 27 European Countries." *Personality and Social Psychology Bulletin*. doi: 10.1177/01461672211002366.

Fileva, Iskra. 2019. "Envy's Non-Innocent Victims." *Journal of Philosophy of Emotion* 1 (1): 1–22. doi: 10.33497/jpe.v1i1.25.

Festinger, Leon. 1954. "A Theory of Social Comparison Processes." *Human Relations* 7 (2): 117–40. doi: 10.1177/001872675400700202.

Hillesheim, Inga, and Mario Mechtel. 2013. "How Much do Others Matter? Explaining Positional Concerns for Different Goods and Personal Characteristics." *Journal of Economic Psychology* 34: 61–77. doi: 10.1016/j.joep.2012.11.006.

Keltner, Dacher, and James J. Gross. 1999. "Functional Accounts of Emotions." *Cognition and Emotion* 13 (5): 467–80. doi: 10.1080/026999399379140.

Kristofferson, Kirk, Cait Lamberton, and Darren W. Dahl. 2018. "Can Brands Squeeze Wine from Sour Grapes? The Importance of Self-Esteem in Understanding Envy's Effects." *Journal of the Association for Consumer Research* 3 (2): 229–39. doi: 10.1086/697082.

La Caze, Marguerite. 2001. "Envy and Resentment." *Philosophical Explorations* 4 (1): 31–45. doi: 10.1080/13869790108523341.

Lange, Jens, Aaron C. Weidman, and Jan Crusius. 2018. "The Painful Duality of Envy: Evidence for an Integrative Theory and a Meta-Analysis on the Relation of Envy and Schadenfreude." *Journal of Personality and Social Psychology* 114 (4): 572–98. doi: 10.1037/pspi0000118

Lange, Jens, and Jan Crusius. 2015. "The Tango of Two Deadly Sins: The Social-Functional Relation of Envy and Pride." *Journal of Personality and Social Psychology* 109 (3): 453–72. doi: 10.1037/pspi0000026.

Lee, Kiyoung, Michelle K. Duffy, Kristin L. Scott, and Michaéla Schippers. 2018. "The Experience of Being Envied at Work: How Being Envied Shapes Employee Feelings and Motivation." *Personnel Psychology* 71 (2): 181–200. doi: 10.1111/peps.12251.

Lee, Jung Ah, and Matthew S. Eastin. 2020. "I Like What She's #Endorsing: The Impact of Female Social Media Influencers' Perceived Sincerity, Consumer Envy, and Product Type." *Journal of Interactive Advertising* 20 (1): 76–91. doi: 10.1080/15252019.2020.1737849.

Levitt, Theodore. 1980. "Marketing Success Through Differentiation—of Anything." *Harvard Business Review*, January. https://hbr.org/1980/01/marketing-success-through-differentiation-of-anything.

Lin, Ruoyun. 2018. "Silver Lining of Envy on Social Media? The Relationships between Post Content, Envy Type, and Purchase Intentions." *Internet Research* 28 (4): 1142–64. doi: 10.1108/IntR-05-2017-0203.

Lin, Ruoyun, and Sonja Utz. 2015. "The Emotional Responses of Browsing Facebook: Happiness, Envy, and the Role of Tie Strength." *Computers in Human Behavior* 52: 29–38. doi: 10.1016/j.chn.2015.04.064.

Lin, Ruoyun, Niels van de Ven, and Sonja Utz. 2018. "What Triggers Envy on Social Network Sites? A Comparison between Shared Experiential and

Material Purchases." *Computers in Human Behavior* 85: 271–81. doi: 10.1016/j.chb.2018.03.049.

Loureiro, Sandra M. C., Maria A. P. de Plaza, and Mehdi Taghian. 2020. "The Effect of Benign and Malicious Envies on Desire to Buy Luxury Fashion Items." *Journal of Retailing and Consumer Services* 52: 101688. doi: 10.1016/j.jretconser.2018.10.005.

Malesza, Marta. 2019. "Relationship between Emotion Regulation, Negative Affect, Gender and Delay Discounting." *Current Psychology* 40: 4031–39. doi: 10.1007/s12144-019-00366-y.

Matt, Susan. J. (2003). *Keeping Up with the Joneses: Envy in American Consumer Society, 1890–1930*. Philadelphia: University of Pennsylvania Press.

Miceli, Maria, and Cristiano Castelfranchi. 2007. "The Envious Mind." *Cognition and Emotion* 21 (3): 449–79. doi: 10.1080/02699930600814735.

Mohr, Inga K., Peter H. Kenning, and Isabella M. Kopton. 2013. "What about Me? Evidence of Consumer Envy and Destructive Envy Behavior." *Advances in Consumer Research* 41: 789.

Moors, Agnes, Phoebe C. Ellsworth, Klaus Scherer, and Nice H. Frijda. 2013. "Appraisal Theories of Emotion: State of the Art and Future Development. *Emotion Review* 5 (2): 119–24. doi: 10.1177/1754073912468165.

Morgan-Knapp, Christopher. 2014. "Economic Envy." *Journal of Applied Philosophy* 31 (2): 113–26. doi: 10.1111/japp.12045.

Nelissen, Rob M. A., and Marijn H. C. Meijers. 2011. "Social Benefits of Luxury Brands as Costly Signals of Wealth and Status." *Evolution and Human Behavior* 32 (5): 343–55. doi: 10.1016/j.evolhumbehav.2010.12.002.

Nozick, Robert. 1974. *"Anarchy, State, and Utopia."* New York: Basic Books.

Parrott, W. Gerrod, and Richard H. Smith. 1993. "Distinguishing the Experiences of Envy and Jealousy." *Journal of Personality and Social Psychology* 64 (6): 906–20. doi:10.1037/0022-3514.64.6.906.

Protasi, Sara. 2016. "Varieties of Envy." *Philosophical Psychology* 29 (4): 535–49, doi: 10.1080/09515089.2015.1115475.

———. 2021. *"The Philosophy of Envy."* Cambridge, UK: Cambridge University Press.

Rawls, John. 1971. *A Theory of Justice*. Cambridge, MA: Harvard University Press.

Rodriguez Mosquera, Patricia M., W. Gerrod Parrott, and Alejandra Hurtado de Mendoza. 2010. "I Fear Your Envy, I Rejoice in Your Coveting: On the Ambivalent Experience of Being Envied by Others." *Journal of Personality and Social Psychology* 99 (5): 842–54. doi: 10.1037/a0020965

Roseman, Ira J. 1991. "Appraisal Determinants of Discrete Emotions." *Cognition and Emotion* 5 (3): 161–200. doi: 10.1080/02699939108411034.

Salerno, Anthony, Juliano Laran, and Chris Janiszewski. 2019. "The Bad Can Be Good: When Benign and Malicious Envy Motivate Goal Pursuit." *Journal of Consumer Research* 46 (2): 388–405. doi: 10.1093/jcr/ucy077.

Sharma, Rashmini, Gurmeet Singh, and Shavneet Sharma. 2021. "Competitors' Envy, Gamers' Pride: An Exploration of Gamers' Divergent Behavior." *Psychology & Marketing* 38 (6): 965–80. doi: 10.1002/mar.21469.

Smith, Richard H. 2004. "Envy and Its Transmutations." In Larissa Z. Tiedens and Colin W. Leach (editors), *The Social Life of Emotions*, 43–63. Cambridge: Cambridge University Press.

Smith, Richard H., and Sung Hee Kim. 2007. "Comprehending Envy." *Psychological Bulletin* 133 (1): 46–64. https://doi: 10.1037/0033-2909.133.1.46.

Smith Richard H., W. Gerrod Parrott, Edward F. Diener, Rick H. Hoyle, and Sung Hee Kim. 1999. "Dispositional Envy." *Personality and Social Psychology Bulletin* 25 (8): 1007–20. doi:10.1177/01461672992511008.

Smith, Richard H., W. Gerrod Parrott, Daniel Ozer, and Andrew Moniz. 1994. "Subjective Injustice and Inferiority as Predictors of Hostile and Depressive Feelings in Envy." *Personality and Social Psychology Bulletin* 20: 705–11.

Solnick, Sara J., and David Hemenway. 2005. "Are Positional Concerns Stronger in Some Domains than in Others?" *American Economic Review* 95 (2): 147–51. doi: 10.1257/000282805774669925.

Starmans, Christina, Mark Sheskin, and Paul Bloom. 2017. "Why People Prefer Unequal Societies." *Nature Human Behaviour* 1: 0082. doi: 10.1038/s41562-017-0082.

Tai, Kenneth, Jayanth Narayanan, and Daniel J. McAllister. 2012. "Envy as Pain: Rethinking the Nature of Envy and Its Implications for Employees and Organizations." *The Academy of Management Review* 37 (1): 107–29.

Taylor, Gabriele. 1988. "Envy and Jealousy: Emotions and Vices." *Midwest Studies in Philosophy* 13 (1): 233–49. doi: 10.1111/j.1475-4975.1988.tb00124.x.

Tesser, Abraham. 1988. "Toward a Self-Evaluation Maintenance Model of Social Behavior." *Advances in Experimental Social Psychology* 21: 181–227. doi: 10.1016/S0065-2601(08)60227-0.

Thomason, Krista K. 2015. "The Moral Value of Envy." *The Southern Journal of Philosophy* 53 (1): 36–53. doi: 10.1111/sjp.12095.

van de Ven, Niels. 2009. The Bright Side of a Deadly Sin: The Psychology of Envy. PhD Thesis, Tilburg University.

———. 2016. "Envy and Its Consequences: Why It Is Useful to Distinguish between Benign and Malicious Envy." *Social and Personality Psychology Compass* 10 (6): 337–49. doi: 10.1111/spc3.12253.

van de Ven, Niels, and Marcel Zeelenberg. 2015. "On the Counterfactual Nature of Envy: 'It Could Have Been Me.'" *Cognition and Emotion* 29 (6): 954–71. doi: 10.1080/02699931.2014.957657.

van de Ven, Niels, and Marcel Zeelenberg. 2020. "Envy and Social Comparison." In *Social Comparison, Judgment and Behavior*, edited by Jerry Suls, Rebecca Collins, and Ladd Wheeler, 226–50. Oxford: Oxford University Press.

Van de Ven, Niels, Marcel Zeelenberg, and Rik Pieters. 2009. "Leveling Up and Down: The Experiences of Benign and Malicious Envy." *Emotion* 9 (3): 419–29. doi: 10.1037/a0015669.

———. 2010. "Warding Off the Evil Eye: When the Fear of Being Envied Increases Prosocial Behavior." *Psychological Science* 21 (11): 1671–77. doi: 10.1177/0956797610385352.

———. 2011. "The Envy Premium in Product Evaluation." *Journal of Consumer Research* 37 (6): 984–98. doi: 10.1086/657239.

———. 2012. "Appraisal Patterns of Envy and Related Emotions. *Motivation and Emotion* 36 (2): 195–204. doi: 10.1007/s11031-011-9235-8.

Young & Rubicam. 2009. "All You Need Is Envy." http://emea.yr.com/envy.pdf.

Wert, Sarah R., and Peter Salovey. 2004. "A Social Comparison Account of Gossip." *Review of General Psychology* 8 (2): 122–37. doi:10.1037/1089-2680.8.2.122.

Wolf, Tobias, Steffen Jahn, Maik Hammerschmidt, and Welf H. Weiger. 2020. "Competition Versus Cooperation: How Technology-Facilitated Social Interdependence Initiates the Self-Improvement Chain." *International Journal of Research in Marketing* 38 (2): 472–91. doi: 10.1016/j.ijresmar.2020.06.001.

Zizzo, Daniel J., and Andrew J. Oswald. 2001. "Are People Willing to Pay to Reduce Others' Incomes?" *Annales d'Économie et de Statistique* 63/64: 39–65. doi: 10.2307/20076295.

Index

"absence of envy" economists, 167–70
abuse of power, 13, 157–58
academic envy
    assessing argument against, 66–69
    collective disadvantage,
        65–66, 70–71
    components of envy, 62–65, 64*t*
    criticism, as epistemic good, 72
    destructive behavior, 71, 72–73
    epistemic effects of, 61–62
    intervention options, 73–74
    relative disadvantage, 68, 70–71
    summary of, 74
achievement through envy
    appropriateness of, 203–4, 217, 229
    benign envy as
        motivator, 116, 219
    emotional experiences as
        motivator, 31
    emulation framing and, 188
    experimental economics
        and, 170–75
    by higher-ranking persons and, 49
    introduction to, 2, 7
    in social relations, 26
Adams, Alison, 200
adaptive envy, 8, 101
admirable immorality, 139

admiring envy, 3, 114
advantage, feelings of, 81
affective injustice, 192
aggressive envy, 134, 208–9
akrasia (weakness of will), 135
Al-Anon, 140
Alpha Go, 15–16, 199, 200–202, 207–12
altruism, 140, 170, 175–76
ambivalence to being envied, 36, 47–48
ambivalent emotional experience, 7
analogical emulation, 119
analogical form of emulation, 11
anatta (no-self doctrine), defined, 97
anger at inanimate objects, 207
apet (envy), 31
applied ethics, 12
appraisal theory, 223
approach/avoidance behavior in being
    envied, 51–52
Aristotle
    accounts of compassion, 95
    on character through role-
        modeling, 112
    competitive emotion, 202
    on envy, 2–3, 96, 182, 203
    phronimos, 119–20
    phthonos (envy), 2, 114
    zēlos (emulation), 2, 114

Aristotle-Nussbaum account of compassion, 95–96, 99, 106n3
artificial intelligence (AI)
- Alpha Go case study, 15–16, 199, 200–202, 207–12
- emotions and, 205–8
- envy of, 209–11
- introduction to, 15–16, 199
- traditional assessments of envy, 202–5

aspirational envy, 36
assessment of proximity, 63
assessment of relative disadvantage, 63, 64
attachment to values, 11

Bannon, Stephen, 129
Becker, Gary, 175–76
behavioral economics, 168–75
being envied, 32–35, 47–52
benevolence, 94
benign envy. *See also* consumerism with benign and malicious envy
- as central motivator, 16
- consumerism and, 217–20
- defined, 183
- "Donkey Objection" analogy, 111, 113–18
- fair competition and, 189
- inspiring envy, 11
- perception of control, 5
- Protasi on, 2, 3
- social rank and, 44–53

Ben-Ze'ev, Aaron, 3, 182–83
Better Life condition study, 34
Birx, Deborah, 129
blame, 13, 142n7, 147–48. *See also* envious blame
Bodhisattva's wisdom and compassion, 98–99
Buddhist no-self doctrine in envy/ compassion dichotomy
- compassionate desire and, 98–100
- envy management and, 100–106
- introduction to, 10–11, 93–94
- overview of, 97–98
- pain and, 99, 104–5
- self and, 94–97
- summary of, 106

Bugkalot village in the Philippines, 30–31

capitalism/capitalist societies, 15, 31, 182, 185–86, 190
catastrophizing in social comparison, 103
catch-up consumption, 172
character through role-modeling, 112
Choosing the Right Pond (Frank), 173
Churchill, Winston, 181
clear-eyed hypocrite, 154
cognitive behavioral therapy (CBT), 11, 100–101
cognitive economics, 171
cognitive profile of envy, 24
cognitive requirements in compassion, 95
collective disadvantage, 65–66, 70–71
collectivistic cultural values, 33
comfortable people, 27
commodity in families, 14, 164, 175–76
community of the Peruvian Amazon, 29
comparison. *See also* social comparison
- first comparison-to-another, 84
- second comparison-to-another, 84–85
- self-comparison, 85–86
- upward comparisons, 83–84

compassion, 10, 18nn6–7, 94–95, 98–100
competence test, 152
competition axis of envy, 224, 225
competition through envy, 7
competitive emotion, 202
concealment, 7, 25, 27–28, 29, 36
conformism, 117–19
consciousness, 97–98, 205
consensus framing, 188
conspicuous consumption, 174–75, 182, 185, 187, 194n7

Index

construction strategy, 65
consumerism, 188–89
consumerism with benign and malicious envy
    benign envy, 217–20
    catch-up consumption, 172
    consumer inequality, 227–29
    introduction to, 217–18
    malicious envy, 217–18, 220–22
    response to being envied, 224–26
    social comparisons and, 222
    summary of, 229–30
couldn't-care-less hypocrite, 154–55
counterfactual thought, 84, 90n9
covetous desire, 24–25, 89n5, 159n5
covetousness, 90n12, 159n5
COVID-19 pandemic, 103
criticism
    as communication, 151–53
    as epistemic good, 72
    as rebuke, 153–57
    testimonial model of, 151–57
    as unfair, 147
cultural perspective on envy, 24–27

D'Arms, Justin, 63, 107n4, 125, 204–5
degradation condition in malicious moral envy, 132
demand sharing, 36
denial, 7, 25–26, 36
desert requirement in compassion, 95
desire that the disadvantage be eliminated, 63–64
despair, 9, 17, 77, 82, 105, 115, 210–11
destruction strategy, 65
destructive behavior, 71, 72–73
destructive envy, 3, 9, 114, 220–21
dichotomous thinking in social comparison, 103
digital assistants, 200
diminution in self-worth, 80–83
disadvantage, feelings of, 81
discounting positives in social comparison, 103
disempowerment, 10, 80–81, 89, 120

disguising envy, 46–47
displeasure, 7, 32–35, 93, 186
distributive justice, 14, 101, 165
disutility in envy, 169, 171
dominance strategy, 44
The Donkey and the Pet Dog (Aesop fable), 11
"Donkey Objection" analogy, 111, 113–18
dysfunctional thinking patterns, 11, 103

economic changes and envy, 28–30
economic envy
    "absence of envy" economists, 167–70
    behavioral economics, 168–75
    experimental economics, 170–75
    introduction to, 13–14, 163–65
    New Household Economics, 175–76
    welfarist economics, 14, 165–68, 177n2
egalitarianism, 30, 36, 181–84
egalitarianism in politics of envy
    emotional regimes, 184–85
    implications for, 189–93
    introduction to, 15, 181–82
    irrationality and, 182–84
    summary of, 193
egocentric considerations, 11
ego-consciousness, 98
embarrassment, 3, 199, 202
emotional regimes, 15, 182, 184–93
emotions
    ambivalent emotional experience, 7
    anger at inanimate objects, 207
    artificial intelligence and, 205–8
    competitive emotion, 202
    despair, 9, 17, 77, 82, 105, 115, 210–11
    empathy, 50, 95, 133
    exemplarity-related, 137
    intensity of, 86
    moral emotions, 27, 43, 112

negative emotions, 11, 113, 137, 224, 226
outlaw emotions, 15, 190–92
self-conscious emotions, 3
as self-defeating, 130
social and cultural context, 6
social hierarchies and, 41
Western theories of emotion, 93
empathy, 50, 95, 133
empirical selves, 10, 84
empowering envy, 30–31, 36
emulation framing, 188
emulation strategy, 65, 71
emulative envy
    artificial intelligence and, 210–11
    complications with, 118–21
    "Donkey Objection" analogy, 111, 113–18, 116*t*
    educational implications, 123–24
    exemplars with, 138
    introduction to, 2–3, 5, 11–12, 208
    moral progress, 111, 112–13, 123–24
    obtaining the good, 208–9
    positive motivation and, 103
envidia, defined, 25
envied good, 131
envied *vs.* envier, 12, 28, 32–35, 47–52, 104–5, 224–26
envious blame
    abuse of normative power, 157–58
    criticism as communication, 151–53
    hypocritical blame, 154–55, 158
    introduction to, 147–48
    jealousy *vs.* envy, 148–50
    testimonial model of criticism, 151–57
envy
    as ambivalent emotional experience, 7
    of artificial intelligence, 209–11
    characterization of, 183
    components of, 62–65, 64*t*
    defined by Protasi, 130–32
    defined by Roberts, 131
    defined by Unamuno, 23
    dual nature of, 5
    functional view of, 217–18
    management of, 100–106
    negative consequences and, 8
    as pain, 17, 47, 63, 65, 98–100, 105, 113, 125n4, 182, 203–5
    Protasi on, 208–9
    as psychological experience, 24–25
    social comparisons and, 96
    social hierarchies and, 42–44, 43*f*
    subjective experience of, 23, 34, 45, 53
    taxonomy of, 3–5, 4*f*
    traditional assessments of, 202–5
    understandings of, 2–3
    unpleasant aspect of, 96–97
epistemic goods, 9, 67, 69, 72
ethics of blame, 13, 147–48, 154
evaluative judgments, 97–98, 156, 159–60
Eves, Richard, 28
evil eye accusations, 29–30, 36
exception-seeking hypocrite, 154
exemplarism in moral progress, 111, 112–13
exemplarity-related emotions, 137
existential envy
    diminution in self-worth, 80–83
    intensity and quality of, 83–87
    introduction to, 9–10, 77–78
    self-reproach and, 10, 82, 87–88
    structure of, 78–80
    summary of, 88–89
experimental economics, 170–75

failure scenario in literal imitation, 117
fairness theory, 166–67
Farmer, Paul, 140
Fauci, Anthony, 12, 129–30, 132–36, 140

Index

fear axis of envy, 25, 224, 225
"fear of envy" index, 34
fear of others' envy, 28–30
felicitous criticism, 152–53
Ferran, Vendrell, 117
first comparison-to-another, 84
focus of concern, 5, 80, 89n6, 208
foolish imitation, 111
fortune-telling in social comparison, 103
Foster, George M., 25–26
Framing Class: Media Representations of Wealth and Poverty in America (Kendall), 187–88
Frank, Robert, 173
free-market capitalism, 189
Friends (TV show), 149–50, 151–52
functional approach to envy, 8, 43, 217–18, 223, 227–30

gamak (desire), 31
Gauld, Tom, 149
Ghosh, Amitav, 26–28
giving (gift exchange), 29
Good, I. J., 201
gossip, 33, 73, 123, 220
gratitude, 11, 17–18, 112, 191
guilt, 3, 105, 112–13

hambre espiritual (spiritual hunger), 23
hasad, defined, 26–27
hate, 27, 32, 93
Hayek, F. A., 181
hedonic treadmill, 219
helplessness, 5, 81, 82, 102
Hendershott, Anne, 181
higher-rank/status people. *See* social hierarchies/rank
honesty, 114, 129, 133, 137
hopefulness, 81, 82, 210
hopelessness, 5, 10, 83, 141, 210–11
horizontal collectivism, 34, 49
hostile envy, 80, 86–87
humility, 11, 102, 122, 155
hypocritical blame, 13, 154–55, 158

ideal self, 10
"I" (ego), 98, 103–4
illness narratives, 28–29
imitative envy, 120
incoherence and ambivalence, 137
individualistic cultural values, 33
individualistic notion of self, 93
inequality impact on well-being, 14
inert envy, 71, 105, 208–9, 210
inferiority response, 42, 77, 81
injustice, 2, 15, 74, 82, 104, 182–84, 192, 204
insecurity, 82, 102
inspired envy
    complications with emulative envy, 118–21
    "Donkey Objection" analogy, 111, 113–18
    exemplarism in moral progress, 111, 112–13
    introduction to, 11, 111
instant gratification, 221
intensity of emotions, 86
Internship condition study, 33–34
interpersonal alienation, 104
irrational envy, 227
irrationality and politics of envy, 182–84
Izquierdo, Carolina, 29

jealousy *vs.* envy, 13, 62, 148–50, 205
Johnson, Allen, 29
joy, 99

Kant, Immanuel, 204
karuna (compassion), 99
Kendall, Diana, 187–88
khandas (aggregates) of matter, 97
Kidder, Tracy, 140
Korean culture, 33

labeling in social comparison, 103
"lack *vs.* loss" model in jealousy *vs.* envy, 148
Lelet, Papua New Guinea community, 28–29

leveling up/leveling down in envy, 5, 132, 134–35, 142n7, 142n9
liget (anger/energy/passion), 31
limited good, 7, 25–26, 36
literal imitation, 116–17
Logan, Lara, 130
Lopez, Jensen de, 32
love
    as antidote to envy, 18n7, 135–36, 142n6
    compassion as, 93
    competition and, 202
    envied *vs.* envier, 104–6
    for non-human beings, 206
    self-worth and, 101
lower-rank/status people. *See* social hierarchies/rank

MacFarquhar, Larissa, 139–40
maladaptive beliefs, 11, 103–4
maladaptive envy, 8
malicious envy. *See also* consumerism with benign and malicious envy
    aggressive envy as, 134, 208–9
    Buddhist perspective on, 96–97
    characterization of, 24
    consumerism and, 217–18, 220–22
    destructive behavior and, 71
    "Donkey Objection" analogy, 111, 113–18
    outlaw emotions of, 15, 190–92
    perception of control, 5
    as radically vicious, 189
    social rank and, 45–53
malicious moral envy
    defined, 130–34
    introduction to, 12, 129–30
    moral ambivalence and, 136–41
    puzzlement associated with, 134–41
    self-defeat and, 134–35
    summary of, 141
marginal disutility, 169
marginal productivity theory, 173

Mbappé, Kylian, 203
media frames, 188
mental formations, 97
meritocracy, 191–92
metaethics, 12
Milinda's Questions (Buddhist text), 97–98
Mora, Fernández de la, 79
moral ambivalence, 136–41
moral emotions, 27, 43, 112, 142n3
moral envy. *See* malicious moral envy
moral grandstanding, 142n9
moral narcissism, 140
moral progress, 111, 112–13, 123–24
moral psychology of envy, 12, 13, 174–76
"Moral Saints" (Wolf), 138
Morgan-Knapp, Christopher, 183
Murakami, Haruki, 61

Napoleon Dynamite (film), 150, 153, 156
narcissism, 42, 132, 135, 140
Navarro, Peter, 130
Naçaawy village in Egypt, 26–27, 31
needy people, 27
negative consumption externality, 14
negative emotions, 11, 113, 137, 224, 226
negative self-assessment, 80
neo-Machiavellians, 192
New Household Economics, 175–76
New Welfare economics, 165–66
non-excludability, 69
non-malicious envy, 2–3
non-rivalry, 69
normative ethics, 12
normative power, 157–58
Nussbaum, Martha, 95

Obama, Barack, 129, 132, 135–36, 140
object-envy, 5, 36, 114, 115*f*
obtaining the good, 208–9
ontological envy, 77
othering, 31

outlaw emotions, 15, 190–92
Overridingness Thesis, 139
Owens, David, 157

pain
    in academic envy, 74, 78
    Buddhism and, 99, 104–5
    consumer inequality and, 227
    criticism and, 147, 159
    displeasure and, 186
    emotions defined by
        Aristotle, 2, 95
    emulative envy and, 209
    envy as, 17, 47, 63, 65, 98–100,
        105, 113, 125n4, 182, 203–5
    inert envy and, 208
    moral reasoning and, 120–22
    pleasure and, 175
    self-comparison and, 10–11
    self-compassion and, 104
    self-deception and, 88
    shame and, 210
    understanding of, 106,
        106n1, 106n3
pan-cultural envy, 25
Pareto efficient, 166
pecuniary emulation, 187
perceived obtainability of the good, 208
perceived undeservedness, 223–24, 228
phronesis (practical wisdom),
    121–22, 127
phronimos (practically wise
    person), 119–20
phthonos (envy), 2, 114
physical form, 97
pity, 10, 18n6
Plato, 119
pleasure, 7, 32–35, 102, 175
politics of envy. *See* egalitarianism in
    politics of envy
positional goods, 17, 66, 183, 222–23
poverty, 186–87
powerlessness, 77, 81–82
prestige in academia, 67–68
prestige strategy, 44

price tag framing, 188
primordial suffering, 99
the priority rule, 67
Protasi, Sara, 71, 105, 130–32, 148,
    182, 205, 208–11
psychoanalytic tradition of envy,
    18n5, 90n11
psychotic altruism, 140
public goods, 69

quiet ego, 102

rank/rank differentials. *See*
    social hierarchies
Rawls, John, 177n2, 185
recently-converted hypocrite, 155
Reddy, William, 184
relative disadvantage, 68, 70–71
rentier capitalism, 191
resentment, 27, 62
response to being envied, 224–26
Ressa, Maria, 203
reward system in academia, 68
Rhetoric (Aristotle), 2, 114
rivalry, 53, 81, 87, 104, 132–33, 213n10
Robbins, Lionel, 166
Roberts, Robert, 131–32
robots, 200
role-modeling, 112

schadenfreude, 1, 12, 62
Scheler, Max, 9, 79
second comparison-to-another, 84–85
Sedol, Lee, 15–16, 199, 201–2, 207–10
self, 89n2, 93, 94–97. *See also*
    Buddhist no-self doctrine in envy/
    compassion dichotomy
self-assessment, 80, 117
self-betterment, 2
self-blame, 147
self-comparison, 85–86
self-compassion, 93–94, 102, 104
self-confidence, 225
self-conscious emotions, 3
self-deception, 10, 87–88

self-defeat, 134–35
self-defeating nature of envy, 105, 209
self-destruction strategy, 65
self-destructive envy, 9
self-destructive greed, 85
self-disclosure, 85–86
self-efficacy, 117
self-enhancement behavior, 33
self-envy, 90n11
self-esteem, 10, 87–88, 89n7, 132–34, 151, 184, 227
self-evaluation, 94
self-focused counterfactuals, 86
self-improvement, 12, 103, 111, 118, 134, 219
selfishness, 32, 63
self-protective behaviors, 49
self-relevance, 89n3, 96, 132–33
self-reproach, 10, 82, 87–88
self-sufficiency, 185
self-transformation, 120–21
self-worth
    diminution in, 9, 78, 80–83, 88
    envy and, 125n9
    as goal-attainment, 101–2
    goal attainment and, 101–2
    of higher-ranked persons, 45
    lack of, 11, 111, 117, 120
    love and, 101
Sen, Amartya, 190
seriousness requirement in compassion, 95
shame, 3, 65, 81, 104–5, 112, 115, 134, 184, 210
signal values, 101
similarity condition in malicious moral envy, 132
similarity requirement in compassion, 95
similar possibilities requirement in compassion, 95
sincerity test, 152
Slote, Michael, 139
Smith, Adam, 15, 186, 188, 190
social class, 36, 188

social comparison
    compassion and, 95–96
    dysfunctional beliefs about, 103
    in envy, 7, 24, 182, 222
    self-relevance conditions and, 133
social equality, 7, 25
social hierarchies/rank
    approach/avoidance behavior in being envied, 51–52
    benign and malicious envy, 44–53
    disguising envy, 46–47
    envy and, 42–44, 43f
    introduction to, 7–8, 41–42
    reactions to being envied, 47–51
    social rank, 44–46
    summary of, 53–54
socialism, 181
social media, 61, 129, 206, 222, 226
social psychology, 2–3, 16
sociocultural approach to envy
    being envied, 32–35
    covetous desire, 24–25
    cultural practices, 26–28
    economic changes and, 28–30
    empowerment and, 30–31
    introduction to, 23–24
    limited good, 7, 25–26, 36
    summary of, 35–37
Socrates, 119
sorcery accusations, 29–30
Spinoza, Baruch, 96
spiteful envy, 132, 134, 208, 210–11
state-envy, 114, 115f
status and envy, 13, 101–2
Stoics, 119, 202
striving actions, 121–22
subjective experience of envy, 23, 34, 45, 53
suboptimal allocations of resources, 65–66
success scenario in literal imitation, 117
suffering, 95–105. *See also* pain
symbolic sharing, 7, 25, 26, 36

Taylor, Gabriele, 3, 79, 88, 114–15

temporary suffering, 100
testimonial model of criticism, 151–57
Thatcher, Margaret, 181
The Theory of Moral Sentiments (Smith), 15, 186
Thomason, Krista, 3
Thunberg, Greta, 140
Tinbergen, Jan, 165
traditional assessments of envy, 202–5
true sharing, 7, 25, 26
Trump, Donald, 12, 129–30, 132–36, 140
trust/trustworthiness, 17, 130, 133
two axes model of envy, 33
Tzintzuntzan peoples, 25–26

Unamuno, Miguel de, 23, 77, 85
undeservedness perception, 223–24, 228
unhappiness, 98, 102
unpleasantness of envy, 182
upward comparisons, 83–84. *See also* comparison

valued good, 131–32, 135
valued object, 13, 26
Veblen, Thorstein, 187
vertical individualism, 36

weak-willed hypocrite, 154
welfare recipients, 191
welfarist economics, 14, 165–68, 177n2
Western theories of emotion, 93
Williams, Bernard, 138–39
wisdom in selfless action, 98
Wolf, Susan, 138

You're All Just Jealous of My Jetpack (Gauld), 149, 151–52

Zagzebski, Linda, 112–13
Zambrano, María, 9, 85
zēlos (emulation), 2, 114
zero-sum beliefs, 25, 28
Z-good, 175

About the Contributors

Alfred Archer is an assistant professor of philosophy at Tilburg University (The Netherlands) and a member of the Tilburg Center for Logic, Ethics, and Philosophy of Science (TiLPS). His primary research interests are in moral philosophy and moral psychology, particularly supererogation, the nature and ethics of admiration, and the ethics of fame. He also has research interests in applied ethics, political philosophy, and the philosophy of sport. He is the co-author of the monograph *Honouring and Admiring the Immoral: An Ethical Guide* (2021) and has co-edited volumes on *The Moral Psychology of Admiration* (2019), *Self-Sacrifice and Moral Philosophy* (2020), and *Emotions in Sport and Games* (2020). He is currently serving as the vice president for the European Philosophical Society for the Study of Emotions (EPSSE) and the vice chair of the British Philosophy of Sport Association (BPSA).

Miriam Bankovsky is a senior lecturer in political theory at La Trobe University (Melbourne, Australia), where she directs the Bachelor of Politics, Philosophy, and Economics program. In her philosophical work, Miriam contributes to what she thinks are important normative debates in political philosophy, drawing on both analytic and continental resources, with a particular focus on economic marginalization and unlawfulness. It is in this context that she was awarded the Australasian Association of Philosophy's Annette Baier Prize for her 2018 article on economic envy (*Journal of Applied Philosophy*). In other work in the history of economic thought, she has primarily focused on the role of families in market-paradigm economics, but this is also a tradition that has included an interesting account of how a family might seek to control envy between members, so as to maximize the family's utility. Bankovsky has published numerous articles on a wide-ranging set of topics in quality outlets, cutting across history, economics, family, and philosophical conceptions of justice. Her book on the family, *The Family, Economics and Ethics: A New History*, is forthcoming.

Vanessa Carbonell is associate professor of philosophy and Obed J. Wilson Professor of Ethics at the University of Cincinnati in Cincinnati, Ohio. She works primarily in normative ethics and has written about moral saints, moral obligation, self-sacrifice, and the socially mediated nature of the moral community. She has additional research and teaching interests in applied ethics, including medical ethics and health policy. vanessa.carbonell@uc.edu

Christina Chuang is a philosopher at Nanyang Technological University in Singapore. Her research interests are in comparative ethics between early modern philosophy and ancient Asian traditions. Currently, she also has three interdisciplinary projects with scientists studying the ethics of quantum technology, ethical data practices in post disaster setting, and the moral implications of sex robots.

Jan Crusius is an assistant professor at the Department of Social Psychology at Tilburg University, The Netherlands. He is also affiliated with the Social Cognition Center Cologne at the University of Cologne, Germany. In his research, he is mainly interested in how specific emotions based on social comparisons such as envy, pride, or admiration determine how people make sense of social hierarchies and navigate in them. He uses experimental as well as correlational approaches to investigate how such emotions contribute to decision-making, social perception, and behavior at individual and social levels of analysis. As an editor of the *In-Mind Magazine*, his goal is to enable psychologists to communicate their science to the public.

Bart Engelen is an associate professor at Tilburg University (the Netherlands) and is affiliated with the Tilburg Center for Moral Philosophy, Epistemology, and Philosophy of Science (TiLPS). His research focuses on the borders between ethics, political philosophy, and economics. He has published on issues surrounding rationality, paternalism, voting, and the role of preferences in economics. Recently, he has focused on ethical and conceptual issues that arise with respect to nudging and behavioral influencing. He has published on how nudging relates to manipulation, rationality, autonomy, transparency, and ethics more generally and how nudges can and should be implemented in health promotion and moral education.

Alison Duncan Kerr is a feminist philosopher and the founding director of the Centre for Research Activism for Intersectional Justice. She was previously the founding director of the St. Andrews Institute for Gender Studies and its related master's program in gender studies at the University of St. Andrews. Her research focuses on philosophy of mind, emotions, gender, AI, and their application in practice.

Jens Lange is a post doc at the University of Hamburg. He has two main research areas. First, he is interested in the role of emotions in the regulation of social hierarchies with a special emphasis on status hierarchies based on prestige and dominance. Primarily, he investigates the diversity of envious reactions of individuals with low social rank and how these reactions are predicted by these individuals' personalities (e.g., the Dark Triad or motivational inclinations) and by highly ranked others' emotions (e.g., pride). Second, he is broadly interested in conceptualizations of emotions and how approaches to the measurement of emotions can inform conceptualizations of emotions. Lange has published his work in leading journals in social and personality psychology as well as emotion research. lange.jens@outlook.com

Ariele Niccoli is currently a high school teacher of philosophy in Florence. His research interests lie at the intersection between philosophy of the emotions, contemporary virtue ethics, and philosophy of education. He has published several papers and chapters, which include "Phronesis as Ethical Expertise: Naturalism of Second Nature and the Unity of Virtue" (*Journal of Value Inquiry*, 2018; with M. De Caro and M. S. Vaccarezza). and the forthcoming chapter, "Emotional Skillfulness and Virtue Acquisition," (with M. De Caro and M. S. Vaccarezza).

Sara Protasi is associate professor of philosophy at University of Puget Sound. Her research interests are primarily in moral psychology, philosophy of emotions, and aesthetics. She has published scholarly essays on love, envy, beauty, pornography, and pedagogy in peer-review journals and edited volumes. She is the author of the monograph *The Philosophy of Envy* (2021). She has been interviewed for articles published in *The Stylist*, *The Globe and Mail*, and *Der Standard*, has been a guest in podcasts and radio shows (*Counterpoint*, *The Philosopher*, *Philosophy Talk*, and *Elucidations*), and has written articles and blog posts for the general public in venues such as *The Prindle Post*, *Aeon*, and *The Institute of Art and Ideas*.

Patricia M. Rodriguez Mosquera is professor of psychology at Wesleyan University, Connecticut. She studies emotions in their cultural contexts using a multi-method approach, with a special focus on how people from different cultures experience having a positive or negative social image. She has published her work on a wide range of emotions about perceived social image (e.g., pride, happiness, anger, shame, fear, sadness) in social psychology, cross-cultural psychology, and emotion journals (e.g., *Journal of Personality and Social Psychology*, *Journal of Cross-Cultural Psychology*, *Cognition & Emotion*). She was lead editor of a special issue on *Social Image* for the *European Journal of Social Psychology* and editor of a special issue on

Cultures of Honor in *Group Processes and Intergroup Relations*. She was associate editor of the *European Journal of Social Psychology* and *Frontiers in Psychology: Section Cultural Psychology*.

Felipe Romero is an assistant professor in the Department of Theoretical Philosophy at the University of Groningen in the Netherlands. His research falls in the domains of philosophy of science, social epistemology, and philosophy of cognitive science. He works primarily on understanding how the social and contextual aspects of research activities affect their epistemic outcomes.

Alan Thomas is a professor of philosophy at the University of York in the United Kingdom. Thomas was previously a senior lecturer at the University of Kent, a professor of ethics at Tilburg University in the Netherlands, and moved to York as a professor and head of department in 2016. He has been a visiting researcher at the University of British Columbia, the ANU, the Murphy Center at Tulane University, and St, Louis University. He is editor of *Bernard Williams* and the author of three monographs: *Value and Context: The Nature of Moral and Political Knowledge* (2006); *Thomas Nagel* (2008); and *Republic of Equals: Redistribution and Property-Owning Democracy* (2017).

Neal A. Tognazzini is a professor of philosophy at Western Washington University. He specializes in moral psychology and the metaphysics of free will. He is co-editor of *Blame: Its Nature and Norms* (2013), and co-editor of two volumes of *Oxford Studies in Agency and Responsibility*. His published work has appeared in *Ethics*, *Philosophy and Phenomenological Research* and *Noûs*, among other venues.

Maria Silvia Vaccarezza is associate professor of moral philosophy at the University of Genova, and secretary of Aretai—Center on Virtues. She is author of numerous monographs, journal articles, and book chapters on several topics in virtue ethics, philosophy of emotions, and philosophy of education. She has recently edited *Practical Wisdom: Philosophical and Psychological Perspectives* (with M. De Caro; 2021) and *Virtues, Democracy, and Online Media: Ethical and Epistemic Issues* (with N. Snow; 2021).

Niels van de Ven is an associate professor at the marketing department at Tilburg University in the Netherlands. His research focuses on the psychology of (consumer) behavior, financial decision-making, and emotions. He studies envy extensively, focusing mostly on the idea that envy might have subtypes (benign and malicious envy). Other work focuses on defining greed and investigating the behavior of greedy people; people's behavior after past good actions (moral licensing), and other emotions or the behavior associated with them like regret or crying.

Íngrid Vendrell Ferran is Heisenberg-fellow at the Goethe University Frankfurt. Her research interests are phenomenology, philosophy of mind, aesthetics, and epistemology. Some of her publications include: *Die Emotionen* (2008); *Wahrheit, Wissen und Erkenntnis in der Literatur* (edited with Christoph Demmerling, 2014); *Empathie im Film* (edited with Malte Hagener, 2017); *Die Vielfalt der Erkenntnis* (2018); and *Beauty* (edited with Wolfgang Huemer, 2019).

www.ingramcontent.com/pod-product-compliance
Lightning Source LLC
Chambersburg PA
CBHW020114010526
44115CB00008B/831